# The Cost of
# FREEDOM

Marla Glen

*with*

Stacey McClain

Book Cover Photo Credit: Alexander Scheuber

ISBN: 979-8-9891557-0-5  Paperback
ISBN: 979-8-9891557-1-2  Hardback

Published by: Chitown Publishing, LLC

# CONTENTS

Preface .......................................................................................v

Stacey's Acknowledgements ....................................................ix

Introduction ............................................................................xi

Chapter 1    What's in a Name?...............................................1

Chapter 2    Discovering Music..............................................6

Chapter 3    Not Like Other Girls ........................................16

Chapter 4    School Days .......................................................21

Chapter 5    Troubles at Home...............................................27

Chapter 6    A Drifter is Born................................................33

Chapter 7    Finding Independence......................................43

Chapter 8    Studs in The City .............................................54

Chapter 9    Making Connections .......................................62

Chapter 10   Bo Diddley.........................................................71

Chapter 11   Nina Simone .....................................................77

Chapter 12   Center of a Star .................................................85

Chapter 13   Playing the Wrong Pipe ..................................97

Chapter 14   New Orleans Blues...........................................104

Chapter 15   The Contest.......................................................112

Chapter 16   My First Band....................................................122

Chapter 17   Revenge in a Clothing Store...........................129

Chapter 18   Sandrine .............................................................137

Chapter 19   Enter Mr. Gonzalez .........................................142

Chapter 20   Catch 22.............................................................153

Chapter 21   More Unanswered Questions...........................160

Chapter 22   Old Friend............................................165

Chapter 23   Going Gold..........................................169

Chapter 24   The Mystery Chocolate........................175

Chapter 25   Mom Learns the Truth.........................182

Chapter 26   Gonzalez Goes Too Far ....................... 186

Chapter 27   The Truth Emerges ............................. 191

Chapter 28   Goodbye Europe................................... 199

Chapter 29   Meltdown............................................206

Chapter 30   Hospitalized........................................ 212

Chapter 31   By the Grace of God and Fans..............216

Chapter 32   More Bad News....................................222

Chapter 33   Out on My Own................................... 227

Chapter 34   Tragic Loss..........................................233

Chapter 35   Trouble in Switzerland........................240

Chapter 36   Following the Money ..........................244

Chapter 37   Time For A Change.............................252

Chapter 38   More of the Same ...............................257

Chapter 39   Another Loss ...................................... 263

Chapter 40   Sabrina................................................267

Chapter 41   Menges................................................273

Chapter 42   The End and More of the Same ........... 282

Chapter 43   I'm Done ... Again!..............................290

Chapter 44   Losing My Mind .................................298

Chapter 45   Hospital Again.................................... 302

Chapter 46   Mr. Badu............................................ 305

Chapter 47   The Fight ............................................ 311

Chapter 48   Teamwork ... Or Not ........................... 315

Chapter 49   Bruno.................................................. 326

Chapter 50   Out With The Old .............................. 331

Chapter 51   Finding Freedom ................................ 339

# PREFACE

Welcome to the pages of my life! In the following chapters, I invite you to join me on a journey through the highs and lows, that have shaped my existence as Marla Glen. This autobiography is a testament to the power of music, perseverance, and the human spirit.

As a singer/songwriter, I've had the privilege of using my voice to express emotions, tell stories, and connect with audiences from all corners of the world. But beyond the stage lights and applause, lie a plethora of experiences to give you an insight as what I've been through.

From the bustling streets of Chicago to the vibrant scenes of New Orleans, to European cities, my life has taken unexpected turns and surprising detours. I've faced challenges that tested me on many levels. Through it all, music has been my constant companion, offering comfort in times of turmoil and a channel for my most authentic self.

This journey wouldn't have been possible without the support of countless individuals who've walked alongside me, believed in my vision, and offered their encouragement. To my family, friends, mentors, and fans – your presence has been the melody to my lyrics, and I'm eternally grateful for your role in my story.

As you turn the pages of "The Cost of Freedom" you'll witness the evolution of a young stud, never wanting to be in the music business, but ended up in the reality of a naïve singer's life. You'll share in the moments of triumph and vulnerability, the anecdotes that make up the fabric of who I am today.

Whether you're a music enthusiast, an aspiring artist, or simply someone intrigued by the relentlessness of the human experience, I hope my journey resonates with you. May my story inspire you to chase your passions, navigate life's twists with courage and faith, as well as find your own harmonies in the symphony of existence.

Thank you for picking up this book and allowing me to share my story with you and embarking on this adventure with me. Let the notes of my life's song guide you through the chapters that follow.

Peace and Blessings,

Marla D. Glen

This book is dedicated to
*My entire family, especially my dearly departed mom, dad,*
*along with the many fans who have been there throughout this journey.*
*A very special thank you to my mother and father of music,*
*the late Nina Simone and Bo Diddley,*
*both who led me in the right direction.*
*Marla Glen*

# STACEY'S
# ACKNOWLEDGEMENTS

*A very special thank you to my mom, family and
all of my friends for
being understanding and supportive.
A heartfelt thank you to those who have encouraged
and hired me so that I could assist Marla in getting out this story,
especially Kym Whitley, Sherri Shephard, Warren Oates
and the late Tim Slevin.*

*I am able to be me because you all have amazing hearts,
and I love you for it.*

*To Marla,
I am grateful that you allowed me to help you get this story out.
My only wish is that you move forward and
do the great things you were born to do.
Shine!*

# INTRODUCTION

As far as I'm aware, there isn't any other musician with a story like Marla's—someone with gold and platinum discs who never really saw any of the money earned and who, at the height of their fame, had to ask favors for somewhere to sleep.

There is so much to tell about Marla, and much of the last twelve years have been spent pulling this book together. Marla felt it was time people truly understood all that had gone on during the previous thirty years. Much has been gathered over many interviews between the two of us, so let me share what Marla said right at the start when I asked why he wanted this book to be written:

"It's all about what happened to me in my career, how it felt to be on the other side of those who sought to manipulate me. I'm tired of people saying that I'm always complaining about the things that were done, so I want to get it all out, once and for all, and then people can read the book if they want to know.

People say I'll never get justice, but for what? You'll have to read the book! —but telling all publicly, risking being taken to court, is what I have to do now. When I spoke to a lawyer about what I had to say and people getting upset by it, he told me that the truth is always a great defense. I have nothing else to offer, but I want the book to explain to my fans what I was going through.

Furthermore, I don't want to be like my good friend Nina Simone, who was talking about her troubles—with some of the same people as me—until her dying day. I want my story to help me never talk about it all again—it's in the book, I've shared it, and that, for me, is part of my new beginning, like with the album I released in 2020, called *Unexpected*. It's about breaking free.

Written when I was just a kid, my song, *Cost of Freedom*, first appeared on my debut album in 1993, but there was only ever going to be one title for this book. Opening up all the old wounds in the way I have and admitting my faults and weaknesses that exacerbated such dire situations are the cost of becoming free of all that went before. And, so many times, the price has been my sanity. But, as best I can, I'm going to tell you all that happened."

It's been a long journey, and, as Marla's cousin, I've been there for most of the story and not just since I agreed to help him write this book. I was there, for example, when he was hospitalized in Pasadena, California, against his wishes and watched as he barely spoke while wondering if the doctor's opinion of Marla being mentally unstable was accurate. That wasn't the case; I discovered it was yet another instance of willful manipulation. I was in the room a couple of times when Marla spoke to different attorneys seeking justice for the past. It was difficult to watch, as nothing really happened when the dust cleared, and the attorneys couldn't help or disappeared. While I'm not a medical doctor, it has always been my opinion that Marla suffers from PTSD as it relates to certain things pertaining to the music industry. When we first began this journey, there were countless times that Marla would cry uncontrollably while trying to get the words out as I asked about certain stories or shout at me, trying to get me to understand the gravity of a certain situation. As the years passed and we got the story out, Marla became better at sharing the many incidents that left an indelible mark in the artist's mind, but there are still certain conversations that come from a place of pain. This is why, no matter how long it took, I had to finish this book because I knew it would help the healing process. I'll leave things there and let you read; it's a story like no other.

Stacey

Stacey McClain, Aug 2023

# HUMANOLOGY

"Look in the mirror, tell me, what do you see?
Are you true to yourself?"

# CHAPTER 1

# What's in a Name?

Considering where I live today, my mother missed the irony when she named me Marla. The origin is German, a shortening of Mary Magdalene, such an important person from the book I read most, the Bible. But when I was born, on January 3rd, 1960, the only significant thing about my name was the moment my grandmother heard it as she held me. She took one look at me before she turned to my mother.

"Nice name, but baby, your daughter is gay."

"Mom, you don't know what you are talking about," my mother replied.

"In time, you will see."

My mother told me that story when I got older, but no one ever knew why grams said that at the time. It turns out she was right, but in those early days, Mom certainly didn't accept what her mother said. She simply focused on nurturing her baby girl.

As my grandmother's prophecy became more and more of a reality, especially in my teenage years, I didn't want the name Marla.

"Mom, I want to change my name."

"But why?" she asked as she looked up from cooking my breakfast.

"Because I want a nickname like my brother."

"Well, Marla, what do you want me to call you?"

I wasn't sure at that moment and said the first thing that came into my head.

"Marvin, or maybe Marco."

These were clearly masculine names, and my mother looked at me like she was going to argue, and then she simply shook her head.

"Well, when you decide, you just let me know."

She was great like that. I'd always be her little girl, but she wouldn't deny me my true identity.

As I began to truly realize who I was, that I wanted to be viewed as masculine rather than feminine, I wanted that boyish nickname. My brother, Armando, had the cool nickname of "Tuggy." Our mother began calling him "Tuggy Man" after a children's book called *Tuggy the Tugboat* Armando loved to have read to him. Eventually, she dropped the 'man' at the end, and the nickname of Tuggy stuck. We have always been close, and today it's still what I always call him.

There were many times I wanted to be just like him. As a kid, he was rough and rugged and mechanically gifted, being able to take anything apart, like toys, electronics, and bikes, and put them back together again. But as I thought about my name more deeply, I decided that if God gave my mother the name Marla for me, changing it would be disrespectful to my mother and disrespectful in the eyes of God. So, that's why I never changed it. Later in life, my mother told me she chose Marla and Armando because of our dad's Mexican / Spanish heritage.

Despite mom giving me that name, I never saw myself as a girl. One of my earliest memories was when I would have been around three or four years old at Christmastime. We had a beautiful tree with lots of tinsel and ornaments, and the house smelled of fresh pine and the cake mom baked as we waited for Santa Claus.

When I woke up on Christmas morning, I remember running

towards the tree and seeing all these carefully wrapped presents. Tuggy and I dived in, and for me, there was what every little girl would have wanted. I got things like dolls, tea sets, girly pink outfits, a play oven, and other girl-defining toys. However, those things didn't excite me as much as my brother Tuggy's little green army men, toy trucks, his G.I. Joe and his train set. I played with my things for a while, but later I spent much more time with Tuggy's toys, which he happily shared.

As I got older, my mother still tried to get me to wear little frilly dresses and girly skirts, but I hated them. Around the age of six, rather than a nightdress, I told my mom I wanted two-piece pajamas because they made me feel more like a boy. I only chose to wear pants, and we would have arguments about it.

"Mom, I don't want to wear some pink dress because it makes me look like a Liberty Bell. Just my jeans are fine."

"This must be some tomboy phase you're going through," she suggested. I'm sure my mother thought I would get past it.

My dad didn't really say much about how I dressed. It didn't bother him at all. He was the more laid-back type of parent—nothing much fazed him—but my mom chose to ignore the signs that I would never be the feminine young daughter she wished she had.

When I was about eight years old, she encouraged me to join the new Brownies group, a Girl Scouts of America division for younger girls starting in the neighborhood. I was always a very bouncy, inquisitive individual with a thirst for adventure. I was curious about everything, and my mother thought this would be great for me and, quite honestly, I did too.

"They go camping, help sell cookies, and there will be a bunch of other girls there to play with."

"Oh wow. I want to do all that!"

Mom took me to the first meeting, held in the local church's basement. We entered a room that looked like it was being used as a

Bible study, with all the chairs facing one direction. We filled out paperwork at a table by the door and then took a seat. There were about thirty other kids there, most of them were my age, and we all waited anxiously for the meeting to begin. I was excited because I knew you could get into the Girl Scouts after you finished in the Brownies, and I loved that they sold cookies. Also, being around a bunch of cute girls was certainly something that I would enjoy!

The woman leading the meeting had a cheery attitude and smiled a lot as she explained how the Brownies got started. She then looked around the room and excitedly explained all the fun things Brownies would get into. She raised her voice to get all the girls' attention.

"Okay girls, I hope you all like camping!

In unison, all the little girls raised their hands and cheered, so she kept going.

"We also have loads of cookies you can sell to your friends and family. Would you like to do that?

"*Yes!*" Came the united response.

"We have great campgrounds where we will take everyone; you can swim, hike, and play games. There are also pins you can win to place on your Brownie uniform. How about that!?"

All the little girls shouted, "*Yes!*"

I was excited and shouting right along with them all, really getting into the idea of being a Brownie. Then the perky woman ruined it all.

"Okay, let me show you what the Brownie uniform looks like."

She picked up a Brownie uniform dress from a table behind her and held it up in front of everyone.

"And you all will get to wear this cute little Brownies' uniform!"

All the girls shouted another huge 'yes' ... except for me. This is where they lost me. There was no way I was going to put on a dress to do anything. I was so disappointed because it all sounded great but putting on a dress was where I drew the line. I grabbed my mother's arm and pulled her towards me.

"Mom, I don't think I want to be a Brownie Scout," I whispered, and after she got over the surprise, she looked at the dress, back at me, and then nodded.

My mother wasn't the type to make me or my brother do anything we didn't want to do. So, I never became a Brownie and later realized it was a defining moment about who I wanted to be, even at such a young age.

If this makes sense, as much as I felt different, I grew up quite normal. My parents always supported whatever I wanted to do as a child, allowing me to grow into the person I am without reservation or fear. It was clear that I was born a bold kid who often made life-changing decisions about how I wanted to be perceived. Resigned to not having the type of girl she had expected, my mom would often say, "Marla, you have to live your own life the way you see fit. As long as it is your choice and you are happy."

My mother's main goal was that Tuggy and I grew up being respectful, kind, and independent. Primarily because this is how she was raised. I remember my mother telling me that someday I would be on my own and need to figure things out for myself. I couldn't wait till that day came, but later on in life, I'd many times wish I had someone to guide me.

My dad often endorsed what my mother said, but having that more easy-going personality, he left a lot of the serious parenting to Mom. If we asked him something, his response was usually, "Did you ask your mother?"

When it came to other things, Dad's explanation of how things worked in the world was pretty simple, like, "You got money, you got friends, if you don't have money, you don't' have friends. Period."

Dad talked a lot about money, and that was where he too missed the irony of what was to come.

# CHAPTER 2

# Discovering Music

My dad was my first musical influence. Born Cortez Glen, my father was tall and handsome, with a deep, smooth voice and personality to match. He was suave and cool. A military man, he worked as a mechanic in the Army repairing tanks in Frankfurt, Germany. After an honorable discharge, he returned to the United States, where he bounced around, taking on odd jobs, such as working at the Chicago Steel Mill. He also had jobs in construction, dressmaking, or whatever he could get to make money.

Dad loved listening to music and playing around with a harmonica. It was something he taught himself while he was in the military. Our home was always filled with music from the radio or record player, especially in the evenings after work or at family gatherings. I remember him playing the song *Ol' Susanna* on the harmonica, and as a child, I thought it was amazing.

He was raised in a large family, and all my aunts, uncles, and cousins would gather together for celebrations. It was always a lot of fun. Everyone would have backyard barbecues, family reunions in Chicago's Washington Park, or birthday parties at someone's house.

Whenever the family gathered, music played in the background, and shortly after the music kicked in, the dancing would begin.

It was the early 60s, and Motown music always filled the air. The Jackson Five, Smokey Robinson and the Miracles, and Marvin Gaye would get people up on their feet or occasionally a little jazz and blues. We would all have a great time. While the kids were playing, the adults would dance and cook good food, and there was always plenty of laughter.

I remember one time when my cousins and I got together and pretended we were a musical group. We were trying to be like the Jackson 5 or the Temptations. We would each take the lead, and the rest of us would make up steps like backup singers. Those were some of the best times of my childhood.

My mother was great at throwing parties, and she also loved music. Born Dell Earlette Byrd, she was a small dark brown woman with a petite slender frame and a smile that could warm the heart of a thousand Eskimos. She was straightforward when she needed to be but handled herself with style and grace. Just like my dad, mom also had a strong relationship with her family, and her sisters and brothers would often come over on the weekends, or we would visit them.

When they met, both my parents lived on the South Side of Chicago, and my mom worked at a record store near 39th and King Drive. One day after my father returned from the military, he went to the shop where she worked. Once he laid his eyes on her, they immediately had a connection. They began dating and shortly thereafter fell in love. They even had cute little nicknames for each other. She affectionately called him Fang, and he called her Doll. Not long after dating, Mom became pregnant with Armando; shortly thereafter, they got married and moved in with each other. One year after giving birth to my brother, Mom became pregnant again and gave birth to me.

Always a close-knit family, one of the first places we lived was at a two-story house at 5549 Lafayette. Mom was outspoken about what she believed in and wanted for herself and us. She was ambitious yet down-to-earth and a strong black woman who did not take "no" for an answer when she wanted to accomplish something.

Like most boys, my brother loved being around our dad. He also loved model cars, practicing Karate, and playing with swords and little green toy army men. Armando and I had a great bond, and I'd say we had a normal sibling relationship. We were only a year apart, so we would play games, checkers, darts, ping pong, put together puzzles, and goof off, laughing at each other's jokes. Like most siblings, we also would have our occasional fights and wrestle and then brag about who beat whom up. Tuggy would say, "You know I beat you; you should just go sit down somewhere."

Feisty, I'd respond, "Boy, I beat you. You just don't want to admit it."

Despite our sibling spats, we mostly got along. We both loved animals, and while growing up, we would always bring pets home, or stray animals, such as dogs, frogs, cats, birds, chickens, and lizards, and we also had turtles and snakes that we would get from the local fish store. In one fish tank, we even had a piranha, which was my father's pet! We kept many of the animals we brought home in the basement of our next house on 95th street. Sometimes we would charge the neighborhood kids a fee or take candy in exchange for them coming to pet our animals.

We rented the old house on Lafayette, but my parents had purchased this one, their first proper home, in an area called Longwood Manor. It was in this house that I spent most of my childhood. I had my own room, and Tuggy had a bedroom built in the attic. My parents were one of the first black families to purchase a home in this upper echelon neighborhood, which at the time was occupied by a majority of Caucasian people. It was one of the more segregated areas of the

South Side of Chicago. Racial tensions were high. We were the third black family to purchase a home on our block and became part of an ever-growing black middle class who bought homes in good districts to ensure their kids went to the best schools.

My dad said to me one day after school, "I love the neighborhood, but I'm sick of the police stopping me every day and asking me if I live here."

"Did they stop you today, Dad?"

"They pull me over almost every day."

When we moved in, we were only a few blocks from an all-white, well-known racist area of Chicago, near a popular mall called Evergreen Plaza on 95th and Evergreen. This was an area where blacks weren't welcomed at all. Black people that ventured into that area would experience being called racist names, or they would get bricks or other things thrown at them out of car windows, or even arrested on a trumped-up charge. After dark, it was much worse. But not long after my parents bought a home there, the neighborhood began to change, and more black families began to move in.

During those years, I always looked up to Tuggy. No matter what he did, I wanted to do it too. I remember how he taught me how to pop the head off of my baby doll's body! When the head would come off, we would both laugh hysterically. It just looked funny to us. When I wanted to play with his toys, I made a deal with him, "Tuggy, if you let me play with your toys, I'll let you pop the head of my dolls."

Sometimes when we were together, we would act like the two stooges, goofy and silly, cracking jokes and playing pranks on one another. Mom would laugh at us being silly, and often she would even play with us. I don't remember her talking to us like we were children, it was always as if she was our best friend, yet she still gave us the parental guidance we needed to go out and make it in the world.

She would always take time to explain things if we weren't clear or if something we didn't understand was going on in the world. Many times my mother and I would sit down and read the Bible together and study it. She told us jokes and took us to museums, concerts, and Lincoln Park Zoo. I know she loved me, but as the first born, I always thought she doted on Tuggy a little more than she did me. It was as if she was protecting him from things in the world, while encouraging me to be independent. It didn't bother me because I had the right 'get out there' spirit. She was creative, and she encouraged us to be creative as well and that helped with my growing interest in music.

Mom's mother "Gram" lived on 47th and Cottage Grove. Mom would take my brother and me to visit often. My great-grandparents lived on a farm in Michigan, and everyone affectionately called them "Mama" and "Poppa." We would visit them every year for summer vacation and had a lot of fun picking blueberries, going to church, and playing in the open fields. Poppa and I would watch Westerns on TV, and I enjoyed watching Mama while she cooked. We loved them dearly, out of all my family, there is one woman who will always have a special place in my heart, and there is no doubt that some of my creative instincts come from her. This was my paternal Grandmother, Ceola Glen.

A very dark-skinned woman, who in her early years worked traditional jobs at Curtis Candy, Loretta Hospital, and for the City of Chicago. Later in life, she found a way to make money by selling items like statues of baby Jesus, candles, and black angels. Grandma Ceola was married to a Spanish man named Nick Glen. Nick was a military man who served in the Army. He was away most of the time they were together. None of my aunts or uncles remembered a whole lot about Nick, except that he was there in the early years of their lives. One day Grandpa Nick and Grandma Ceola got into a fight, and after that, Nick never returned home.

Essentially a single parent who raised her children alone, Grandma Ceola lived in a housing project called Ida B. Wells. The projects at the time were a beautiful place to live, with everything being brand new and flowers planted in each of the courtyards. Ceola, with a firm hand, managed to handle raising all six kids with the help of her mother, Margaret Wilson. Margaret was from Homer, Louisiana, and she was one of the nicest individuals around.

During the time Ceola was raising all her kids in Chicago, it was segregated with a lot of racial undertones, more so than during my mother and father's time. Ceola always told her children she wanted them to do better than she did in life and get decent jobs. Dad shared with me a conversation he had with his mother, telling him that because his skin tone was a little lighter, he could get a better-paying job. She told him never to marry anyone with dark skin, so his children could have a better life. This was the mentality of many people like Grandma Ceola because growing up in the south, they watched darker- skinned black folks have a more difficult time getting ahead than lighter-skinned ones. This was certainly a historical stigma that came about because of the slave owners who segregated their slaves by making the darker-skinned ones work the more menial tasks like in the cotton fields. The lighter-skinned slaves, who were usually a child born of a union between a slave master and a slave were given special treatment.

Grandma Ceola simply wanted a better life for her children and grandchildren. At some point, she came along with her mother, and father to Chicago. Their minds were set on improving our family's lot. She was a voracious reader who taught herself how to speak Spanish and French. As a child, I remember the times she would speak French to me and make me count in French. Unknowing, the irony of where I would later live.

Grandma Ceola was one of the few women in the Ida B. Wells housing project who had an upright piano. As with the languages, she taught herself how to play without any lessons from anyone, and clearly, a lot of my musical roots come from her. As my mother played music throughout the house, I would pretend as if I was some of her favorite singers, such as Sam Cooke, Nat King Cole, Johnny Mathis, and many others.

Music had always been a part of my life to the extent that I would always imagine I was a member of a band. I was one of those kids that used to beat on items throughout the house, pretending that any piece of furniture in the house was my personal drum set. My mom loved clothes, so we had a lot of clothes hangers at home. At the bottom of a coat hanger was always a long, round stick-looking item used to hold pants in place. I would use these as my imaginary drumsticks, or I'd use my hands and pretend I was playing congas.

Tuggy would watch me and be amazed when a song came on the radio, and I was able to keep up with the drummer playing along with the song.

"How are you keeping up with that song?" he'd ask. I'd laugh and reply, "I can just feel the rhythm, Tuggy. I feel that rhythm."

Dad worked quite a bit as a conductor on Amtrak, so he was gone for long periods. Getting to spend time with him when he was home was always special, and I'd urge him to play *Ol Susanna* on the harmonica, entertaining Tuggy and me. I always wondered how he made the harmonica sound like it did, and he would give it to me to try. I could only get a few notes out, and none of them were correct, but things were going to change.

Around this time, when I was five, one of my mom's friends, Lucille, asked her to help her with a birthday party for one of her children. My mom helped host it, and there were balloons for a handful of kids from the neighborhood. Lucille was the girlfriend of Muddy Waters, and he was at the party giving out plastic toys. I got a plastic harmonica and was so excited about it. It was a smaller version of my dad's harmonica and came with a list of color-coded instructions on how to play it. One of the songs was "*Ol' Susanna*" and I couldn't wait to learn it so when dad came home, I would be able to show him.

I wanted to be as good as him so he would be proud, and I practiced so much that I was often out of wind. I could not put it down! I'd sit in the corner of the kitchen and practice for hours, before and after school and on the weekends. I don't know how my mom and Tuggy put up with it! Finally, Dad came home, and the moment he put the key in the door, I ran to get my harmonica.

"Dad! Dad! You're home! I got something to show you."

Mom came to the door to greet him, gave dad a kiss on the lips, and said, "Hey Baby, welcome home. I guess Marla has something to show you."

"Hey there, what's going on in here? Let me sit down first," Dad said and smiled as he took off his jacket.

He took a seat in the kitchen, and my mom stood in the doorway. I stood in front of them both; then, I put the toy harmonica to my lips as he and mom listened. As I began to play, a big smile came over their faces. Mom had heard me all the time, but Dad was so surprised I played the song to perfection. I didn't leave out one note. When I finished the song, they applauded, and I smiled. My mom turned to dad and said, "We have ourselves a young musician here. She's a natural and baby, we have to nurture her."

"That was amazing, Marla!" my dad said and gave me a big hug.

I learned how to play every song on the instruction sheet and was so happy I knew more songs than Dad. There were also times we played together and had such fun doing it that I began to think of myself as a young musician. I'd dream of performing on stage, but then, around the age of seven, I saw on television that one of my favorite bands, the Doors, got arrested. I didn't exactly understand why it happened, but at that point, I decided that if going to jail was a part of being a musician, then I didn't want any part of it!

I began thinking of other jobs that I wanted in life. My Uncle Johnnie was a police officer, and I thought it would be great that I'd become one too. I particularly liked that policemen wore really cool uniforms. But despite me making that decision at such an early age, I still enjoyed music. My mom kept telling my dad that I needed to learn another instrument, and she insisted he take me over to my Uncle Juan's place for guitar lessons. Uncle Juan was nicknamed Uncle Dell, but no one knows why.

I would hop into Dad's green Thunderbird and make our first stop at the local grocery store to grab a few snacks and beer. Uncle Dell always greeted us with a smile, and while he was my first music teacher, he never played professionally. Like his mother, he was self-taught, but he certainly knew more than I did. As my dad would begin barbecuing, Uncle Dell would give me instructions and then leave me to practice. He had a big Spanish guitar, and it was almost bigger than I was. In my first lesson, he had me wrap my arms around it and practice moving my fingers, showing me how to move them to make simple notes. He would give me a chord to play over and over again. I would be playing for hours while he and dad sat in the backyard, barbecuing and chatting over a few beers. Each time I'd go visit, Uncle Dell would show me something new, and I'd work on it until I got it right. He would say to my dad, "Marla is a natural."

Every weekend we went to Uncle Dell's, I learned a lot. I wanted to play more and more, and I asked Mom if I could get a guitar for Christmas. Mom was always quick-witted with a response, no matter what I would ask her, and she quickly said, "Are the dishes washed?"

"They will be."

Of course, I did the dishes promptly.

Christmas time came, and I could barely sleep on Christmas Eve. I kept wondering if I would get my own guitar. When morning came, I woke up to run downstairs and saw there was no guitar under the tree. I was happy about the toys I received but was really hoping I got my guitar. Then the doorbell rang, and my mother said, "Marla, get the door."

I went to answer it, and there was my dad holding a brown Spanish guitar encased in a cardboard guitar box. Dad said with a smile, "Merry Christmas, baby!"

*"Thanks, Dad!*

I was grinning from ear to ear as I grabbed my new guitar by the neck and ran around the house with it.

"Aw, man, this is so cool! I got a guitar! I got a guitar! Thank you, Dad!"

He nodded and replied, "Thank your mother, too."

I hugged them both, and I immediately began to play it. In the box was a sheet of paper describing the different guitar parts. A 45rpm record came with it, providing step-by-step instructions on how to play it. I sat in the living room, placed the 45 on the portable record player, and listened as the man explained how to play. I can still hear the voice that said, "Put your first finger on the first fret. Put your 2nd finger in the second fret on the second string ..."

I quickly learned to master that guitar from my lessons with Uncle Dell, listening to the record and practicing all the time. I took my guitar everywhere I went and played until my fingertips got sore and then went hard. The guitar didn't come with a strap on it, so I made one and tied one end of the string on the side of the guitar, then I tied the other end on the neck of the guitar. I'd carry it everywhere as if it was like a baby that was glued to my hip, and sometimes I even slept with it. I wanted to be cool and carry it over my shoulder like Elvis Presley did in some of his movies. I practiced and practiced, and eventually I created my first song, *Love across the Railroad Tracks*. It had a lot to do with a girl I liked at the time. I let my mother hear it, and she cried with joy.

# CHAPTER 3

# Not Like Other Girls

My first crush was on an older girl by the name of Carolyn, she was twenty-six, and I was fifteen, but I was around eight when I began to notice girls. I'm not sure anyone else at home knew about this, and Tuggy was always a little clueless about his surroundings and usually in his own world. I'm sure he just saw me as his little sister but knew I never liked to wear dresses. He was happy I wrestled with him and played my guitar. But I was becoming more aware I was not like the rest of the girls, and I first admitted it one day when Tuggy asked me if I liked a boy called Kevin who lived down the street.

I flat out told him, "No, Tuggy. I don't like boys; I like girls."

Tuggy was taken aback for a moment and didn't say a word, but from that day, we never even spoke about it. It didn't change our relationship at all, and he just accepted me for who I was becoming without any questions or concerns. There were still several incidents that showed my mom was in denial about my lack of femininity, but by the time I reached my teens, I absolutely knew, and I was okay with it, even when others weren't. I remember meeting this beautiful young girl named Kim and inviting her to hang out. She had flawless skin, light-colored eyes, and a definite feminine look. We had planned to hang out, so Kim came to the house. Mom answered the door and saw that Kim had on a T-Shirt with the words "I'm Gay" on the front.

"*Marla!*"

I had already entered the front room. Mom continued, "There's someone here to see you."

Mom was polite, but I caught her glancing at Kim's shirt when I came to greet them. She looked at me and said, "So, where are you going?"

"Downtown, just hanging out."

Mom looked at the both of us and said, "Okay. Well, have fun."

Just before Kim headed out the door, Mom turned to me.

"Marla, don't forget the new bra I bought you," she said.

My breasts weren't even developed to the size of quarters, so I was really mad about that and lashed out.

"Mom, why do I need to wear a bra when I don't even have any tits?"

I was so embarrassed, I ran to my room, but then I overheard Kim.

"Mrs. Glen, Marla's a stud; she doesn't need a bra. I doubt that she's going to wear it."

Kim left the house, and I heard the door shut as I was looking for the damn bra. Mom called, "Marla, I'm sorry! Go out and have a good time with your friend."

I came out of my room, and before I headed out the door, I stopped, looked at my mother, and said, "Thanks, Ma. I'll see you later."

When I got outside the house, Kim gave me a T-shirt that matched hers, and I immediately put it on. We smiled and headed towards the bus stop holding hands. I considered this the first real silent "up yours" to anyone who didn't like how I decided to live my life. I really liked Kim, and her family always accepted me; I was learning that my family just needed a little more time with their understanding of how God made me.

The conversation about me being gay continued to come up with Mom, especially during my teens. I think she thought I was just going through a phase. However, like most teenagers, I would constantly get phone calls and sometimes talk for hours at a time. All my phone calls would come in from girls my age. One time, the kitchen phone rang, and Mom answered it before I had a chance to. Mom called me down to the kitchen, where the phone hung on the wall,

"Marla, it's for you!"

I ran to the phone and grabbed it from Mom's hand.

"Thanks, Ma."

This time before she handed me the phone, she looked me in the eye and said, "Marla, every time I pick up the phone, it's for you, and it's usually some girl. So you really are gay?"

Without hesitation, I nonchalantly replied, "Yeah, Mom, now can you please give me the phone?"

Mom simply walked away, and when I got off the phone, Mom came back into the kitchen.

"Look, I understand that being gay is your choice ..." she said in a serious tone, and I thought I was in for a lecture.

Then she made an ugly face by squishing her nose upwards with her finger and twisting her mouth. Holding her face in this crazy contorted way, she then said, "Just do me a favor, don't bring any ugly girls home and say, 'Mom, this is my girlfriend.'"

We laughed so hard, and all I could say was, "Okay, Mom. I promise!"

Mom was trying to be cool, but I could tell she still wasn't exactly sold on me being a stud. With that in mind, I'm pretty sure I unintentionally pushed the limits when I came home one day and shared with her that the girl I had been dating had become pregnant. This was Carolyn.

"I'm gonna be a father," I told her.

"Oh my God, Marla! What in the world are you talking about?"

"Well, it's not my baby, but she's my girlfriend, and she doesn't want to have anything to do with the real father. So, I want to step in and be the father. Her dad wants me to be the father, too."

My mother raised her eyebrows, but she didn't say much.

"Mom, I know that I can take care of it. Just don't say 'no.'"

Mom said nothing; instead, she took a deep breath and shook her head.

Over the next few weeks, I was there for every doctor's appointment. I would help her with what she needed while her stomach was growing like crazy. One evening, she and I sat on the sofa, and her dad entered the room.

"You have been the most responsible of any of these other people Carolyn has been with. I'm glad you are here."

"I'm glad you said that. This is my baby right here."

As I sat right next to her rubbing her belly, talking to the baby inside her tummy, I began to develop strong feelings for this unborn child. I felt like I could take on this responsibility, even though my only job at the time was a few babysitting gigs and a paper route. I knew I had to step up to the plate because Carolyn was on drugs, and she told me the baby's father was on drugs as well.

Months later, she had the baby, and I felt so proud. She bought the baby home, and it was a beautiful girl she named April. I changed diapers, babysat, and did what I could after school to help take care of the baby. Mom even let me bring her over to the house a few times. However, I began to suspect things were becoming too much for Carolyn to handle. I knew something was wrong because she had been quiet for a few days. One afternoon, she came over with April and told me the news that her dad said she had to give the baby up for adoption. I was heartbroken. I loved them both.

My mom and Carolyn had a strong relationship, and I know they often talked without me being present. Mom had a bleeding heart for women in this sort of situation, and I later suspected they had talked about the baby and came to a decision without talking to me.

"For real? Are you going to?" I asked.

"Yes, I think it's best for the baby."

I was not happy, and my naive self replied, "Aw, man. I wish you didn't. I think we can make it work. I'll get another job."

Carolyn was not her usual perky self, and I could tell she didn't know what to do.

"Marla, it's not even your baby."

I grabbed her hand and replied, "But I feel like it is. I don't care if it's someone else's baby. I think we can make this work!"

"No. I'm going to do what my dad said. I'm giving the baby up for adoption."

We both looked at each other in silence. As a teenager, my hormones and emotions were all over the place, and it truly broke my heart. I was sure I was ready to be a dad, and now it wasn't going to happen. After Carolyn gave the baby up, we slowly drifted apart. I'm sure my mom was relieved and probably did a happy dance somewhere in the house when I wasn't looking. But she never said anything afterward. Instead, she was sympathetic and understanding. I later realized that I truly wasn't ready for a child, but in the moment I wanted to be. I truly loved them both.

# CHAPTER 4

# School Days

One of my earliest memories of school was being in kindergarten. I felt deep frustration reading along with the class as we studied the nursery rhyme, Jack and Jill. I went to Holy Angels Catholic School on the South Side of Chicago, and in class one day, my teacher Sister Cicely showed our class a picture of Jack and Jill. The picture revealed a boy and a girl going up a hill. The class looked at the picture as we read along with her, as she taught us the nursery rhyme.

"Jack and Jill went up the hill to fetch a pail of water, Jack fell down and broke his crown, and Jill came tumbling after."

When Ms. Cicely asked if anybody had any questions, I anxiously raised my hand and said, "Why isn't Jack's head broken in the picture?"

Sister Cicely replied, "Jack didn't break his head."

I told her, "Jill's head should be broken, too, because Jill came tumbling after."

"No, Marla, no one's head is broken in this picture."

The kids began to giggle at me as I tried to explain it further.

"Well, there is no crown, so they must be talking about their heads," I persisted.

By now, almost everyone was laughing, but I was very serious and could not understand why Sister Cicely didn't understand what I was saying. She became very annoyed with me as she pointed to the classroom door.

"Marla, you need to leave this classroom, clowning like this."

"Why do I have to leave when the picture is wrong?"

I didn't understand why I was in trouble, and she never answered my question. I had been taught many things by my mother before sitting in that classroom. I remembered that, as my mother and I sat to read the Bible together, she taught me that your head is your crown. I knew my mother was right, so why didn't the teacher who was paid to teach us understand that the crown can be your head? Jack and Jill didn't have any injuries in the picture, so the picture to me was inaccurate. Sister Cicely didn't know what she was talking about, and I was obviously a deeper thinker than she was, even though I was only five years old. She treated me as if I was a problem child, and this type of situation continued to happen to me quite a bit as I grew older.

In the Chicago Public School District, they would test 3rd graders to determine how they were academically developing. I took this test and passed it with a very high score. Afterwards, it was determined that I was intelligent enough to skip 4th grade, so they placed me in 5th grade, and ironically, I ended up in the same class as Tuggy.

He really hated I was in his class, but I loved it. And if that wasn't fun enough, one day in class, when our regular teacher was out, in walks Mom! My mother often filled in as a substitute teacher, and when she walked into the room, Tuggy and I were both shocked. She entered the classroom, and when Tuggy and I both looked up, she put her finger to her mouth before introducing herself to the class.

Mom had been a substitute teacher since we were in kindergarten; however, even outside of the classroom, she was a teacher at heart. We were instructed never to call her mom while in school; we were only to call her Mrs. Glen. Mom then treated us like the rest of the kids, and even when we got home, she made us do our homework and complete assignments no matter how long it took.

I was the type of child that many people would call a busy body. I talked a lot, asked many questions, had more energy than the average kid, and was always creative. When I was in middle school, I was placed in what was called a special education class. It was a classroom where kids were labeled dysfunctional and ranged from being blind, deaf, or in some ways slow learners. This class was put together for kids considered unfit for a regular classroom or labeled "retarded" before we called it special education. Some of the kids in this room were unable to talk because of birth defects, others were in wheelchairs, and some were savants. I had loads of energy, a little nerdy, and classified as hyperactive. The classroom had a window for administrators to peer in, to watch students play and interact. Being a part of this class, we were often teased, chastised, or talked about among other students in the school. I was in these classes during the sixth and seventh grade, and sometimes I would walk up to my teacher's desk, and they'd say, "Yes, Marla, did you need something?"

I'd look at them and ask, "Yes, I wanna know why do I have to be in this classroom? There is nothing wrong with me."

The teacher would just stare back at me, and not say a word.

I did really well in these classes because I felt if I could show I was smart enough, I would get out of the class, and they would put me into a normal classroom. Another part of being in that class were appointments with the school psychiatrist and doctors. These people would tell you how you were supposed to live your life. While sitting in one of the psychiatrist's offices, I remember her saying, "Don't you want to have children and a family in our community? You should try to excel to be independent."

"One day I will be, but I'd have to get out of this class first."

Being in this classroom technically labeled 'special', I felt it was anything but that, because the teachers made you feel stupid and not very special at all. My mother tried to convince the teachers and administrators that I didn't belong in these classes, but it didn't change anything. When that happened, I naturally got upset again.

"Mom, I know I'm not like those kids; some of them can barely talk. Why do they keep me in this class?"

"Marla, just be patient; it's going to change."

She then knelt and looked me in the eye.

"Baby, I just need you to buckle down, go along with what they say, and do the work given to you. You understand?"

My mother never lied to me. I had a lot of trust and faith in her because of that. She was also a teacher, so she understood the system and how it operated. She placed high values on learning and school in general and instilled in Tuggy and me many things that still stick with me today, like being kind to others, not being afraid of hard work, saying your prayers, and "say what you mean and mean what you say."

I could talk to my mother about anything, and no matter what I wanted to know, no question ever went unanswered. Mom wanted us to grow up to be freethinking individuals, and it was important for us to talk of whatever we were curious about. It's because of her patience with us, it made me feel free to explore my musical gifts.

Outside of what we learned in school, she also made us learn the names of all the states. She talked to us about world issues, but one of the most exciting things she taught us was how to ride the city trains, called the Chicago Transit Authority (CTA).

The CTA is one of the finest transportation systems in the world, and the trains take you from the north side to the south side of Chicago with ease. You get a view of the city, from the fancy streets of the north side, to behind the back streets of the ghettos, all throughout downtown. Mom took both Tuggy and me on our first train ride when I was about eight, and as we all went through the turnstile, it made me feel like a grown-up on a journey to who knows where.

As we watched the doors open and close at each of the station stops, I saw all different types of people get on and off the train. This was such an adventure, being on this train making its way through inner Chicago where there was always something to see. From downtown to the north side to the south side, and in between each stop was a different part of the city that had a life all its own. We saw back porches showing the backs of buildings, windows of old brick buildings, and vacant lots with weeds or just dirt. Downtown there were tall buildings, amazing architecture, great parks, and people everywhere. There was so much to see, and riding this train made me realize that the world was much bigger than my own backyard. One of the things I remember while traveling downtown was seeing men on the streets playing instruments for money; sometimes, it would be a saxophone or trumpet, but as they played on the sidewalk, people would toss money in their hats. I thought this was the coolest thing and imagined being out there with my harmonica or newly acquired guitar.

I was eleven when I began taking the train by myself. I'd go see friends in different parts of the city and took my guitar with me everywhere I went. I kept seeing people playing for money, and by the time I was 13, I felt confident enough to play some music on the streets of Chicago. I'd find a busy spot and begin to play and sing. I'd play all over the city, playing my own original songs, from downtown, to the North Side, South Side, Hyde Park, and South Shore.

I'd always wear a newsboy cap, which was rather big for my head. I'd place my cap on the ground and make a few dollars. As soon as I'd get two or three bucks, I'd sometimes use it for cigarettes or beer. It was just fun money for me. I remember being on the North Side, at a park near Lake Michigan. I liked playing on the weekends, early in the morning near the beach, in a park area just before the lake. There were always a lot of musicians playing together in the same spot.

One summer, I got to the park early, and while playing and singing my songs, a blonde lady wearing a yellow summer dress came up to me and listened for a bit. I never looked up at her face, but I could tell she was moving to the tune I was playing. At the end of my third song, she smiled, then handed me a five-dollar bill.

"Wow, that was really great. You're going to be somebody one day; you're really talented."

I put my head down and shyly said, "Aw, I'm not that good."

The woman quickly took the five-dollar bill out of my hand and began walking away. I was a bit shocked, but of course, there was nothing I could say or do, and I thought, "Well, I blew that."

She walked quite a distance before she turned around and came back. When she stopped this time, she looked me in the eye as she handed me the money again.

"I'm going to give you this five-dollar bill, but the next time someone pays you a compliment, you should simply say thank you."

"Yes, Ma'am," I quickly replied.

I took the money, and she walked away. Ever since that day, whenever someone would give me a compliment, I just did what she said.

# CHAPTER 5

# Troubles at Home

After getting my guitar, I acquired congas and proper harmonicas, and like others in the family, I taught myself by listening to the radio and copying what I heard. Alternating instruments, I would emulate tunes from the radio my mother listened to, such as music by Elton John, Neil Young, The Doobie Brothers, Earth Wind and Fire, Led Zeppelin, The Rolling Stones, and The Moody Blues.

Listening to music made me yearn to write my own songs and play around with lyrics. I would spend hours writing music on the guitar and practicing the songs I developed; my room was such a great place for me to be creative. I had an Indian head statue that I called George on my dresser and fifty hats on the wall from different places I'd visited. I loved wearing hats wherever I went. My mom let me stay in there for hours, and words and chord arrangements would pop into my head, and I would write them down.

By now, I had about fifteen to twenty songs all written while I was in my room, but one of the first was *Repertoire*. This was written back when I was about eleven, inspired by what I saw going on in the news. This was 1971, and there was a lot of discussion about the Vietnam War, and it was reported that sixty percent of Americans were against it. Being young, I was completely confused about how people not that much older than me were going to war to fight for things they had nothing to do with. I kept asking my parents questions and even looked for answers in the Bible to better understand it all. Writing this song offered me an outlet at the time, and I always hoped the masses would someday hear it. It was eventually released on my 1995 album, *Love and Respect*.

### <u>Repertoire</u>
You're living your life of pleasure by
living in this world
Everything seems to turn out wrong
because it is no pearl
They say they'll do this, and they will
They'll say they'll do that but
come on people
Let me tell you
where it's at
I'm going to write myself a repertoire
'cause I'm tired of being caught up
in the middle of a war 'cause
I'm going to tell you all
what you've been waiting to hear
'cause no better time than now
Let me show you where it's at.

Music was consuming my mind, and while I didn't have an issue with learning, there were times my focus was a bit off at school because of it. While in grammar school at Wendell E. Green, I would always be thinking of lyrics while in class. My teachers often caught me daydreaming or writing.

"Marla, what are you doing?" a teacher would say, and I'd look up from writing lyrics.

"Oh, I'm just writing."

"But the assignment isn't about writing anything right now."

Knowing I could get in trouble, I'd politely ask if I could just finish what I was doing. I was told to focus on the lesson, but there were so many things I wanted to write about. New lyrics came to my mind every day, and writing helped me a lot because oftentimes I felt misunderstood, and music felt like the best outlet by which I could explain things that happened to me, around me, and worldwide.

Thinking about music wasn't the only problem, and my being exuberant and hyperactive sometimes led to me getting into trouble. One time, my mom had to come up to the school for a meeting with the principal and two of my other teachers. My mother had to take time off from work, and they didn't give her any specifics why she had to come out to school on my behalf. On the way to the meeting, my mother told me not to say a word. Mom sat in silence and listened to each teacher relate a different complaint. They told my mother, I often didn't pay attention in class, staring into space, and I was disruptive. My mother took a moment, and before she said anything, she looked at each of them in turn.

"I can tell you one hundred things my child does well at home. There is nothing wrong with my child. Marla helps me around the house, does homework, and my child is never disobedient, so stop judging based on your standards. Mr. Davidson, when I walked in here, your toupee was cocked to the side. Ms. Thornton, I smell alcohol on your breath, and Mr. Paxton, your eyes are red, which means you probably smoke weed, and trust me, I know what that looks like. Sounds like you have your own issues to deal with, so leave my child alone and stop asking me to come up here for this nonsense."

It was during high school that things began to fall apart at home when my parents began having issues in their marriage. My mom did her best to keep up a good front, but it was clear that she was becoming increasingly unhappy. My dad was gone a lot, and music offered an escape, taking my mind off wondering what the future might bring. I wanted them both to be happy but hoped it would be together.

Instead, they began to argue more, and my dad was gone so much it became apparent he wasn't coming back. Mom had two jobs, working at Merrill Lynch and a part-time job at Western Union, so she had a conversation with me and my brother. She sat us down in the kitchen one day when she got home from work,

"Look, I got a note from your dad saying he's not coming back. So, I need you guys to help out a little more around here. Marla, make sure the dishes are washed and pick up around here as much as you can. Tuggy, you're now the man of the house, and I need you to make sure the trash goes out of here when it's full. But don't take me and your dad's problems out in the world with you. We will be fine. You live your life."

But that still didn't help me feel better. I hated that my parents were going through a separation, but I also understood that these were adults' problems. Mom made good money, so even with dad gone, we did okay. Still a good-looking woman, she would also occasionally model for Evans Furs, a popular department store in Chicago. She also rented a small storefront in the South Shore area to paint portraits. Mom was full of creative ideas to make money, but despite all she did, I felt the need to help out. I began doing odd jobs like hanging out at the grocery store, helping people to the car with their bags, or babysitting, and I had a paper route to deliver papers around the neighborhood. I'd always give the money to Mom to help out with bills.

No matter what my parents were going through, Mom always remained positive, and it wasn't too long before she began dating a man called Thomas. He was tall, goofy looking, with a big forehead and big bulging eyes. He had a bit of a deep voice, and sometimes he stuttered a little. I thought he looked like big bird from Sesame Street, and Tuggy and I both felt he wasn't smart enough for mom. He would say big words but use them incorrectly. Mom was far too good for him, but he seemed to make her happy.

After a few months of Mom dating this dude, it was clear he walked around and pretended to be intelligent. Neither Tuggy nor I liked him, and one day it really hit home, how weird he was.

"What kind of music do you pacifically listen to? he asked me one time.

I just looked at him and said you mean, "Specifically?"

"I never heard of that band."

I laughed, and Thomas then said, "What's so funny? Don't laugh at me because I don't know that band."

I wasn't sure if I could take him seriously, but he came over one day before my mom came home from work and tried to tell Tuggy and me he and Mom were going to have a baby. We laughed because we knew she'd had an operation and had told us she'd never get pregnant again. He was around longer than Tuggy and I expected him to be, and sometimes he was at our house when Mom wasn't. One afternoon, I came home from school, and like most teenagers, I'd play loud music while doing household chores, and it was something I'd also do often to relax. Our main stereo player was in the living room, and I was playing Led Zeppelin while doing the dishes. There are simply some groups that are meant to be blasted loud, but Thomas turned the volume down.

"I don't like you listening to this music," Thomas shouted.

"You can't tell me what music to listen to," I snapped as I turned it back up again. How in the hell could he not like Led Zeppelin?

He turned it down again and said, "I said, I don't like it. It sounds like devil music."

I turned it up and stood in front of the record player.

"Leave it alone, Thomas!" I don't care what it sounds like to you, and this ain't even your house.

"I don't care! You need to be respectful."

He managed to push me aside and turned the music back down. His eyes got big, and he put his finger in my face.

"If you touch that dial again, I'll cut you up into bits and pieces and put you in the basement."

I stormed into my room, opened my closet, and started tossing stuff in my backpack. I was mad as hell. Within minutes, I left the house and didn't look back. It was getting dark, and I was still pissed. I was mad at Mom for dating Thomas, mad at Dad for being gone, and mad at Thomas because he was too stupid to understand that music was my escape. I wandered around the streets for hours and found myself in an unfamiliar neighborhood. I was not fourteen yet, but for some reason, I wasn't scared. I ended up being picked up by the police, and once I got home, I had to face Mom.

"Marla, what the hell happened? Why did you leave?"

"Thomas gets on my nerves, Mom. He didn't want me to play my music and threatened to cut me up and put me in the basement."

Her mouth opened in shock.

"Marla, you should've called me to tell me this. You don't just leave. I don't ever want you to think you can't talk to me, you understand me?"

I nodded, and within a month, Mom and Thomas broke up.

# CHAPTER 6

# A Drifter is Born

In my freshman year at Morgan Park High School, I joined the band. I didn't love everything about it but being able to play music while attending school was still cool. The instrument my music teacher assigned to me was the clarinet; I was excited about learning how to play it. We were also being taught how to read music, and that made it even more exciting. The band met a couple of times a week after school, and I couldn't wait to perform at one of the games until they gave out the uniforms. It was a dress. Immediately I knew performing was out of the question. Instead, I only attended rehearsals and made excuses when it came time to perform.

When it was warm out, if we got an early start, Tuggy and I could walk the few miles it took to get to school; otherwise, we took public transportation. It was only a few miles from where Mom and Dad had bought our first house, and we were one of the few black families to live on our block. Our neighborhood was predominantly white, and so was Morgan Park High School, so there was a racial undertone at the school. Black students were moving into the community, and a few were bussed in, but we were still very much a minority.

However, the tensions this caused didn't bother Tuggy and me because of how we were raised, taught that no matter what color you were, what mattered the most was how you were being treated or how you treated people. With this in mind, I was my own person. I dressed differently, often wearing hats, sometimes coveralls, boots, hooded capes but never anything too fancy. I was oftentimes silly but serious when I needed to be. Because of this, I made friends easily, and had friends from all different races, walks of life, and cultural backgrounds. I was easy-going and didn't look for trouble.

Students of the same race would hang out together, but I had both black and white friends. This made things awkward at times when my black friends would see me hanging out with white students; they felt it was a sign of betrayal. They would ask if I was a honky lover and tell me, "Them white folks don't care nothing about you; stop hanging out with them."

It was equally as awkward hanging out with my white friends, I would be sitting with them at lunch, and they would say things like I wasn't like them other niggers. Sometimes, it would be after they said derogatory things about the black kids that they'd realize I was among them. I didn't know what to say, it was awkward, and I felt torn between the two races.

Of course, racial issues weren't the only things I had to navigate. I looked like a boy, so my identity was oftentimes an object of ridicule. I kept my hair in a short afro, always wore slacks, never wore makeup, and none of my clothes were girly. For gym class, I would wear boy shorts and T-shirts instead of the regular one-piece short jumper that girls wore. I would hear people whisper behind my back or say mean things when I went into the girls' locker room while preparing for gym class. Many of the girls would question me, asking if I was supposed to be in there. I'd overhear them whispering that the lesbian made them uncomfortable, and I'd tell them I wasn't a lesbian but a stud. Or sometimes, I'd just smile and say, "You look good; you should give me your phone number!"

Before they could answer, I'd walk off real cool with a smile on my face. Humor was always a way to get people to lighten up. I didn't care that people were confused about my identity; I was comfortable being myself no matter what people said. What did make me uncomfortable was being bullied.

All throughout high school, there was this one boy who constantly bullied me. His name was Billy, and he was a medium height curly-haired white boy who did his best to make my life a living hell. He would tease me, chastise me, and provoke me every time he got a chance. When walking through the hallway, he would either give me menacing looks or try to trip me while I wasn't looking. He would stand in front of my locker and make it difficult for me to get into it. One time he threw snowballs at me with rocks in them, and all I could do was yell at him to stop.

No matter what I did or said, things worsened until I began going to the principal's office to report every incident I had with him. Every time he pushed me, tried to trip me, or said something harassing, I reported it. I was in the principal's office almost daily, but nothing was done. Around the middle of my senior year, I decided I wanted to put this problem to rest—I would extend an olive branch to Billy, thinking somehow we could be friends.

It was a day that students were required to turn in books, and as I was on the way to my locker. I saw Billy standing there with two friends. I took a breath and got up enough courage to approach him.

"Look, I don't know if I did something to you, but if I did, I apologize. I just want to drop this whole thing 'cause it's almost graduation time. Let's shake hands and just be friends."

I then reached out my hand to shake on it. Within seconds, Billy the bully got up in my face.

"Look at this fucking Nigger Bitch! Stop biting out of my ass!"

His friends stood for a moment laughing at me, and then they all walked away, heading to class.

Humiliated, I turned to my locker, feeling my frustration building as I got a few books, then headed back where Billy went. By now, he had walked to the stairwell, and without hesitation, I crept up on him and whacked him on his head, causing him to fall down the stairs. He got up, looked around, and began chasing me, and I kept running until I got to the principal's office. By the time Billy reached me, I had told the people in the office what happened. When Billy reached the office, and because we both caused such a ruckus, they called the police.

Even with the police and school officials present, while they were looking over all the reports I'd made, he kept taunting me, mouthing racial epithets. They instructed Billy to stop, but he kept doing it. I was fed up that all the authorities were doing was discussing things, so I got up and socked the bully square on the nose. Billy squealed, and blood went everywhere as they rushed to help him. I quickly left the office and didn't stop until I got to my locker. I took my clarinet and left the building. It was the one thing I didn't want to leave behind, convinced I would be banned from returning.

Shortly after the incident, my mom was notified that I was no longer allowed back in the school. My teachers arranged for me to study at home, and my mom was happy they still made it possible to get the work done. She had known I was bullied, and she never told me how to deal with it, but she told me what options I had. She wanted me to begin making my own decisions because I was getting old enough to do so.

When the police investigation was over, the bullying incident landed in court, and my mother and I stood before a judge, where I had to explain what had been happening to me. The judge looked over a stack of paperwork in front of him and then lifted his head.

"Looks like Billy has been involved in similar incidents, and if you press charges against this boy, he will be in some serious trouble. Marla do you want to press charges?"

The school year was practically over, and I wasn't going to get my time back. What was done was done. I looked up at the judge and said, "No, Your Honor. I'll just let it go."

For some reason, I didn't want to be responsible for him going to jail. Billy looked shocked, and his mother came over to hug me. She said she was sorry for what he put me through and thanked me for not pressing charges.

The later part of the school year I spent at home, my mom had started a romance with a man named Calvin. Mom told me they met at an art exhibit, where she won the highest prize for her drawings. Mom was a really good artist. Calvin took second place, and they struck up a conversation. Mom was soon incredibly happy when he completely swept her off of her feet.

Other than being an artist, Calvin was a tall, attractive bus driver who lived in the South Shore area of Chicago. While Mom loved Calvin, and he was much better than Thomas, neither I nor Tuggy really got along with him, mainly because Calvin wasn't comfortable with Tuggy or me living at the house. He felt we were old enough to be on our own. Tuggy and I did our best to adjust to Calvin being in the house because we wanted to see Mom happy, but we both had disagreements with him.

I had a decidedly independent spirit and was coming and going from the house unsupervised by now, so it affected me less than it did Tuggy. I wasn't quite 18 yet, but I was close enough that Mom convinced Calvin to let me move into his studio apartment because he was hardly there. I was very excited at the prospect of my first taste of living independently and determined to be responsible about having my own place.

Including my brother and a few friends, I only had the occasional visitor in my cool little bachelor's pad. I didn't want to bring too much attention to me living there, as it was a very prestigious area. Located on South Shore Drive, it was in a tall building, and the apartment had a bit of a view of the city. Natalie Cole and The Staple Singers resided in the area along with several other musicians and blues artists. Sometimes I'd step back into being a child and do silly things like ring Natalie Cole's bell and run after hearing her voice answering from the intercom!

I still had my paper route, so oftentimes my day began at 3 am. Although I was gone from my mother's house, I was still under her supervision. I hadn't graduated yet, so I was still doing schoolwork. I would visit friends in my spare time, but I also started going to the North Side of Chicago to perform at some open mic nights.

When I left the apartment, I'd often come back to find that Mom had been and cleaned up the place, leaving care packages full of toiletry items or food. I wanted to be independent, so this was frustrating, but I didn't say anything about it. I was responsible for paying $600 a month for the apartment, so along with the paper route, I worked a few other odd jobs, like bagging groceries or helping people move to keep money in my pocket.

I still wanted to become a police officer, but as I began to explore all the North side clubs, places like, Kingston Mines, Biddy Mulligan's, and Wise Fools, music was becoming important. I had started to sing, but I was doing it for fun and didn't take it seriously until one evening I invited Tuggy to a club called *That's Life*. When we got to the door, there was a guy you had to talk to about getting stage time.

"I'd like to get a spot to go on," I asked.

The guy had a smirk on his face and said, "Okay, I need to see if you can sing. Can you do Michael Jackson's, *I'll be there?*"

Tuggy watched and didn't say anything. I knew the song, but I didn't know the words. I tried anyway, and the tune came out, but I just couldn't pull it off. I had been focusing on my own songs. The guy tried to make jokes about it, and Tuggy and I walked away from the club. Once we were a few yards down the street, Tuggy stopped me.

"Marla, that guy was trying to insult you."

I shook my head and told him, "I don't want to look at it in a negative light. Just because I wasn't his cup of tea doesn't mean I won't be someone else's. I'll go somewhere else to sing my own songs."

"Oh, okay, that's a good way to look at it," he replied, and from that moment, I was serious about singing.

There were several open mics throughout the city I would frequent, but there was one place I particularly enjoyed called Jewtown. Originally it was labeled Jewtown because several Jews owned businesses in the area, but years later, they renamed it Maxwell Street to be politically correct. I'd been going there for several years.

As a family outing, my mom and dad would take Tuggy and me to Jewtown, and we would have some of the best Polish sausages I have ever had in my life. They grilled them with onions, and you could smell them a mile away. It was a vibrant place with all types of people, gritty with culture, and full of flavorful food and music. There were several blocks of vendors selling every item you could think of, and hundreds of people would crowd the area to eat and haggle about prices when looking for deals and bargains.

Jewtown was a breeding ground for many jazz and blues musicians, who would play on makeshift stages. The music could be heard from several blocks away, and I had fallen in love with going there in my mid-teens. There were times I went without my family, and I would hang out and watch bands play all day. Sometimes, I'd take my clarinet and harmonica, and I'd play along as I watched. I still had a small-framed body with wiry arms and legs. I wore an apple hat pulled down partially over my eyes, and when I played, rarely did I talk to people. I would also hide behind the speaker and play along, trying not to draw attention to myself.

One day while hiding behind one of the speakers playing my harmonica, one of the musicians took notice and asked me to join in with them! I was a bit shy about it, but I gladly went up and began to play along with the older guys who had been clearly playing their instruments for years. I didn't join in with the harmonica, I played with my clarinet, and it felt good to be there.

After going to Jewtown regularly, I ultimately gained the respect of the elder musicians in many bands. One guy that grew exceptionally fond of me was a blind steel guitar player named Arvella Grey. He was an excellent musician, and to collect his many tips, he would use a safety pin to attach a plastic cup to his shirt. In exchange for music lessons, I did odd jobs for him, like running errands, making phone calls, or washing dishes. He was like a grandfather figure who I always listened to when it came to wisdom and music, and he treated me like a son. Arvella gave me a lot of pointers on playing the guitar and prepared me for working at open mics.

One of the things he helped me with most was playing the blues. I had been spending a lot of time with my Caucasian friends, who listened to a lot of honky-tonk music, and I felt I needed to learn more and understand more about the blues. Arvella would take me to a different part of Jewtown, and we would stand on a corner. As he played guitar, I played my clarinet or harmonica, and we complemented each other as people would gather around, watching us and dropping money in his cup.

After sharing a few corner sessions with him, Arvella asked me,

"Hey, listen, the money here is good, but we need a fresh new group of ears. Why don't you and I travel to Detroit?"

"I can do that. When do we go?"

My time was my own, and most of my work for school was done. I could use the extra money, and I told my boss at the newspaper stand I needed a few days off. We took the Amtrak, got separate rooms at a small hotel, and traveled to several areas of Detroit playing on street corners throughout the city. Arvella was a meek, yet wise, musician, and because he wasn't able to see, his other senses were stellar. We would draw crowds that would toss 10's, 20's, and even $100 dollar bills in the blind man's cup, and sometimes we would place a hat on the ground. I would stand and play along, watching as people tossed money all day. One day after a street session, we went to our nearby hotel rooms and made plans to get up early the next morning. Before I left his room, I took a one-hundred-dollar bill out of a huge stack Arvella had on the dresser, went to my room, and went to sleep.

The next morning when I went to Arvella's room, he was counting the money. I never realized how good he was at doing that until that moment, touching the corners of each bill and placing them carefully in one stack. While I stood watching him, he said, "There's money missing here."

"Really? Missing?"

How did he know? He counted the money again as I stood, speechless.

"There was a hundred-dollar bill in here."

I sighed, and I'm sure he heard it. He tilted his head and listened as I stood still.

"Marla, did you take it?"

A blind man busted me, and there was no way I could deny it.

"I did, but I was going to give it back."

"Hand it to me," he said.

I reached in my pocket and gave him the money back.

Embarrassed, I quickly said, "I'll meet you outside."

I worked harder after that incident, trying to gain back his confidence in me. Living with what I did was much more difficult, but he seemed to forgive me because he didn't mention it afterwards and continued to treat me with kindness. Our friendship continued, and he truly inspired me to play better and keep things honest. As life and gigs came and went, we eventually drifted apart. However, this sparked a sense of adventure in me, gave me the confidence to travel while playing music, and gave me my first taste of being a drifter. Years later, my first album had a track called *Travel*, inspired by my time with Arvella.

# CHAPTER 7

# Finding Independence

Even though I completed my studies outside the classroom, Morgan Park High allowed me to walk with my graduation class, and I received my diploma. Not long after that, I really got annoyed with Mom coming into my apartment; it wasn't like being on my own. I left the apartment and stayed on friends' couches, slept on a park bench or two, and many times I just stayed up all night wandering about the city trying to figure things out. I began drifting, usually on the north side of Chicago, because I needed money so I could get my own place. My paper route wasn't enough, so I needed to look for jobs. I thought about going back home, but Mom and Calvin seemed so happy together that I didn't want to disturb them, and Tuggy was now doing his own thing. I had no idea where my dad was, so I felt I was old enough to be able to make it on my own.

I did everything I could to make sure I didn't bother anybody, so instead of going home, I decided to go to Pacific Garden Mission. It was a homeless shelter that provided a warm bed, warm meals, and the Word of God. I was greeted by a missionary who told me the rules.

"It's important you make up your bed, make use of our showers, go to Mass, and there should be no profanity or disrupting anyone's peace; also make sure you keep your area clean."

Those were pretty much the same rules I had at home, so this was easy. I nodded in agreement and told him, "No problem."

I got settled in and felt safe there. I especially enjoyed that there was a church on the premises. The shelter was full of people down on their luck. Some of them were drug users, alcohol abusers, or people like me in transition. While at the shelter, when I wasn't out looking for a job, I would study the Bible or play my harmonica or guitar. One afternoon, one of the missionaries approached me and asked, "Do you have a job?"

"No, but I'm looking."

He sat me down in the office and helped me with the paperwork for Government Assistance, and shortly thereafter, I began receiving food stamps and a small amount of money. I wasn't there very long before someone stole my watch that I had taken off at night, and that made me move a little quicker about improving my situation. I worked a few odd jobs and finally found a position working at McDonald's. I saved enough money to leave the mission and found an efficiency apartment. It was a former hotel that had been repurposed as small one-room apartments with no kitchen. I liked the location because it wasn't far from the open mic night places and a few of the gay clubs. When I wasn't working at McDonald's, I would go to some bars with free food for happy hour.

No matter where I went, I was never without my harmonica or guitar. My circle of friends were artists or musicians of all different races and backgrounds. Making friends with people of different ethnicities was never an issue. My friends were as mixed as the crowds I played for. The blues and jazz clubs of Chicago had great crowds, and it was a perfect training ground for new musicians. I only played my harmonica at the open mic nights in the blues clubs and my guitar at the jazz ones. There were also occasions where I would jam with friends in their apartments or parents' basements or on the street. We played all kinds of music, from Country to Bluegrass to Honky-Tonk.

I enjoyed being on my own, no matter how challenging it sometimes got. I always remained positive, and I knew God would make a way. When I missed my family, I would occasionally go visit Mom, and each time I went, it was clear that Calvin did not really want my brother or me to stay at the house. I began to stay away longer and longer but when I walked into the house, Calvin would immediately question how long I intended to stay. I would just laugh it off and ignore him the best I could.

After being away for several months, I saw my Auntie Thelma and I told her where I was staying and gave her the main phone number where the manager would answer. When I got back the following evening, I got a message from the apartment manager that my mother had called, and I rang her back.

"Marla, where have you been? I've been worried."

I could hear the stress in her voice.

"I'm okay Mom, just living my life. How is everything with you and Calvin?

"Well, I'm fine. But I have not heard from you. I want to come and see you."

"Mom, I'm okay!"

"I know, but I need to see for myself. Give me the address."

Within a few days, my mother was standing in the middle of my tiny room, hugging me close for dear life. She took a seat, and we began to chat.

"So, you're good?"

I looked her in her eyes and said, "Yeah, I don't know why you think I wouldn't be."

"Well, I am your mother, so I'm gonna ask these things."

Mom then reached down in her purse, pulled out a joint, and handed it to me.

"I got you some weed."

"Thanks, Ma. I was running low."

I began looking for a match, and Mom continued to watch me as I lit it.

"So, are you doing anything else? Coke? Pills? What about—"

Before she finished, I jumped in.

"No, Mom, just weed. I might have a few beers, but that's about it. I remember what you told me. I'm not doing anything hard, and I'm never gonna do anything like heroin or anything hard like that. I promise you that."

My mother's shoulders relaxed as if the weight of the world had lifted from her. I'm not sure what Thelma told her, but after that talk, she seemed to lighten up. She told me more about Calvin, and I told her how happy I was that she found love. We discussed my job at McDonald's and how I was looking for more work. We talked about Tuggy and laughed about some childhood memories. Not too long into the conversation, she got up and opened my closet, and her mouth dropped.

"Marla, what are all these men's clothes doing in here? Are you wearing these?"

I was surprised by the question.

"Mom, I'm a stud. What do you think I should wear?"

She was speechless, and so was I, unsure why she asked. We'd had this conversation about me being gay, and I needed to make the conversation lighter.

"Mom, I know the clothes aren't that fancy, but my friends Ham and Trent are showing me how to dress better."

"So, you don't want to wear anything other than these?"

It was apparent that my mother had not quite come to grips that I was a stud.

I just looked away and said, "No Mom. I'm not."

She sighed, took a seat, and we continued to chat. She seemed more relaxed and began 'mothering' me.

"You eating okay?" You need me to fix that pocket that's coming off on your jacket? Let me know if you need anything, okay?

"Mom, I'm fine."

"Well, I just need you to keep in touch with me more often, okay?

"Of course, Mom."

It was the only way I could answer, but it was good to see her, and we parted with a warm hug, both understanding my need for independence was strong. I wasn't her baby girl anymore.

It wasn't long afterward that I met Rhonda, an amazingly beautiful black woman who was slender and had such an amazing smile that it could melt the heart of the world. She was a sexy, articulate, smart older woman who worked as an operating room nurse at a Chicago Hospital. We hit it off immediately and began to see each other every single day, and I would often visit her at her apartment on Michigan and Broadway. I was nineteen years old and over the moon in love the moment I set eyes on her. She was so damn sexy that I never wanted to leave her side. She was about eight years older than me, but the age gap didn't seem to matter. Rhonda was mature in every way, and because her job was so mentally exhausting, I believe she welcomed the silliness of my youth and personality and the laughter we shared.

However, no matter how silly I was, I was extremely thoughtful when it came to our relationship. We talked about everything, from how we grew up, our families, hopes, and dreams, and I always told her I loved her. When she shared all the stressful things going on at her job, I simply wanted to take her problems away so she could relax. We spent a lot of time together, and after a year or so, and because I was there so much, we both agreed that I should move in with her, and I did. With each passing day, I fell deeper and deeper in love with her, and there was no doubt that she was in love with me.

If a patient died on the table, especially if it was a child, she would always be deeply affected and come home depressed or oftentimes crying. So, no matter what I was doing, I would always try to be there when she arrived, to cook her a good meal, buy her ice cream, rub her feet, or simply talk her through the ordeal. I simply loved just being there for her. We felt very connected to one another, and as a result, our sex life was amazing!

During this time, I juggled several jobs. I'd get up at 3:00 am and hop on my motorbike to work my newspaper route, then I'd come home, change clothes to work at McDonald's, and afterward, I would go to work as a security officer. Sometimes I would also pick up an odd job here or there by working at a local hotdog stand or asking store merchants if they wanted their windows washed or the front of their store swept. I was hustling to keep money in my pocket, and as long as the job was legal, I'd take it.

When Rhonda was at work and I had evenings free, I would hang out with my best friend, Ham, at some of the local gay bars on Broadway Blvd, in an area of Chicago they called Boys Town. My buddy Ham would participate in pantomime contests, and I would do some of the local open mic nights.

I learned a lot about how to treat a woman while living with Rhonda. After some time, she eventually introduced me to her mother, who was also a nurse and overly protective of Rhonda. Rhonda's mother usually had something to say about whom Rhonda was dating. Despite me being very respectful to Rhonda's mom, it was clear that she did not like me at all. I couldn't understand this until one day Rhonda told me why.

"Marla, it has nothing to do with you. No matter how you treat her, she is not going to like you."

"But, why? I didn't do anything to her."

"My mother always had hopes of me marrying a wealthy man, preferably a doctor. Dating someone like you is just not in her plan."

Realizing it was a losing battle, I got overwhelmed.

"Well, I'm not planning on going anywhere, so I hope she gets over it."

Rhonda briefly looked at me, leaned over, and gently kissed me on the lips. It made me feel as if everything was going to be fine, and I wanted to love her even more for it.

There was no question that Rhonda made significantly more money than I did, and she had a taste for expensive things. Some of the things she loved were going to fancy restaurants, receiving expensive gifts, and Victorian Styled Furniture. I saved every bit of the money I had to get her whatever she wanted. I wanted to shower her with whatever she wanted, whenever I could. This woman was perfect for me.

Aside from being beautiful and accomplished, she also had a photographic memory. Rhonda could remember anything and everything she ever laid her eyes on. It was impressive and cool. One night, we were walking the streets of Chicago's north side, and Rhonda got a glimpse of a man walking down the street opposite us. She pointed and said, "Marla, I think that guy is your dad."

I looked, and while the man resembled him, I really couldn't tell. I shook my head and said, "I don't think that's him. Why would he even be down here?"

"Well, he looks like the picture you showed me."

"I don't know, but we should get a closer look."

My dad has this swagger about the way he moves, and my brother and I have a very similar walk. We watched him for a few moments, and he did walk like my dad a bit, but I was still unsure. He turned into one of the bars, and we followed him.

As we crossed the street, we could see from the window that he took a seat at the bar. He then sat at the bar and began laughing and talking to a bartender. It had been eight years since I saw my dad, and I was extremely hesitant to approach this man that looked like him.

We entered the bar, and Rhonda said, "Go over there and say something."

I squinted and watched him for a bit, and then I got enough courage to get closer.

"Dad?"

The man kept talking, and I got closer and said it a little louder, "Dad, is that you?"

He turned around, and it was indeed my father; it took a second or two, and he said, "Oh my God, hey baby!"

He opened his arms, and we shared a long hug before I introduced him to Rhonda. We had a few drinks together, and the reconnection with my dad was just what I needed; I was so happy to see him. Over the next few months, I would make frequent visits to his place, and we chatted and got caught up on each other's lives. It didn't matter why he left; I was simply happy he was back in my life.

On my 21st birthday in 1981, Dad came over to our apartment, and he was grinning from ear to ear as he handed me one of my favorite desserts, a small cheesecake, and he placed a large number one candle on top of it.

"Happy Birthday, Baby!" he said,

It was such a special moment to even have him around on my birthday after being estranged for so long, but then he asked me to go into the kitchen and grab him a beer. I was reluctant, comfortably eating cheesecake.

"Dad, it's my birthday, and I have to go get you a beer?"

"Do as you are told."

I got up shaking my head, and when I entered the kitchen, I saw a huge bouquet of balloons on the balcony and attached to them were twenty-one individually wrapped birthday presents. That night, Rhonda, Dad, and I had a great time.

Over time, it was clear Rhonda's mother was becoming more unhappy with our relationship. She had become even more disrespectful and would say nasty things about our relationship or me. Her mother would often catch me alone, and say things like, "You can't do nothing for her, why don't you leave her alone?" Or, "If you don't leave her alone, I'll find a way to make you do it."

Things got out of hand one night when four Chicago Police Officers came to our door.

"Are you Marla?" one of them asked when I opened the door.

"Why, what do you want?"

One of the police officers grabbed me and pulled me out of the apartment. I was fighting them, not understanding why they were harassing me. The four policemen stood in the stairwell, and I pushed one of them; the rest fell like a domino effect. After they regained their composure, they grabbed me, took me down the stairs, carried me out the door, and placed me in the back of a police squad car. They then began to ask me very personal questions.

"How do you have sex with Rhonda?"

I was angry and shouted, "That's none of your damn business."

"You know she doesn't really love you."

I got upset and told him, "How you know, you don't know shit."

They then threatened me.

"If you don't leave her alone, we are going to find a way to lock your ass up."

"You're mad 'cause I'm giving her what you can't? Do what the fuck you gotta do, then."

After that, the police drove me to the police station and locked me up on false charges.

I began to realize that this was some sort of plan staged by Rhonda's mother so I would break up with Rhonda. I was heartbroken, but I didn't want to go through such hassles to love a woman. After I was released from jail, I split the time between my mom's place and dad's because I really needed to talk while dealing with the heartbreak of it all.

I could not get over what had happened and wanted to make amends with Rhonda, but I was pretty sure I was no match for her mother. After three years together, I broke up with Rhonda completely, and it was one of the most painful heartbreaks I had ever experienced. After a couple of months, Rhonda came to see me at my dad's; she shared with me how she felt.

"Marla, I'm so sorry. Mom admitted that she set that whole thing up with the police."

I could not hold back the tears and said to her, "All I want to do is love you. Why is it even her business?"

Rhonda was crying too.

"My mother will never understand the love we have."

I grabbed her and held her close. We both cried and agreed it was officially over, and she left. I felt a hole in my heart I didn't know how to fix. I worked a lot during this time to keep my mind off things but had to quit a couple of jobs because I couldn't focus. Eventually, my dad helped me get another job, working in drywall, and I could get my paper route back.

I continued to hang out with my friend Ham, who planned to go to New York. Ham invited me to join him, but I wasn't up for it at the time. However, after a few days, I felt even the idea of being in the same town with Rhonda was bringing me down, and leaving Chicago might be the best way to get over the heartbreak. It was as if there was a voice inside of me telling me it was time to move on. One day I just went and got a Greyhound ticket to New York. Time to drift for a while.

# CHAPTER 8

# Studs in The City

When I arrived in New York, I was looking forward to exploring the city to keep my mind off things. When I finally got off the greyhound bus, I found a payphone and called Ham. Delighted to hear I'd made it, he told me how to get to his place on the subway. Once I got there, it was like we never missed a beat. He was staying with a lady friend who had invited him, and he introduced me. She was just like a lot of the women that Ham dated, thick in the waist and cute in the face. She was nice and cordial, and I was just happy to see him. Ham already had a job in security waiting for him, and he said he would try to hook me up. We finished drinking a few beers, and I headed out. I didn't want to impose on my friend and his new lady, so after I left, I went to try to figure out how to get things done on my own.

After a few nights of sleeping in a park or two, I finally found a shelter to stay in and received government assistance until I could find a job. Whenever I found myself short on cash, it didn't last long because I had my harmonica and guitar with me. I'd place my hat on the ground and play my heart out, just long enough to get me something to eat, buy cigarettes and weed, and I'd usually have a few dollars left over.

I played in Times Square or Central Park, and my favorite thing to eat was a falafel sandwich and a cold beer. New York food differed from Chicago food, but I enjoyed discovering new places to eat. One time I ran into a group of tourists and played along as they sang the *New York, New York* song. I rarely called home because, once I called Mom and asked for fifty dollars, she said, "I'll give you twenty-five, and you come up with the rest on your own. I think after her last visit, Mom had gotten a little used to me being on my own.

After a few weeks in New York, one of the guys at the shelter instructed me to go to the public assistance building. He informed me that they had found me an apartment. It was a furnished single unit, in the Bronx on 167th and Clay Avenue.

The five-story apartment building was within walking distance to Yankee Stadium, across the street from a park, and the unit was just big enough for one person. I didn't have many possessions, but once I arrived, the building manager suggested I pay to put a full-length, ceiling-to-floor bar lock on the door for protection, along with bars on the windows. It was the first thing I purchased before I bought anything to decorate the place.

I had not found a consistent job yet, but as luck would have it, one day, when I left my building, I noticed a construction company nearby, and people, mostly women, were picketing outside of it. I went over to ask what they were picketing for, and they told me they were protesting the lack of women being hired on construction jobs. At the time I inquired, a small ruckus broke out, and the crowd began pushing. Within minutes, I found myself at the front of a line and entering a trailer, ready to ask for a job. Once inside the office, I stood in front of a tall guy with a big mustache.

"Are you guys hiring or what?"

"Yes, but only females."

"I'm a female."

The guy looked at my ID and said, "Okay, let's see what we can do. We'll take you on a week's trial."

I filled out an application, and he told me I'd be working demolition. The company gave me a tool belt, a helmet, a sledgehammer, and anything else I needed to get started. It was one of the few times I didn't mind telling someone I was a female. I wasn't ashamed because I needed that job badly, and it paid well. This was about survival and being able to take care of myself; the job paid $500 per week, more than any of the Chicago jobs I ever had. I was 22 years old and clearly had more of a masculine demeanor, but they needed to fill this diversity job, so it was a win-win situation for both of us. The job entailed hammering down walls in old, abandoned buildings, and it was hard, and I ached at night, but I didn't care. I worked for a few weeks, and once I got myself settled, I connected with Ham again.

Over the next few months, Ham and I would hang out as we did in Chicago. One evening we went to one of the famous girly clubs in Manhattan. I had never been to any kind of club where the women were completely naked, but once I got there, I ain't gonna lie, I enjoyed the hell out of it. Most times, I couldn't help but stare or sometimes blush. Watching naked women was one thing but handing over money was another.

The money I had been making was too hard to come by for me to just hand it over for the entertainment of watching naked women. I paid a few dollars in tips for the girls on the stage, but I didn't want to blow it all like I saw some guys doing. Ham was having a great time tossing money at women, but I was not as bold as him, still a bit shy when it came to dealing with women, especially in public. I wandered off looking around and came across private rooms with huge glass boxes and curtains. From across the room, I watched as some guy was talking to a woman inside one of them; as I stood there, Ham approached me.

"Man, you got to do this," he said, pointing to a coin box on the wall next to the glass container.

"How does it work?"

I had an idea but asked anyway. Ham lit up with excitement as he told me.

"You put quarters in this box, and the curtain goes up. A chick comes out, and she will do whatever you want. Go ahead and put a quarter in it."

I looked around at all the boxes.

"Nah, I'm good."

"Marla, man, you're boring as hell. I'm going back over to the stage."

Ham walked off, and I kept looking at the glass, then at the box. I will admit, curiosity did get the better of me.

I reached into my pocket, pulled out a couple of quarters, and put them in the coin box. Just like Ham said, the curtain came up, and a woman came out. She had dark hair, wearing a candy apple red negligee, and she laid on a round bed. I waved, and she giggled.

"You like what you see?"

I stood there blushing and shrugged my shoulders.

"Don't be shy; I can't bite you from in here."

I walked a little closer, and she began touching her breast.

"Would you like me to take my clothes off?"

I stammered over my words, "Uhm, well, no. You don't have to."

She seemed surprised, but I did think I should keep talking to her. I did pay her, after all.

"Are you cold in there?"

She smiled and said, "No, but I warm up quickly when I start to move. Should I dance for you?"

"No, you don't have to."

She gave me an odd look, and I added, "I bet you get bored in there."

As the conversation continued, the meter ran out, and as the curtain eased down, we waved goodbye to each other. I've never been motivated by just watching someone naked, not really been into porn, but a good conversation is harder to come by.

I loved hanging out with Ham, but I had begun to make other friends. I'd jump from borough to borough traveling from Manhattan to the Bronx, to Harlem, to Queens and Staten Island. New York was growing on me, and I also began to really vibe with New Yorkers. They took a certain pride in their city and felt the need to tell me how great it was, especially after discovering I was from Chicago. No one called me Marla, only Glen, and people thought that being from Chicago, you were automatically associated with being a gangster or a badass. It seemed they respected Chicagoans, and I welcomed that, but I certainly didn't have that gangster mentality in me.

Another reason why people thought I was gangster-like was that I had a huge gap in my mouth. When I had braces as a pre-teen, the bone marrow in my front tooth dissolved, and by the time I had gotten to New York, the tooth was coming out and started dangling, so I just took it out. Eventually, receiving public assistance that included dental benefits helped to get that fixed, and it made me seem less of a badass to be able to smile without trying to cover my mouth. While I didn't mind being called a badass, I did mind how a few of my experiences unfolded while living in the city.

While hanging out near Central Park at a jam session, I met another stud named Diane, and everyone just called him D. When D and I met, we instantly connected. He had two kids and a woman in his life whom he called his wife. Most studs called their woman their wife. It didn't matter that it was illegal for them to get married; they skipped the legal stuff, made their own vows, and to them, they were married.

When I visited D and his wife, it was always fun, and the kids would call me Uncle Glen. They hired me as a babysitter, so they could get out and nurture their relationship a little, and we became great friends. One evening D and I decided to go out and crash a nearby party. When we arrived, we found some weed and decided to go half a block away in a nearby park to smoke it. While sitting on the bench, we heard gunshots, and D sat perfectly still.

"Don't move!" he said, and I followed his instructions, and while sitting there, we heard more gunshots. A minute or so later, a man ran by us with a purse, and following behind him was a couple, and the man protecting his lady was firing shots at the purse-snatcher. They whizzed right by us and kept going. I felt lucky that day; it was really too close for comfort. I was sweating and said, "Let's get the hell out of here."

The relationship with Ham went sour when I got caught up in an argument he had with his lady friend, where they got so heated neighbors called the police. I was happy to get out of there, and it was a while before I reached back out to him when I was still in New York. I kind of kept to myself most of my time after that, but there were times I would cook dinner at my apartment for my friends from my construction job. Maybe eight of us would hang out after work at the park, and inevitably someone would ask if I was cooking.

We all worked the 2$^{nd}$ shift, from noon to midnight, and it was like a close-knit little family. We laughed and joked with each other all the time, and if anyone was short on cash, somebody would lend them money until payday, and we helped each other with job duties as well. There was one guy in our group called Peanut, who also did demolition. He was tall, a bit seedy, and menacing if you got on his bad side. I got along with him for the most part, but I wouldn't exactly call him my friend.

Late one night, long after work was over, I got a knock on my door.

"Who is it?"

"Marla, it's Peanut, open up the door."

He had a sense of urgency in his voice, but there was no way I was going to be alone with this damn near seven-foot dude, late at night.

"Man, I got company. I'm not opening the door."

I didn't want him to think I was alone, and to try to seem convincing, I imitated my voice by raising it an octave and said, "Who is that?"

Peanut knocked louder. "Open up, Marla. I've been shot."

"And you came here?"

There was no response.

"Man, I'm not opening up the door. I'll see you tomorrow at work," I said.

I heard his footsteps as he walked away, but moments later, I could see him hanging around from outside my window. I lifted the window and yelled, "Peanut, I'm not letting you in here. I told you I got company."

Shortly thereafter, he disappeared, but Peanut didn't show up the next day at work. I told our little group what happened, and they all said they would have done the same thing and not let him in. A few days later, we found out that Peanut got arrested for raping a woman, and they found her beaten and left for dead. This was the last straw for me when it came to living in New York. I'd had enough, decided to leave, and booked a ticket back home.

When I arrived in Chicago, I went to see my mom, and she told me that she and Calvin were now engaged. While Calvin wasn't my dad, I was still happy for my mom. We had a great visit, and she told me that Tuggy had moved to California with the Ball family, who lived two doors down from our house. Mom and I were both happy about this because Tuggy, now 23, wasn't doing much at home, and he and Calvin never really got along. The Balls were a large family, and many of them were musicians. At a young age, Leroy and Larry Ball were working with Earth Wind and Fire and other bands that toured. Tuggy had been helping the family for years with little odd jobs, and I sometimes babysat for them. Tuggy going with them was a win-win situation for everybody. Mom knew the Balls well and trusted them to ensure Tuggy would be okay.

I went to stay with my dad until I figured out what I wanted to do, but I didn't want to just live off him. I wanted to help him out with bills, so I picked up my old paper route since I always kept a good relationship with the owner. I also landed a job in security and a job at McDonald's on the north side of Chicago. I always juggled more than one job at a time.

I had no idea what I would do next, but I had always thought about going into the Army. One morning, I decided to take the exam, but I got a horrible migraine. The test went by quickly, and they told me I missed passing it by one point. I had my heart set on joining the Army, but when I retook the test, I again got a migraine. I knew God was involved and accepted the only thing left for me to do was music.

# CHAPTER 9

# Making Connections

While I juggled a few jobs and tucked away some money, whenever I could, I went to the park to play music, hung out with friends at open-mic nights, or attended guitar parties. Growing up, I went to guitar parties in my neighborhood hosted by an Irish American family named the O'Neals. We would sit around and listen to each other, mostly people my age, and there were several of us from different cultural backgrounds. Almost everyone did experimental drugs, such as LSD, cocaine, and speed. It was the mid 70's, and we were a group of easy-going, free-spirited hippy kids. Many were the sons and daughters of doctors, lawyers, politicians, and other upper echelon members of Chicago's elite, but we all had plenty of fun, and nothing ever got out of hand. I never had more than weed.

One of the guys I met during this time was Trent. We were about the same age and got along so well because we weren't afraid to be ourselves. He was an openly gay guy with a flamboyantly big personality and always dressed to impress. His dress style was like that of a fashion model, while I was still loyal to my tennis shoes and T-shirts. Trent invited me to many house parties, and on Saturday nights, we would sometimes go to a club called "The Warehouse," which was always packed.

If going there, he insisted that he dress me in a tie and a white shirt, so I would be more presentable by his standards. I just went along with it because I will admit, I did usually dress in a way that resembled a twelve-year-old boy. After putting on the upgraded clothes, he would look me up and down and say, "Now that's the type of man I would want to be seen with; if I were a real woman, you would be in trouble!"

One evening, Trent invited me to a party being thrown for Whitney Houston. Trent always went to classy parties, but this wasn't the type of affair I'd usually go to. I was excited about going because Whitney was one of the hottest artists at the time. The party was located in Hyde Park, on a rooftop filled with all types of partygoers, including neighbors, socialites, and a few celebrities. Whitney's own entourage of people surrounded her, and she looked absolutely flawless. I walked around for a while but didn't talk to many people. One time Trent came over and told me I should go and say something to Whitney. She was a star, so I didn't know what to say to her.

"She looks busy; I'll try to say something to her later.

Trent kept pushing. "You know she's your type."

All I could say was, "Oh yeah."

After that, I noticed there was a stud in her entourage that stayed close to the superstar most of the night. But that didn't matter; I was still incredibly shy and could never have approached someone like Whitney. I was just happy to admire her from afar.

I hung around the party, ate food, and watched other people have a good time. Then I noticed a different woman who was very attractive, tall and slender with long auburn hair and light brown eyes. Even from a distance, she had amazing sex appeal that had me staring at her. She seemed to be by herself, so I plucked up the courage to go across to where she was standing and make small talk.

"Cool party, huh?"

"It's alright," she said with a smile.

"Since you are not having a good time, you should give me that plate of food you're holding."

We both laughed, and she passed the plate in my direction.

"Here, you can have it; I ate what I wanted."

"C'mon, I was just kidding. So, who invited you to the party?"

While I waited for her to answer, I couldn't help looking at her face as the moon lit up her beautiful smile. It was obvious I was staring.

"I'm dating a boxer, and he told me about it. He said he was coming, but I think he lied."

"If I were a boxer, I wouldn't let you out of my sight. I'd beat up all kinds of people for you."

She giggled, and as we kept chatting, I learned she was a model named Janet. We talked all night, and I had no idea why this beautiful woman wanted to spend time with me, but she laughed at my silly jokes, and we had a good time. We found a quiet corner and smoked a joint, and, as the party was ending, we exchanged numbers. I called her the next day, and soon we were hanging out together almost every day. I continued to flirt with her, but she insisted she only wanted to be friends. She had a silly side to her like me, and I found myself doing whatever I could to make her laugh.

One evening, I shared with her something I'd been thinking about ever since my mom told me where Tuggy had gone. I wanted to go drifting again.

"I'm planning to go to California."

Without hesitation, Janet said, "I want to go!"

"You would just leave Chicago?" I asked, surprised at her immediate response.

"I don't think my modeling career is going anywhere here, and California seems like a good place to start over."

"So, let's go and figure it out," I replied, and just like that, I had a traveling companion.

Within a few weeks, we got our Greyhound bus tickets and excitedly headed to California. We stayed together in a few Long Beach area hotels, but after a week or so, Janet started to venture out on her own and be gone for days. When she returned the first time, she had a lot of money in her pocket.

"Where did you get this money from?"

She stared at me and hesitated before she answered.

"I found a boyfriend, and he gave me the money."

"Well, are you going back out to be with him?"

"Probably."

"But will you be coming back?"

"Don't worry about me," she said with a smile, "I'll contact you when I have time to hang out again."

I was worried about her, and even though she wasn't my girlfriend, I still cared about her, but she was free to do whatever she wanted, and I was happy she was having fun. Eventually, I found out where Tuggy was staying with The Ball family, and we all had a great reunion. The place I was staying was a little run down, so Tuggy helped me get a better room to stay in, and I left a note for Janet saying where I'd gone to.

After a few weeks in Long Beach, I eventually ventured out into other areas of Los Angeles and landed a job at a security company in Hollywood. While I'd moved with music in mind, I was still trying to figure out what I wanted to do, and I had thought becoming a security guard was a pathway to becoming a police officer. At least I got to wear a uniform!

The job required a mandatory three-week course, and I had to go to a shooting range to get registered to be able to carry a gun. That was fun; it turned out I was a very good shot, so I was eligible for my gun permit and passed the course with flying colors. I saw a future in security and wanted to work at concerts, events, banks, and warehouses. The company gave me an option to carry a gun, and I opted not to do so, but instead, I happily carried my baton. I also had my badge, handcuffs, and a two-way radio.

Music remained a thing I would do outside of work, but even wearing my uniform, I'd take my guitar with me everywhere I went, carrying it over my shoulder. Once settled into the security job, I juggled other part-time jobs as I had in Chicago but always found time to get to open mic nights. I found the best ones in the Hollywood area, where the events were always packed with a lot of up-and-coming musicians. And free beer!

I would go back and forth between LA, Long Beach, and Hollywood, visiting Tuggy and the Balls. Leroy Ball was already working in the music industry, and he would sometimes get me studio gigs, where I would sing background when the artists were looking for a person with a deeper voice. I loved getting those gigs because I'd get paid well in cash, getting a fee of $800 per song. It was totally fun, and the highlight wasn't just the money; it was getting a free meal and hanging out watching celebrities record their songs. One time I met Jermaine Jackson, and I briefly sat next to him as he practiced on a piano in one of the studio rooms. I was awestruck but not bold enough to ask for an autograph. He didn't say much, but he was really nice, and being in the same room with him was cool.

I loved being in a musical environment and doing the Hollywood open mics had started to get interesting. The more I'd show up at the same clubs to perform, the more people began to approach me, asking who I was or where I was from. Many were fellow musicians, but some identified themselves as music producers. This was so different than the open mic nights in Chicago because no one in the industry ever showed any interest. I wasn't sure if they were legitimate, and since this was just a hobby to me, it really didn't matter.

While hanging out in Hollywood one day, as I walked past a shoeshine stand, I happened to run into Janet. I had not seen her in a while, and it was good to reconnect. She told me she'd found another boyfriend and had moved in with him. When I asked where she lived, she evaded the question but said we should hang out together again.

So, we picked up where we left off, but no matter how many times I asked her where she lived, she never told me. Eventually, I let it go, simply pleased to see her when she came to my open mic night performances. We traveled throughout Los Angeles, Hollywood, and surrounding areas, eating at great restaurants and enjoying the city. When I had time off from my job, we would venture out, exploring California's beaches and parks and eventually taking more adventurous excursions like jumping on the Greyhound bus and traveling up and down the California coast, even as far as San Francisco. I would always take my guitar and harmonica, and sometimes I'd just stop somewhere and play for Janet because she loved listening to me.

One beautiful summer day, we took an excursion to San Diego. As usual, I had my guitar and my harmonica. We had just gotten off the bus and were traveling through a park near a university campus when Janet stopped and pointed to a sign advertising a Bo Diddley concert in a couple of days.

"We should go down there."

"Why? It's not for two days," she replied, we had only planned to go there for a day.

"Doesn't matter. Let's just go check it out. My mother plays his music around the house. I just want to go, and we'll get by."

Janet eventually agreed, and we went to see where it was. It was midafternoon when we arrived at the university to see about tickets, and as we got closer, I could hear a harmonica playing from the one of the buildings. As we reached the stage, already set up for the concert, I could see and hear a young boy playing a great blues number. No one was in the auditorium, and I smiled as I listened to him play; he had the same style I did. I had never heard anyone play like me, so I was excited to listen. I stood in the doorway until he stopped playing and approached him,

"Wow, that was good."

"Thanks," he said, and his face lit up with a smile.

I pulled my harmonica out of my pocket, and the young boy looked at me as I blew into my harmonica a little, making a sweet noise.

"Mine is a C, is yours?" I asked.

"Yeah, mine is C too. You want to play together?"

"Sure," I replied.

He jumped down from the stage and said, "okay, but let's go outside away from here; they're gonna do a sound check soon."

The kid headed out of the auditorium, and I followed. There was a nearby empty construction site, and the workers had dug out a huge hole in the ground. Janet stood nearby, holding my guitar, as the kid and I walked down into it and began playing our harmonicas. He began playing first, and I dropped my backpack and jumped right in. The acoustics of being in that hole sounded great, and it was amazing as the music echoed around and around. Out of the corner of my eye, I could see Janet smiling and nodding her head to the music as we gave our own mini concert, jamming and both playing with passion. I would stop occasionally and let him take the lead, and then moments afterward, he would do the same with me.

Within about five minutes, a crowd had started to gather, and I was more than surprised to see Bo Diddley with what must have been a few band members. They had obviously followed the sound, walked up, and watched us. After we finished, Bo Diddley wearing thick dark-rimmed glasses and speaking in a heavy Southern accent, yelled down into the hole, looking directly at me.

"You can play the harmonica real good.

While slightly out of breath, I smiled. "Thank you, sir."

"Wait a minute, is you a boy or a girl?"

I looked at him and sighed. "I don't want to talk about what I am, sir."

The two of us walked out of the hole, and Bo Diddley continued asking me questions. He noticed the guitar I'd now put on my back.

"So, you play that guitar as well?

"Yes, sir."

He took a pause and asked another question, "What about singing; you sing too?"

"Yes, sir."

"Good. I'd like to hear it. Why don't you come to my hotel tomorrow at 3 pm? I'm staying at the Hyatt up the street. Bring your harmonica and your guitar and be prepared to play. Let's see what you can do. I'll treat you to a good meal."

A big smile came over my face.

"Yes, sir!"

Along with the kid who they obviously knew, he and his band members walked back into the auditorium. The kid and I waved goodbye to each other until they were out of sight. Super excited, Janet and I began jumping up and down laughing.

"Oh my God, this is so good!" she squealed.

"I know! I can't wait 'til tomorrow!"

Janet and I hung out that evening and enjoyed walking around town. In celebration, we got drunk and ended up sleeping in a park on benches until the next morning.

The next afternoon, Janet and I went to the hotel suite, and Bo Diddley and another guy sat and listened as I was asked to play and sing several songs. He didn't ask me much about playing my harmonica. I guess he had heard enough. When I was done, he said to me, "Would you like to come work for me in Florida?"

Without hesitation, I said, "Why, sure! Of course, I would!"

He reached in his pocket and handed me a few dollars.

"Here are a few dollars for traveling. My guys will get you a bus ticket."

I took the small stack of bills and said, "Thank you, sir."

He looked at me and nodded.

"You've got something. So, I want you to go stay at the ranch, and I'm going to pay you a hundred dollars a month to watch my studio equipment. While you are there, I want you to practice on that guitar."

All I could do at this point was nod. I had thought he was giving me a job to work with his band. I didn't know what watching a studio meant, but this was Bo Diddley, and surely he knew more than I did? He must've seen the confused look in my eye.

"I can trust you to be there?"

"Yes, sir. I'll go."

I persuaded him to let Janet come with me even though he said she looked like she could be trouble. I got the information to secure the bus tickets, and Janet and I left San Diego and headed back to Hollywood. I quit my jobs, and she quit her boyfriend, and within two weeks, we were drifting off on a Greyhound bus to Florida.

# CHAPTER 10

# Bo Diddley

Janet and I arrived at the small Greyhound station in Jacksonville and were picked up by Bo Diddley's son, Anthony. We got on the road to Gainesville, and in a little over an hour, we arrived at the McDaniel Ranch, named for Bo Diddley's real name of Ellas McDaniel. However, I learned that McDaniel was a name he had given himself because his given last name was Bates. We finally arrived at the ranch, and it was huge. When Anthony stopped the car, I was so excited that I jumped out and began running in circles with my hands up, shouting, "Yeeehaaa! This is so cool!"

Trees and grassland spread as far as the eye could see, and a ranch-style home was surrounded by several trailer homes parked several feet away from the house. The whole setting was amazingly beautiful, with dingo dogs, goats, rabbits, cats, and chickens adding to the vista. Living there were Bo Diddley's children, Michael, Anthony, Evelyn, and Tammi, and many of his grandkids. Everyone slept in their individual trailer home, and the only person who slept in the house was Mr. Diddley himself along with his girlfriend. At the time Janet and I arrived, we stayed in the same trailer, and later we were each given our own trailer.

Everyone was welcoming and being there felt like being with family. After I settled, I was given a key to a big barn sitting next door to the house. The barn had been remodeled and turned into Bo Diddly's music studio, and it was my job to keep an eye on it, making sure no one went inside to mess with anything. He told me to call him Bo Pop, and he made good on his promise to pay me a hundred dollars a month.

"I'm mostly worried about my grandson, Mark. He calls himself a DJ, and he's always fooling around in my studio," said Bo Pop when he gave me the key.

He was not wrong about Mark, who always tried to get into the studio to mix some of his songs. I'd be watching television, and Mark would stand over me, asking for a key. I always said 'no' until he discovered my Achilles heel and muttered the magic words when Bo Pop had gone on the road for a while.

"I got a couple of joints I can give you," he said one night as I sat on the steps of my trailer, picking at my guitar.

I looked up. He had my attention.

"You can have them, and I'll only be an hour."

Getting something to smoke while on the ranch was difficult, so I quickly gave in.

"Alright, boy, one hour and that's it. I swear, you better not tell anyone I did this either."

"I swear I won't."

He reached out his pinky finger, and I grabbed it, sealing the deal. I went to unlock the door, but not before putting my hand out, where he dropped two joints right into the palm of my hand. Before walking off after I'd let him, I said, "Okay, this gets you one hour."

I closed the door and left to smoke my weed, returning an hour later, and Mark reluctantly came out.

This happened every few days, or maybe a week would go by, and

I'd let Mark work an hour or so, and then I'd lock the door after he left. Sometimes I'd accidently put the key down somewhere, and Mark would sneak his way into the studio, and I'd have to chase him out once I discovered him in there.

When Bo Pop returned from the road, I saw him go into the studio, and then he was soon banging on my trailer door.

"Okay Marla, tell me the truth ... Who's been in my studio?"

He was like a dad to me; he had a big heart, and we all loved him, but he was aware I wasn't a very good liar. When he looked me in the eye, waiting for me to respond, I probably gave myself away with the uncomfortable expression I had on my face. I couldn't take the pressure of lying to him, so I just let it come out.

"I let Mark in for a bit," I said as he stood looking down on me. He shook his head and called out to Mark.

"Mark! Mark! You come here right now! I told you not to go into my studio!"

Bo Pop seemed to be so stern, but he never really punished anyone. He just threatened to, and he went right back to being his jovial self. Despite me snitching on Mark, we all got along like one big family.

There was plenty to do and great food on the McDaniel ranch, and oftentimes, when we didn't go into the nearby town of Gainsville to get something to eat, Bo Pop's eldest daughter Tammi would cook for everybody, especially when Bo Pop was home from a tour. It was like a celebration when he returned to the ranch, and we would barbecue by digging a hole in the ground, placing hot coals at the bottom of the hole, then placing foil and food items in the hole and cover the foil with all the dirt. When the food came out, it was always tender and perfect. From his tours, Bo Pop would always bring toys, souvenirs, and lots of candy to give everyone on the ranch. We would stand in line to get what he brought, and it felt like it was Christmas. They were exciting times.

In one of the neighboring towns, an establishment would pay people by the pound for tree moss. Anthony and I began going out early in the morning and picking moss off trees and turning it in for a profit. We made big money picking moss, and the process was easy. We would get up around 3:00 am and drive into the woods. When we found a good tree, we took long sticks with nails and stuck it into the moss, sometimes in the middle of a tree's branches. We'd then twist the stick, grabbing the moss, and we'd keep rotating until we'd hear a huge crack of the branches, and then pull a beard of moss off the tree.

Anthony had a small car, so we would get as much moss inside as possible. We'd pick moss all day, and by evening, we would turn it into cash at a local barn. There was always a line of people waiting, but once we arrived, they always invited us to the front of the line because they knew we were from Bo Diddley's ranch. Bo Pop was always supportive of all his kids and extremely encouraging when they were doing anything positive. When he came home and heard that we'd been hustling up cash by picking moss, he asked us a bunch of questions.

"So how much money have y'all been making picking moss?"

"We've been doing a lot, sometimes about a hundred and fifty," replied Anthony.

"Yeah, and sometimes one-eighty," I chimed in.

We were excited about this, and it showed. Within a week or so after we had this conversation with Bo Pop, he got Anthony an old school bus for us to continue picking moss in. We were so excited. We took the seats out of the bus and headed out again to pick moss. We quickly began making around five hundred dollars a day, and even on slow days, we made about three hundred dollars.

As promised, Bo Pop also helped to nurture my musical talents. Each time before he left town, he would have a talk with me about music, telling me what to work on while he was away. He wanted to make sure I practiced every day and told me to have a new song mastered by the time he got back. Every day in my trailer, I picked up my guitar or harmonica, working on writing new music. I wouldn't just work on one song; I'd work on a couple. I didn't want to disappoint him, and sure enough, when he got back to the ranch, he would look down at me over those glasses and ask, "You got any songs?"

With a smile, I'd say, "I sure do!"

A song I wrote, which never got recorded was entitled, *Moss Picking Time*. Another one entitled "*Personal*" was released on my first album, *This is Marla Glen*, and one other song I wrote while on the ranch was *I Told Them, Snitch, Thief, and a Traitor*. The inspiration for writing this was when I was being called a snitch from telling on Mark when he broke into the studio. We laughed and joked about it at the time. Also, when everyone was asleep, I would sometimes sneak out at night and take roaches out of the ashtrays. If I put them all together, I'd have at least half of a joint. Although no one caught me, they suspected I was the one who took them, and someone laughingly called me a thief.

One afternoon when they had a barbecue, I gently kicked open a screen door to where everyone was and shouted the lyrics while playing the guitar ...

*Let's all get together and have some fun. Hey Hey ...!!*
*Let's all drink lots of booze and barbecue and party out the day ...*

As I sang the rest of the song, they were laughing hysterically through it. It was family fun on the ranch, and the laughs and good times were plenty. Like any family, they had their issues and fights as well, but they would work it out and keep things moving.

However, while I was enjoying my time on the ranch, Janet seemed to get in trouble, and she never really fit in. Bo Pop was not happy with Janet being there in the first place. One day, when we'd been there for about 18 months, Bo Pop told me that Janet needed to leave. He wouldn't give the details of what kind of trouble Janet was getting into, but I suspected it was of some sexual nature with one of the guys there. Bo Pop just told me she had to go. I understood, because Janet could be a handful.

I didn't want Janet to go back to California by herself, so I decided to leave with her. She was my friend and always had my back, so it was only right for me to travel back with her. Bo Pop didn't hesitate and got us both Greyhound tickets headed back to California. I promised I'd keep in touch, and he wished me luck with my music career. He'd guided me about playing the guitar and writing songs, and for this I will be forever grateful, not to mention, I thoroughly enjoyed being around his family.

# CHAPTER 11

# Nina Simone

After a long bus ride, Janet and I made it back to California. This was now 1987, and I was 27. I went back to the security company, got my old job back, and briefly stayed with the Ball Family until I could get my own place. I found a hotel room in the Hollywood area, and every month or two, I would find a different and better spot to live. I wanted to be close to both the open mic nights and my job. I was happy to get my security job back, and after that, I vowed to make sure I never left a job without leaving an open door for the possibility of coming back. It was always in the back of my mind that I could be a police officer someday, and the security job seemed to offer a pathway to get that. I'd get excited about taking my uniform to the cleaners, and getting it back fresh, pressed, and without a wrinkle. I would shine my shoes to the point I could see my reflection.

One evening after work, I was walking down the block home when I noticed a lot of police cars, including the SWAT team, holding up traffic. There were loud sirens, helicopters flying overhead, and television broadcasting trucks along with reporters capturing what was going on. This wasn't an ordinary occurrence, and many of the tenants on my block were outside looking around trying to see what was happening. Cars were backed up, causing a traffic jam, and nobody could move. On the news, it was being reported that a sniper on a Hollywood roof had been taking shots at people.

Rather than going into my building, I stood around with some of my neighbors wondering what would happen next. As usual, I had my guitar on my back, and a tall black guy got out of a black sedan and approached me, pointing to the guitar.

"You know how to play that thing?"

"Yes, I do," I replied, wondering if he wanted me to join a band. "But I really only play my own music. Mostly things that I wrote."

"Do you know Nina Simone?"

That was not the next question I was expecting and it kinda threw me for a moment.

"Well, yes, I guess I do because my mother would play her records. Isn't she the lady who sang the song, *To Be Young Gifted and Black*?"

I sang a bit of the song, and he affirmed that it was indeed hers.

"She's standing in the crowd right there. I'm going to introduce you to her, but I need you to pretend you don't know who she is."

I shrugged my shoulders, "okay."

Next thing, Nina Simone heads toward me with a grimace on her face.

"I gotta pee. You gotta a toilet?"

"Yes ma'am. Follow me, I'll show you where it is."

I must be in a dream, I thought, because I'm showing Nina Simone the way up to my small unit, and where the bathroom is. As I opened the door, I breathed a sigh of relief that I'd left the place mostly tidy. She came out of the bathroom looking relieved and pointed to the security uniform I was wearing.

"Are you a police officer?"

"No ma'am, I'm a security guard."

She noticed my guitar now laying against the wall and pointed to it.

"Do you play that thing?"

"Yes ma'am, I also play the harmonica too and sing some."

She briefly looked around at the small unit. There was just a tiny closet, and a bed with one nightstand.

"How much do you pay for rent here?"

Where was this conversation going?

"Three hundred a month," I replied and let out a short laugh.

"Well, you can pay that to me. I have a much better room you can stay in. Would you like to come work for me? I need someone who wears a badge."

There was no hesitation when I said, "Yes, Ma'am."

She smiled. "Great, my driver will give you the address, and we'll see you soon."

It was almost the end of the month, and I had not paid my rent yet, so I could move quickly. Within a couple of days, I took the one suitcase I had, gathered my things and arrived at her place. Instead of paying my landlord, I paid Ms. Simone. I didn't think of it until later, but I was paying to work for her, but I also got food, as well as the room, and I still kept my other job, so I didn't mind.

Her condo was in a high-rise building called the Franklin Towers, located on Franklin Boulevard in West Hollywood, within walking distance from where I was working. When entering Ms. Simone's building, there was a modest lobby and a doorman named Bon Jovi—no relation to the band—who would greet you. He was a dark-haired guy in his 30s who was very charming and had a baby grand of a smile.

Once I arrived at Ms. Simone's unit, she opened the door to show me where I'd be sleeping. It was a modest two-bedroom place, but she had room for a baby grand piano in the living room. After I'd put my guitar in the room and unpacked my suitcase, she was very clear and precise about what she wanted.

"I'm out of town a lot, and I know the building has security, but I need people to know I'm not the only one here. I need you always to wear your uniform."

"Yes, ma'am," I replied, and that was that.

Even as we grew closer, it was always "Ms. Simone" or "ma'am," and I never called her Nina. When I wasn't working my security job, I would do whatever Ms. Simone needed, especially when she was in town. My duties included driving her around, making phone calls, and running errands, housework, and any other small job she needed done. Simply put I was her live-in personal assistant. I never asked her about her work, nor did I talk about music or ask any personal questions. Since the first day the driver told me to pretend I didn't know her, I did just that. I never uttered a word about who she was or what she did. I had grown up in the presence of BB King—his girlfriend was one of my mom's best friends—and Muddy Waters and never fussed about celebrity status, so I wasn't star-struck. I was simply honored to be in her presence and to work for her. More importantly, I knew my place when it came to her. She was my elder, and I was raised to treat them with the utmost respect.

On my days off, I would head out into the Hollywood area, but I still checked in with her to occasionally make sure she didn't need anything before I got back to the apartment. At the time, she was twice my age at 54, but essentially, I treated her as if she were my grandmother, making sure she was okay, and I dared not talk back if I didn't like anything. There was only one time when I felt like I needed to speak up, when she was looking for me and shouting to Bon Jovi.

"Where is that lesbian!?"

I was in earshot and frustrated. I quickly said, "Ms. Simone, please don't call me a lesbian. I just like women."

Of course, she said it whenever she felt like it.

There were those times when she would snap at me for no real reason, but I knew things were troubling her in the music business. I saw the frustrating pressure of being a celebrity, and even in my room, I'd hear the phone calls where she would cuss people out, shouting at a promoter or her manager. The problem often centered around her not getting her money.

Sometimes, I was asked to make phone calls for her, and she told me I needed to repeat exactly what she wrote down to whatever promoter, manager, or music executive was on the other end of the phone. I would stand in front of her, holding the note until the person picked up the call.

"Hello, is this Carlos? I have a message for you from Ms. Simone." I'd hold the paper in front of me and read it verbatim.

"Fuck you; I want my fucking money. It's been three weeks since you said you were going to pay me. Send me my goddamn money, now."

I felt uncomfortable saying what she wrote, and I often wanted to laugh while reading it, but she was sitting listening to me, so I had to be serious about it. She certainly was. I never made any comments on the calls or asked her what she was screaming about. But I didn't need to; it was clear. It was all about money or other exploitation issues in the music business. Later, I would know all about those first-hand.

She needed to make many phone calls to discover that her management team intercepted money, so sometimes money came through, and sometimes it didn't. The calls would be to Africa, Switzerland, Germany, and other places. Most times, after I'd deliver the message, the person on the other end of the phone would laugh, and in a serious tone, I would simply say, "This is what she told me to tell you, and I'm just delivering the message."

I would also make calls to some of her friends, especially to South

African singer Miriam Makeba. They were so close they acted like sisters, but sometimes I would be caught in the middle of their playful phone banter. I'd tell Ms. Simone that Ms. Makeba was on the phone, and she would look at me and say loudly, "Tell her I'm not here."

Of course, I'd repeated it, and Ms. Makeba would respond with, "Tell her I heard everything!"

This would go on for a while, and it was very awkward at first, but I knew they were joking with each other, and I just played along, and we all ended up laughing. It kinda made me feel at home.

I would see Ms. Simone when she had good days and bad. When she was frustrated about something, she would pace the apartment, shouting about what was bothering her. I felt I was the only person taking the brunt of her problems, but I understood some of the things she was going through and realized her frustration was not aimed toward me; I just happened to be there. But she was also eccentric, and quite often, she did whatever she damn well pleased.

"Prepare the Bentley, Marla. I have some things to do," she told me one hot summer's day when the temperature was already well over 100°f. I struggled to get the car started because the battery was not charging well, but I eventually pulled the car out in front of the building, and she came out in a full-length fur coat. I could not understand it, but I dare not question it. She told me to take her to the nail salon, which was only a few blocks away. I waited in the car, but when Ms. Simone finished her appointment, the car battery was dead again. She went back into the salon and watched me try to flag people down, but not one car stopped.

After a few minutes, she wandered out, walked into the traffic, and opened her coat, revealing her completely naked body. Within seconds, several cars stopped, causing a minor accident, and we got the help we needed. It was something I'd never forget. She was always a force to be reckoned with, and in most cases, she got things done the way she wanted them.

It took a while before she completely trusted me, and there were times when I knew she was testing my loyalty. She was very particular about smoking, and I was not allowed to smoke in the apartment at all. She did allow me to smoke on the patio, but smoking weed in her place was out of the question. One evening, during a St. Patrick's Day weekend, I went to a local bar and lounge. The establishment was giving out plastic keychain trinkets that resembled a small pipe with a four-leaf clover on it. I brought the trinket home and left it on my nightstand. The next day I ran a few errands and returned to the apartment to find her standing in my room. She was holding the trinket in her hand, and before I got a chance to say anything, she gave me a look of bitter disappointment and said, "You've been smoking that shit in my house, haven't you!? This is the proof right here!"

"Ms. Simone, what are you talking about? That's a toy. I got it from a bar, they were celebrating St. Patrick's Day, and it's not even a real pipe." I showed her, and she could see that the pipe did not have a hole in it. Then I noticed my mattress was missing.

"Errm ... where is my mattress?" I asked.

She replied with a perfectly straight face, "Well, I already threw it out the window."

I noticed the window was open, and I couldn't help but laugh. I shook my head and crossed to the window. Sure enough, my mattress was on the ground seven stories below.

"How did you do that?"

She didn't answer that question but said, "Well, since this is not what I thought, you can go down and get your mattress from downstairs."

I looked back at her, and she shrugged before we both began

laughing hysterically at the situation. I went downstairs and had Bon Jovi help me bring the mattress back up to my room.

Her final test came after a year or so of living with her when she told me there was a broken curtain rod in her bedroom. She was leaving to run a few errands, so I had two hours to fix it. I went into her bedroom to find stacks of money laid out over the entire bed, which was up against the wall, where the curtain hung, so I had to climb over the bed while trying my best not to disturb the intricately laid out cash.

By now, I had learned she didn't like things disturbed, so I did everything I could not to touch the money, while in the process of fixing the curtain rod. When she returned, she went into her room and stayed there for almost two hours. I am guessing she was counting it. She came into the living room where I was watching television.

"Well, I'll be damn. You can be trusted."

"Yes, Ms. Simone, I fixed the curtain just like you asked."

"I was talking about the money, child."

"I tried everything I could not to touch it because it looked like you had it in some sort of order."

She shook her head and said, "Well, okay then. Go ahead and watch television for another hour, then you can do the dishes."

"Yes, Ma'am," I replied and smiled to myself. I had learned my lesson with Arvella.

# CHAPTER 12

# Center of a Star

I lived with Ms. Simone off and on for several years and loved the time I spent with her at the Franklin Towers; there was rarely a dull moment. Bon Jovi and I became friends, as occasionally he would run errands for Ms. Simone as well. We would share stories, and there was a room in the garage where he would allow me to hide when Ms. Simone got upset about something and shouted like there was no tomorrow. She didn't know about the room, and we would both hide in there until the coast was clear!

There were also times when she needed the condo to herself for a while, and she would hand me a few dollars and tell me stay away for a few days. I would either go stay with a friend or my brother and the Ball family until she said it was okay to return. Once, as we sat in the living room, she told me she needed me gone for a few weeks.

"Is there some place you can go?"

"I could always go to Bo Pop's ranch."

"Who is Bo Pop?"

"Bo Diddley."

More than surprised; she was not convinced that I knew Bo Diddley.

"Bo Diddley? You actually know Bo Diddley?"

"Sure, I stayed on his ranch in Florida."

Her mouth dropped, and then she said to get him on the phone. I went to my room, got my phone book, and then made the call. We said 'hello' and had a few words before she asked that I give her the phone.

"Is this the real Bo Diddley?"

When she realized it was really him, she said, "Well, I'll be damn, it really is you!" She'd been convinced I was making it up. They began a long conversation about music and being on the road, and Ms. Simone eventually said, "Marla is staying with me, but I need the child to go somewhere for a few weeks. Can you send for her?"

Bo Pop agreed, and the next thing I knew, I was on a bus headed back to Florida for a few weeks. This occurred every few months or so after that, with me being shuffled back and forth between Bo Diddley's Ranch and Ms. Simone's condo. Both of them encouraged me to play music and write new songs, and I felt honored as I listened to them share their music experiences. Most of all, I was happy they fed me well and cared for me.

When I first moved in with Ms. Simone, she was unaware I was going out to the open mic nights and performing. I didn't share that I went around to local open mic nights, or much of my music abilities to play instruments with her. Eventually, she found out that I was playing at a club in the Hollywood area, doing an open mic, and she just showed up.

When she arrived at the club, the owners fawned over her, rightfully treating her as the star she was. They sat her front and center. I was in mid-conversation with someone when I saw her enter and was totally shocked to see her there. Artist after artist went up, and I was sweating buckets. I took my turn and sang the three songs I was allotted and afterward, the crowd gave me a standing ovation. Ms. Simone was the only one who did not stand up, nor did she clap.

*Oh boy, I'm really going to hear it when I get home. What could she be thinking? What is she going to say?*

I was so unnerved by Ms. Simone seeing me perform that I waited until almost 4 am before returning to the condo. Scared to death, I didn't even go into my room. I slept on the sofa with my clothes on. The next morning, she went out without me seeing her, but she came back by mid-afternoon while I was doing chores. She pottered around for a few minutes, putting some groceries away, and it was as she was going into her room, she finally spoke to me over her shoulder.

"By the way, last night, you were great," she said, and I let out a huge sigh of relief.

The next time music was mentioned between us was a short time later, when she returned from tour, and I was in my room playing my guitar with the door closed. It was the early morning hours, and I was trying to work on a new song. Ms. Simone came home while I was playing, and she quickly swung the door open and pointed to the guitar in a commanding voice.

"Bring that thing with you and come into the living room. Now."

She scared the hell out of me, but I followed her instructions and simply said, "Yes, ma'am."

Upon entering the living room, she pointed to the sofa and said, "Sit down! Play!"

I played one song, stopped, and she looked at me and told me to play another one. And another. Sometimes she would sit with her eyes closed; other times, she would just watch me play. I kept playing all the songs I had written for about an hour and forty-five minutes.

"That's it. I don't have any more," I said.

"I had no idea you could play like that and sing. And you can do a whole show." I realized she intended to have me sit and play all my songs, to see how much material I had. I responded, "I guess so, Ma'am."

"Well, okay. Off you go to bed."

I went back into my room but didn't sleep. It was an awkward situation to sit in front of her and play, and I hadn't looked up from the guitar much. I just kept going. I felt our friendship was changing because I was used to listening to her, but for a change, she sat and listened to me.

It was much easier being able to talk to her about the music industry after that. After performing at one of the Hollywood open mic nights, a guy said he wanted to talk to me about a career in the music industry. I told her about this when I got home. As an entertainer, she would be much savvier than I was when it came to talking to these people. I was young and naïve about the music business and didn't have a clue how to spot some of the shady characters that hung out on the open nights, partly because I didn't focus on who was watching me. I was only interested in playing music, making cool friends, and getting free drinks.

"I won't go with you, but I want to hear the conversation. Some of these people are snakes, and you need to be careful who you talk to and what you tell them. I think you should record them."

"Should I ask him any specific questions?" I asked.

"Just be yourself and listen to what he has to say. We'll talk about it later."

I did what she requested, and before I left that night, she helped me tape a recorder to my chest. I had been using the small device to record my songs so I could be better at practicing them. I went out to the club and met the guy after my performance. His name was James. He was a tall dirty blond Caucasian guy wearing a suit jacket with his jeans. He was probably in his 30's and had a nice smile. When he was ready to talk, I told him I needed to go to the bathroom, where I started the recorder. When I came out, he was patiently waiting, and because it was loud in the club, we went outside.

He asked if I wrote all my own songs, and as the conversation continued, he seemed very interested in my music. He also seemed a little anxious, and he kept his hands in his pockets a lot. He then pulled a cassette tape out of his pocket.

"I know you do your own music, but I want you to listen to this. He then pushed play on the small cassette player and said it was a song sung by a guy with lyrics about windowpanes and teardrops. I listened for a few beats and said, "Oh, that sounds good. Is that your song?"

"No. It's a song I'm going to get recorded for a company I'm working for. They're in Nashville. I'm hoping that you would be interested in going to Nashville."

I wanted to make sure I heard him correctly and played dumb.

"Nashville? What's in Nashville?"

"A record company I'm working for. Can you listen to it and try to sing it for me? I think your voice would be great for this song."

He stopped the tape and handed me the cassette, and I agreed to give the song a shot. I left the club and returned to the condo, Ms. Simone and I sat down to listen to it. When the tape ended, Ms. Simone paused for a minute and then looked directly at me, her expression totally serious.

"He was trying to steal you. Go back and tell him, no, you won't go. No matter what he offers you, you tell him no. And never sign anything!"

The following week, I told him I wasn't interested.

"You know, I thought about it all, and I don't want to go to Nashville. I think I only want to do music as a hobby."

The guy really tried to convince me that I was making a mistake.

"Look, you can really turn this into a career. You have something, and you can make a lot of money. You should really think about it. I can make this happen for you."

"It all sounds nice. And I appreciate you trying to look out for me, but my mom doesn't want me to go."

He didn't have a solution after that. I thanked him for the offer, and we said our goodbyes.

Quite a few other people approached me at different open mic nights, but I didn't really follow up, nor did I give them much attention. I politely listened and just kept doing what I was doing. I was comfortable being a security guard, but I was beginning to think I wasn't going to be a police officer. I was happy wearing a badge, and carrying a stick, and it still allowed me to have fun in California, so I just put it to the back of my mind until I figured it all out.

Months later, Ms. Simone returned to the condo after being out all day. She called me to come out of my room. I entered the living room and took a seat, hoping I wasn't in trouble. She folded her arms and again looked me squarely in my face.

"I had a meeting today."

She occasionally met celebrities, so I responded, "Oh good, with who, Stevie Wonder, Michael Jackson?"

Her expression changed, and she shouted, "No! It was to talk about you, Motherfucker! They are watching you!"

"Who? Watching me for what?"

"They are watching you when you go into those clubs to perform for your free beer. They are there."

I was clueless, and she continued, "You know who they picked?"

"No, who?"

"Tracy Chapman."

"Oh yeah, I know that name. Well, who was the meeting with?"

"It was with music executives. They asked me who would be better to sign a deal with, and I told them Tracy."

"Oh, okay. Good then."

That was how much ambition I had, and I was never sure if that pleased or frustrated her. I do know she was worried about me getting ripped off, but the business side of the music industry never interested me. Not paying attention meant I would eventually pay a very heavy price.

I didn't ask her much afterward. I just assumed she recommended Tracy over me for whatever reason she thought was best. I didn't know who Tracy was, but Ms. Simone told me she played guitar and sang. I was fine with it because I didn't take my musical gifts seriously enough to care about developing a career around music. I knew I had something special, but at this time in my life, doing it part-time, and getting free beer, while making new friends was enough for me. I also really loved my job as a Security Officer, but I kept playing and creating new songs because it was fun and interesting.

Ms. Simone would always give me a timeline to complete tasks she needed doing. One day, before she headed out of the condo with her big floppy hat and glasses, she said, "I'm headed to the pool, and when I come back, you'd better have written a song about me—you have two hours."

I was shocked and almost panicked. I had grown accustomed to having written songs for Bo Pop after he was gone for several days, but two hours was a quick turn-around. Talk about pressure! To try to have a song for a woman who was particular, picky, and sometimes hard-nosed about things was going to be tough. Not to mention, it was not something I had ever thought about.

Initially, I didn't want to do it. I was thinking of telling her I couldn't come up with anything. However, after calming myself down, I began writing a hard rock tune but decided to break it down to something more melodic. When she arrived back from the pool, she entered the condo and immediately said, "Okay, Marla, let me hear it!"

Within the two hours, I came up with both lyrics and music. I placed the lyrics on the sofa and strummed my guitar to the melody, and I sang the song, *Center of a Star*, which would appear on my 1997 album, *Our World*.

## Center of a Star

Oh the center of a star
Oh you know who you are
I'm seeing the other world
Seems so strange

They can't wait to get close to you
'cause through your mind they can see
They all know that you're angry
Yet in their hearts they know you're the queen

The center of a star
You know who
You know who you are
Oh yes I've seen the other world
And yes it is so strange

You put me in the right direction, Nina
And the time has come to carry on, Nina
And I know I can say in my heart
For the queen who never left me to roam
And knowing she gave me home

Nina Simone
Simone

Look at them now
They think they know you

They know what you're saying, Nina
But they don't know what you mean
Your spirits rise
Your spirits rise
Now they don't know you
But what they're lacking now, Nina
Is the eyes to see

The center of a star
You know who
You know who you are
Yes now I'm seeing the other world
Yes yes and it seems too strange
It seems so strange
Yes it is
It seems so strange
Yes it is

Oh the center of a star
You know who you are
You were right
You were right Nina
I'm seeing the other world
It seems so strange

She listened and said nothing. She just stood in front of me, with her mouth slightly open. I think she was in shock.

"What? Is it okay?" I asked.

I was reading from the lyrics and had messed up the words a few times. I didn't ask her again if she liked the song because if she didn't, I know she would have said something. Eventually, she told me to play it again, and I did, this time without missing a beat. She stood listening, and when I finished, she said, "You're going be a star, and you're going to meet all the people around me."

I smiled and said, "Oh yeah?"

We never spoke about the matter again until one afternoon, we were lying side by side on her bed, looking at the ceiling and talking about life. Both of us fully clothed, we laughed and shared thoughts about the smallest things, like why life must be so complicated. Each was honest and insightful, a conversation like a son or daughter would have with their mother. In the midst of our conversation, I felt something hard underneath the pillow and pulled a Bible from under it.

"Oh, Ms. Simone, I keep my Bible under my pillow, too."

"Good, it gives me a bit of comfort in this crazy world."

We then ventured off into a spiritual conversation about God and the Bible. She shared stories and life, examples of things she had experienced in the music business as well as outside of it. Out of respect, I'd rarely interrupt her. But eventually, I said, "If I'm going to get into the music business, it's going to be with God."

She chuckled and said, "Oh, so you're going to go the long way, huh?"

I didn't know how to respond to that, nor did I really understand what she meant. Without another word, she went to sit at her piano and played Frank Sinatra's song, *My Way*. When she'd finished, she gave me that square in the face look again.

"I believe this song is against God because Frank did it his way and not God's way."

I thought about the lyrics and took in what she said. It's a moment I will never forget.

Another day, we were having a lighthearted conversation on the balcony when she shed some light on why she allowed me to stay with her, other than her needing assistance.

"Do you want to know one of the main reasons why you are here?" I wasn't sure if she meant on Earth or in her condo.

"Why I'm here?"

She pointed towards the bedroom and said, "Go into my bedroom and grab that stack of photos on the shelf."

I did as I was told and grabbed the photos. On the top of the stack was a picture of a little black girl. My mouth dropped with surprise, and for a moment, I thought the little girl in the picture was me. I walked into the living room and handed Ms. Simone the stack of photos, and said, "Ms. Simone, this girl looks like me."

"Exactly, that is the point. I believe that you are my spiritual child. I think you are strong enough to get through this thing they call living as an artist."

I didn't really know what she meant at that moment, and no words she ever spoke could prepare me for what was to come.

# FEET ON THE GROUND

*Not Knowing where I'm going
but I'll make it somehow*

# CHAPTER 13

# Playing the Wrong Pipe

In the latter part of the 1980s, Ms. Simone went on an extended tour. With her gone, it gave me a lot of time to myself working on my music, doing the clubs, and that's when my life fell apart. One Friday night when my security guard shift was over, I met this woman on the way to the bus stop. It was a nice evening, and I had just gotten paid and needed to get my hands on some weed. I struck up a conversation with this woman who was walking my way, and after we passed a few pleasantries, I asked her if she knew where I could get some smoke.

She smiled and said, "I can take you to a place where you can get anything you want."

Only a few blocks away from where we met, she took me to a house that wasn't anything special, but it was in a nice neighborhood. The only thing I distinctly remember is that it was a pale green. The woman introduced me to a guy who was obviously some sort of dealer; on a nearby table were several pipes that looked like weed bongs. I looked around, and there were a lot of people sitting around smoking out of these same glass pipes. People were coming up to the guy and paying for the drug then going into the house to sit and smoke. At first glance, I again thought they were bongs, but the scent in the place was not weed. It smelled like chemicals.

"What is that they're smoking?" I asked.

"You want to take a couple of puffs?" she asked, and I nodded my head.

When I was a teenager, I did a little Purple Microdot and some Orange Sunshine while experimenting with my friends, but it wasn't anything serious to me. So, I figured it couldn't hurt if I took a couple of puffs off the pipe she handed me ... my first pull was incredible. It was the most beautiful feeling I had ever experienced, so good that I kept smoking until the sun was coming up. And all my money was gone.

By now, it was seven in the morning, and I left the house quickly, having no idea about what the fuck just happened to me. How could I have been in there all night long?

Crying and confused, I needed to tell somebody what happened, and I walked quickly to my friend Bon Jovi's place; I knew he'd not speak about what I'd done. He answered the door, and through my tears, I started rambling about the woman, the house, and the pipes.

"I can't believe I smoked all night long. I don't want to be addicted to this shit. I just can't do it."

After giving him more details, Bon Jovi told me it was crack. I had never heard of it, and Bon Jovi, who rarely used profanity, was pissed. Bon Jovi was always professional, but right then, he looked plain angry.

"That bitch! I can't believe she did that to you! Who is she?! That is how they get you."

Bon Jovi told me I could stay at his place and sleep it off while he went to work, but I couldn't even think straight. I didn't know if I needed to sleep or stay awake. What I did know was that I wanted some more crack. I left, went back to Long Beach to where I was staying, and tried not to think about it. But the urge was too strong to try to forget how it made me feel. This feeling was unreal.

One day after work, I went back to see if I could find the house where I'd smoked crack, and while I initially didn't do it every day, it slowly became a regular habit. I still went to work, but no matter where I went afterward, I would meet someone who smoked crack too.

I began to notice that people were selling their TVs and jewelry, losing their jobs, and doing whatever they could to get it. I hated what I was doing and got even more scared after a few months went by and I began to lose weight. I was in denial, but I knew I was addicted.

By now, there were many places I knew where I could get more crack and smoking it through the night became the norm. I began to stop doing the things I'd normally do, like playing my harmonica at open mic nights and taking on small jobs. Instead, I would hang out with my new addict friends that smoked crack.

I tried many times to put that pipe down, and sometimes it worked, and sometimes it didn't. I thought if I put it in my cigarettes or weed, it would be less of an effect, so I tried it that way, but I would soon go back to smoking the pipe. I never smoked at work, and while living in Long Beach with friends, I was doing it but, hiding it. I told myself I had to find ways to get distracted, and I started going back to performing at the open mic nights again.

One day I walked into a jam session at a club in Long Beach and the place was packed. What had attracted everyone was this black dude sitting on the stage with a sax playing his ass off; he was one of the best I had ever seen. The crowd was really feeling him and cheering him on, and when the band broke, I approached him.

"Hey man, what's your name? You play the hell out of that sax!"

He shook my hand and replied, "Walter Gentry."

"My name's Marla Glen, and I play the harmonica," I told him.

"Well, now, we should make some fine music together, Marla," he said with a grin.

He had the most infectious of smiles, and that alone made me feel better. When it came to my slot, I called him up to join me and boy did that go down well with the folks in the club. We jammed, and immediately became friends because we had so much in common regarding music. Not only was he talented, but he was down to earth and had a real good spirit. He was just what I needed, and I began to feel that, with him in my life, I might just get out of the hole I'd dug for myself.

Walter and I began to hang out a lot at the different open mics in Long Beach, in Hollywood, and at any other places we could find, and being with him felt like being with family. He told me he was raised in the church, and you could certainly tell. He didn't use drugs at all; he was about as straight as they come and would rarely drink a beer. I respected him a lot, and so it surprised the hell outta me when I found out he was selling drugs.

Neither of us knew the mid-80s would be labeled the time of one of the biggest drug epidemics in America. Crack and cocaine were rampant at the time when I found myself right in the middle of it. And so had Walter, but on the other side. Once I got over the shock of what he was doing, he let me in on the real reason why.

"So, you sell it, but you don't use it? What's up with that?" I asked when I found out. We were sitting in a club, waiting to go on together.

"I'm only doing this to make enough money so I can buy me a truck. Then I'm gonna stop and quit this place," he said. "Too much bad shit goin' on around here, and I need to get myself someplace else. You know, Marla, I had a girlfriend who died from smoking crack. It's too dangerous to play around with, and you gotta quit."

"Walter, this is just a temporary thing for me," I answered, and he just looked away. While those words came out of my mouth, deep down, I knew I was truly addicted. He turned back to me and looked me in the eye.

"I'm not going to watch you go down that same road, Marla. Believe me, I'm not."

Walter and I continued to work a lot of the open mic night gigs, and we were getting side gigs from that. I would mostly play my harmonica, or sometimes I'd play my guitar, but we began to hang out even more. Whenever I had some free time, Walter would pick me up and take me to an open mic night, always keeping his eye on me. Sometimes, he would drop me off, and after he left, he would double back a few minutes later to check on me. He was doing whatever he could to make sure I wasn't using crack, and I tried to honor his efforts by behaving myself. But there were times when we were on the phone, and he could tell I was using.

*"I'm coming over right now to get you!"* he would yell into the phone before the call went dead.

He wouldn't take "no" for an answer, and our friendship grew even more. He was somehow always around when I needed him, or even when I didn't. When he came around to where I lived, or we were out somewhere, he always seemed to find a way to distract me from using crack and got me to focus more on my talents. Walter made it clear that he had a plan, took the music seriously, and saw me as part of that.

We began to get even more side gigs that paid more than the occasional tips or the free beers at open mic nights. A friend I knew from Chicago was hiring both of us to do background singing or studio work, and some of those singing gigs would pay anywhere from 50 to 100 dollars. The studio work paid a minimum of eight hundred dollars, and sometimes over a thousand. It was good money, but we both really enjoyed it.

One evening, Walter invited me over to his house, and I began rolling a joint. That was always a regular thing for me, and he never nagged me about that, and sometimes he would even give me weed. Then one day, while we were hanging out, he saw me add crack to my joint before I sealed it.

"How many times do I have to tell you that shit ain't good for you!" he berated me.

"I only add it 'cause I like the way it tastes with the weed," I said, knowing it was lie.

I don't think he understood how addicted I had become, but I had really been trying hard to use it less over the past few months while hanging out with him.

"Well, if you're gonna smoke that, I'm goin' out for a while," he said.

He got ready to leave the house, and I was just about to say I'd go with him when he placed a large bag of crack he had been selling on his table. Walter looked at me and said, "I'll be back."

I watched him go out the door and sat and stared at the bag.

When he came back an hour later, the crack bag was still in the same place, untouched, with nothing missing. He looked at me and tried not to smile.

"You didn't take anything out of this bag. You ain't no damn crack head."

"I told you; I just like how it tasted in my weed. And, I didn't have no weed," wishing I could say I agreed with him. It had taken everything I had not to smoke myself into a coma.

"Well, if you keep on just tasting it, then one day you won't be able to resist the slightest temptation, never mind a big one."

I simply nodded my head. Walter was my friend, and I didn't want to do anything to ruin that. I respected him, and I knew he respected me ... for now.

After a few months of us hanging out, while I did my best to keep clean, he did exactly as he said he would do when I met him. He saved up enough money to buy a truck free and clear. One of his first stops was coming to pick me up in Long Beach, where I stayed with the Balls. When he rolled up, I was right in the middle of rolling up a crack laced joint. When someone told me Walter was outside waiting for me, I put the joint down and went outside. There he was in his shiny new truck, grinning from ear to ear. He yelled at me from the driver's seat.

*"Alright, Marla, pack your things; we are going to New Orleans to play some music!"*

That was it. I ran inside and put everything I thought I needed into a duffel bag. I went right back out to his truck where Walter handed me a bag of weed and a set of brand-new harmonicas, along with a harmonica belt. I couldn't believe it.

"There will be so many gigs in New Orleans; you won't have time to put crack into your weed," he said before he put the truck into drive, and we were off. That laced crack joint never got smoked, and it was the last one I ever rolled.

We hit the road on our way to make good music and lots of cash, and I knew how lucky I was. To have ended up in the crack house, smoking like there was no tomorrow, was the craziest thing I could have done. Now instead of chasing the pipe, I would chase music, and thoughts of being a police officer were gone.

I'd had two major stars of the music industry grooming me to be a better singer-songwriter, and I couldn't throw that away. They saw something in me that I didn't see in myself. Neither of them knew I was using, and if they had, they would have dropped me in an instant. They never did find out, and Ms. Simone was still away when I left. I wrote her a letter when I got to New Orleans, but I got myself out of that huge hole thanks to Walter.

# CHAPTER 14

# New Orleans Blues

Walter's new truck provided a steady ride as we traveled east across the country. We stopped to eat at some great places along the way, and the idea of drifting again, playing music here and there, seeing new places and faces, helped keep my mind off the shit I'd gotten into back on the west coast. I slept a lot as he drove, and sometimes I would be playing the harmonicas Walter had given me. I smoked a joint or two, but music usually provided a good distraction for thinking about adding anything to the joint. While he was driving, I just played old tunes as he hummed along, his fingers tapping on the steering wheel.

We traveled through Arizona, New Mexico, and on into Texas, getting in and out of cities as quickly as possible, before again heading down long stretches of empty road, seeing only a few farms here and there. I wondered what the folks who lived there did when they needed to go to the store. It seemed like a lonely existence and nothing I would want.

I'd set out on this great escape from my problems, not knowing anything about New Orleans, and when we finally got there, it was awesome, not like any city I had ever visited. It was everything Walter had described, colorful and busy with a vintage feel to it as if we'd stepped back in time. People were hanging from balconies, watching all the folks below walking the streets; they were everywhere. I could tell most were tourists because they carried cameras, and many traveled in groups of three or more. The locals hurried around them, looking frustrated. The best thing was walking down Bourbon Street, and I couldn't believe how many clubs there were, all on the same block lined up in a row, and I longed to know what was going on in each one.

I couldn't wait to see how we'd get to playing in the street. As soon as Walter parked the truck, we made our way through the crowd and found a spot to place my guitar case on the ground. We began playing to the never-ending crowds of people, and with Walter playing the sax and me on the harmonica, we immediately began making good money. People would stop and listen, then drop coins or dollar bills into the guitar case; it was like being in a musician's playground!

We spent the first few days looking for a decent place to stay, but finding a hotel room at a reasonable price was not easy, so we slept in the truck a few nights. One time, when we decided to grab a bite to eat, he wanted a burger, and I wanted Cajun food, so we decided to split up. When I got to where we said we'd meet later, he never showed up. I hung around for a couple of hours, but no Walter, so, thinking I'd circle back later, I began to explore the city. People were friendly, many of them were musicians, and no matter where I went, there was always something going on. He still wasn't around at our meeting point later on, but I knew I would catch up with Walter eventually. Quite happy to be on my own, I found some cheap hotels, met a lot of people, and hung out on Bourbon Street, going in and out of clubs.

As I drifted about town, I liked talking to different people and making new friends. I wasn't worried about much because before New Orleans, I had drifted about California, New York, and of course, my hometown of Chicago. One afternoon, while I was wandering around, I stumbled on a lake where many people were hanging out. Right in the center of them all was a guy playing congas. I quickly made my way to this crowd that had a multi-cultural mix of people hanging out like hippies, and all I needed to do was pull out my harmonica and join in. Not only was it such a beautiful vibe, I also made a few bucks. Afterward, I went back to Bourbon Street to grab something decent to eat to celebrate my good fortune that day.

The food in New Orleans was so damn good it made you want to slap somebody. Dishes full of shrimp and crawfish were always good, but my favorite was gumbo, and I could eat it all day, and to top it off, the food was cheap. Most of the dishes I ate often had an amazing roux with celery, onions, and bell peppers. They were well seasoned with Cajun spices that would instantly lure your nose into hunger. After every meal, I'd shake my head and just smile. That awesome food sure helped me beat down the cravings for a pipe, and I was more than happy smoking a joint if I found some weed that day. Smoking after dinner was simply relaxing.

I also learned how things were done there regarding the music, particularly with the clubs that had open mic nights. Because so many musicians came and went regularly, most of the clubs had a high staff turnover, and they didn't get paid a salary; we worked for tips and stage time. At most of them, you could walk in, tell them what instrument you played, and that you also needed to work. Someone would toss you an apron and hire you on the spot, having you collect glasses and plates until your time came to perform on the stage.

Some places didn't need you to help out, so you could perform at more than one club at a time if they'd tell you approximately when your name would get called. There were always places to jam, and I loved being there and meeting a lot of musicians. As the bars emptied for the night, many of them would throw parties and barbecues. We would stand around eating and talking while we shared stories and information about gigs and opportunities. I never had a problem making friends, and there was never any jealousies or backbiting.

One evening I walked into a strip club and got to chatting with a couple of strippers while I waited for a slot. I mentioned I was looking for a more stable kinda job, and one of them gave me a lead for a strip club manager looking to hire someone. It was right on Bourbon Street and a little bigger than some of the other clubs. They had many mirrors on the walls, several tables surrounding a stage, and of course, the bar where I approached the manager.

"Someone referred me and said you were looking for help."

"We are."

"What do you need someone to do?"

"Clean the mirrors, wipe down the pole, run errands, and just act as security if any of the guys get out of hand with the girls."

"Not a problem," I said, and the job was mine.

It didn't pay much, but it was regular work and earned me enough to eat and find a regular place to sleep, but only at a seedy hotel with one bathroom for all the ten rooms on each floor. The mattress was better than sleeping on the ground, and the door fell off the closet each time I opened it, and I won't say what the bathroom smelled like, but I was grateful to have it.

The hours for the job allowed me to keep performing at several open mic nights, either before or after my shift, and I loved it. I was really starting to feel like my old self again, and I knew Walter was right. Regular music had replaced my desire to add crack to my weed and cigarettes, and I just didn't care about it anymore.

A few weeks went by, and one afternoon, when I had a day off, I was walking down the street to join the first open mic when I heard the smooth sounds of a saxophone playing to a small crowd that had gathered around to enjoy the music. As I approached and could hear more clearly, I recognized the style of playing and knew it was Walter.

Wailing away and giving a great show, he would occasionally nod a thank you to those who tossed tips in the saxophone case, but when he looked up, he caught my eye and the huge grin on my face. His eyebrows shot up in surprise, and he almost missed a note before he ended the song and told the folks gathered around that he was taking a break.

"Walter! Walter! I found you!" I said, and we hugged.

"Marla! How've you been? You wanna go somewhere and eat and chat?" he asked.

I couldn't resist the crowd's energy, and without hesitation, I shook my head as I pulled out my harmonica from my pocket.

"Hell, no man, I wanna start jammin'!"

Together again, we gave a mini concert for a crowd that kept growing, and they were all completely engaged in the performance. We complemented each other so well while playing some great bluesy tunes and kept it going while people consistently placed dollars into his saxophone case. The crowd became more and more enthusiastic, and we played harder. As we continued, I tossed my hat on the ground, and the crowd began placing money in my hat as well, and the pot of money was building like crazy.

Eventually, we stopped, thanked everyone, and headed for a beer, where we split some of the money and the rest we used for the rent for an apartment Walter had found. When I told him where I was living, he said he had a spare room. He'd been playing in the streets and had saved enough money to get the apartment, but the great money we made that day would definitely help. He said he had a girlfriend, and some days they'd want the place to themselves, but I was welcome to stay. I respected his privacy, so that didn't bother me. I'd always find a place to lay my head, so I moved in the next day. He was such a great guy, and I was so glad to meet up with him again.

One day after an open mic session that had gone down really

well with a large crowd, a small-framed fast-talking Jewish guy, who truly had the gift of the gab, approached me asking if he could be my manager. His name was Steven Katz, and he had a heavy New York accent, with a big-time city personality, and said he was the son of a government official.

"Marla, you can do better by getting paying gigs, and I'm gonna help you get 'em. You just focus on the work and getting paid, and I would only take a small commission."

He seemed to know what he was talking about, and I had often seen him at open mic nights talking to different artists, but I didn't really know him and guessed he told this spiel to everyone. I told him I was happy with what I was doing and watched him wander off to talk to another musician. I didn't really feel comfortable with this guy, but he tried to convince me to work with him every time I ran into him. He tried so hard to win me over; one day, he even bought me a new guitar. It wasn't an expensive one, but I was surprised, and after that, I thought maybe this guy could help me. I now thought more seriously about seeing what he could do.

A few conversations later, I insisted that Steven do things properly by giving me a contract. Within a day, he arrived at the club where we arranged to meet with a single one-page contract, and he handed it to me and asked me to look it over. I read it, but I didn't really know what was appropriate in this situation, so I didn't sign it. I just told Steven that I would work with him. Neither of us ever mentioned the contract again.

He invited me over to his upscale house in one of the best neighborhoods of New Orleans, where I met his girlfriend, Priscilla. She was gorgeous, but with every bit of beauty was a nasty side, and she turned out to be one of the biggest bitches I had ever met. No matter what I'd say to her, she would just give a piercing look without saying a word. Sometimes she would just completely ignore me. She called herself the 'Queen of Bourbon Street', and pranced around like she was untouchable. I'm guessing it was because of Steven's stature as being the son of a government official since sometimes I would see them with bodyguards as they traveled around New Orleans. The two of them together exuded white privilege.

One night, Steven told me he had set up a show that paid $200. I was excited and agreed to do the gig, and I went to the club to perform. Playing and singing my songs, some written under the tutelage of Bo Pop and Ms. Simone, I drew a great crowd, and the club owner was delighted with my performance.

After I got off stage, he said, "Great job! I'd love to have you back someday."

"No problem, so do I get paid from you?"

He looked surprised.

"No, Steven has your money. I paid him already."

I had expected to get paid directly by the club and planned to give Steven his cut after I got paid. Of course, I went looking for him, but I didn't feel good about this. I first went to the fancy house where I had met him one time, but of course, there was no answer. After a few days of not being able to find Steven, I went back to Bourbon Street looking for him. He was nowhere to be found, so I kept performing at the open mic nights and working at the strip club, but I did get some more paying gigs myself. Eventually, I caught up with him, and he made his excuses and paid me some money and got some more gigs, but I was always having to chase him down.

Because of our hectic schedules, I would rarely see Walter, and there were times he needed the place longer than expected. It was cool, but I began to want somewhere more stable. One evening when I was partying with a group of musicians, there was a house where I met this black guy named Kenny. He was a bass player, and there was a nice woman with him named Sylvia, who played the guitar. Kenny and Sylvia had only recently found this house to live in, so I asked if there was a spare room. They were pleased to have someone join them, and I moved in the next day.

My new place was a nice house with a big backyard, but best of all, it was walking distance to Bourbon Street. There was no rent to be paid because we were squatters. The owners were nowhere to be found, so the three of us took advantage of the situation. Many houses in New Orleans were vacant, and several of my musician friends squatted until they got evicted. We simply took over the property, had jam sessions, and lived in the house as if it were our own, treating it with respect.

One day while walking in the neighborhood, we found two stray dogs and brought them home. I named them, Teensy and Pupsy because they reminded me of two stray dogs Tuggy and I found when we were kids. After having them for a while, the dogs wandered off again, and I cried for days. Now, when I saw those two cute pups after Sylvia picked them up, I smiled and thought to myself, "Teensy and Pupsy finally came back to me."

Those dogs helped me feel like I had a piece of home with me, and Kenny, Sylvia, and I kept them in the backyard. They would bark whenever someone came near the house, and I figured they would be a great warning for us when the owners came back!

# CHAPTER 15

# The Contest

One evening when I came home, Kenny asked me if I was excited about being in a local contest.

"I don't know anything about being in a contest."

"You must've submitted yourself in order to be in it!"

"I have no idea what you're talking about, man."

After we kept going back and forth, I finally asked him, "Where did you see the flyer?"

"They are plastered all over town. Giving the contest venue and time and who's in it."

I was more than confused because I knew I didn't enter myself in any contest. I had to find out what the heck was going on, and I left the house looking for one of the flyers. I finally found one taped to a local storefront window, so I took it back home and showed it to Kenny.

"Is this what you're talking about?"

I showed him the flyer, and he seemed to be annoyed when he said, "Yeah, that's it.

Kenny had been in town longer than I had, and he played a lot of gigs trying to gain exposure. Now my name was on the flyer and not his.

"So, are you going to do it?" he asked me again.

"Well, yeah, I suppose I will. I don't know how I got in it, but I am gonna do it."

Contests were held all the time in New Orleans, and the prize was usually several drink tickets. Kenny surprised me again when he pointed to where the flyer mentioned a special prize, but there were no details.

"I overheard the contest's winner would be invited to perform overseas."

Kenny knew people, so it's possible it was true. I'd never imagined going overseas except when I wanted to join the army and doubted I'd win.

"Okay, well, I'm still gonna do it."

I later discovered that someone from the New Orleans Hard Rock Café entered my name into the contest, but I never found out who. The Hard Rock was one of the very first clubs where I performed when I arrived in New Orleans on an open mic night, but more importantly, it was one of my recent paying gigs. I played four songs and got four hundred dollars. Someone must have enjoyed it, but why didn't they speak to me?

I'd have time to do four songs in the contest and settled on adding a new one I had been working on. When I got home one night, I watched the late news and saw all the images of people tearing the Berlin wall down, and I was overcome with emotion. I grabbed an old envelope and sat there with a pen in hand, writing lyrics as tears ran down my face. I called the song *Believer,* and it appeared on my first album.

## <u>Believer</u>

Like a believer
We are out to find

Like a believer
We are living our minds

Like a believer
We don't waste any time

Like a believer
We stand our ground

I just can't understand this
Why it's so hard

To take each other by the hand and
And say that I love you

Like a believer
We can't let this go

No more war, no more war, no more war
Just say that I love you

This world is in trouble
We got to find a way

To come together
And make a better way

I can't understand this
No
Troubled the world
There's no time for children

And their hearts
Just look at their eyes

Can't you see you're tearing
Them apart
So I ask you believe us
Don't waste any time

Let's stay together and
Save our world

I just can't understand this
Why it's so hard

To take each other by the hand and
And say that I love you

Like a believer
We can't let this go

No more war, no more war, no more war
Just say that I love you

This World is in trouble
We got to find the Way

To come together
And make a better way

I can't understand this
This World is in trouble

We got to find the way
I can't understand this yeah

I just can't understand this no
I just can't understand this

On the night of the contest, when I walked in, other contestants were performing already, and the smokey, low-ceiling blues bar was packed full of people. I told someone my name was on the list, and I had to wait until a few more musicians took the stage before it was my turn to perform. I had the guitar that Steven purchased for me and went up on stage and gave it my best shot. I played four songs. I began with singing *Believer*, then I played *The Cost of Freedom*, added a cover of Neil Young's *Old Man Take a Look at My Life* and I ended with a personal favorite called *El Train Blues*.

The crowd seemed to be into it while I was performing, and immediately after I played the last note, they took to their feet and gave me a great standing ovation; I'd never seen anything like it. As I looked around the room in awe, I noticed four people in a booth off to the side, whispering to each other and writing notes, so I guessed they were the judges.

I watched a couple more acts who didn't seem to go down as well as I had but was sure there'd be several better than me. I left the club and headed out to another one on Bourbon Street where I had put my name on an open mic list earlier. Before I got halfway down the street, a young man stopped me, and I recognized him as one of the judges.

"*Wait! Wait! Where are you going? You won! You won the contest!*" he shouted with a French accent. It was quite common to hear that around the city.

"Oh right, great! Keep the free drink tickets for me; I'm going to another club. I'll get them tomorrow."

He rambled on about something, but I did not know what he was talking about. He then repeated, speaking more slowly to cut through the accent.

"You won the special prize!"

"Yeah, but won what? What's the prize?"

He didn't answer but began to ask odd questions.

"Do you have any responsibilities, family? Anyone here that you are accountable for?"

I didn't know why he wanted to know this information, so I said, "What difference does that make?"

He then began to explain.

"My name is Jean Claude. I am hosting a big festival in France called the Foire de Exposition. We are choosing winners tonight who will be flown there, and we will pay for everything. You're a winner!"

I was shocked but managed a grin.

"France? Cool! Well, when do we go?"

"Do you have a passport?

"No," I replied and thought there went my chance.

I must have looked somewhat crestfallen, but Jean Claude put a hand on my arm.

"Don't worry. Meet me at the club tomorrow, and I will pay for you to get a passport, and we can talk details."

He gave me his phone number, and I put it in my pocket.

"Okay, good. To sort everything, I'll meet you tomorrow at nine."

I nodded and began to head back down the street again.

Jean Claude shouted, *"Where are you going? Do you not want to go for a drink to celebrate?"*

In mid-stride, I called back, *"I signed my name on an open mic list. I don't want to miss my turn!"*

With the phone number in my pocket, I left to do my next show and blew the house down!

The next day, before I was scheduled to meet Jean Claude, I went looking for Steven again because my money was running out again, and there were several gigs I'd done that he hadn't paid me for. I went to most of the clubs on Bourbon Street where I might normally find him, and he was nowhere to be found. Upon leaving one of the clubs, I saw his girlfriend Priscilla through the crowd. I made my way toward her and touched her on the shoulder.

"Hey, where is your boyfriend?"

She looked in my direction and kept walking. I sandwiched my way in between a few people, touched her on the shoulder again, and said, "Wait a minute, I'm talking to you."

Before I got a chance to say her boyfriend owed me money, two of her bodyguards, who I had not noticed before grabbed me and started pushing me around. I began pushing them off me.

"What are you doing? Leave me alone! Her boyfriend owes me money!"

Priscilla turned around, and, in a sarcastic tone, said, "I don't know what you're talking about."

I looked her in the eyes and said, "You know me. Tell your boyfriend I need my money."

I was still grappling with the two guys holding me back from her while I was shouting the entire time. Next thing I knew, the police arrived, grabbed me, and within minutes dragged me away from the crowd and towards the street. I was crying and mad as hell, but no matter what I told them, they didn't want to hear it. They threw me in the back seat of their squad car and carted me off to the local precinct.

When I arrived at the New Orleans jail, the booking officer looked at my license, then looked at me, and the questions came. I had been through this before.

"Well, you look like a boy..." He paused, looked back at my license, and looked at me again. "... but your license says female."

I tilted my head to the side, agitated with this entire experience. "What difference does it make?"

By now, I was accustomed to people either giving me strange looks or questioning my gender. I really didn't give a fuck what he thought. I knew who I was. My God accepted me, so did my family, and that was all that mattered to me.

"Since your ID says female I'm locking you up with the women." I smirked and thought, *That's perfectly fine with me.*

No one knew I was in jail. I didn't call anyone, and I was still mad about Steven keeping my money. It dawned on me that I would lose the opportunity to go with Jean Claude and perform in Europe, but there was nothing I could do about it.

While in the cell, one of the guards approached me when he heard me singing a song I was trying to write.

"You a musician?" he asked.

"Yeah, I like to write and play music, why?"

He told me that there was a recreation break, and I could get an instrument.

"Great, can you get me a guitar?" He nodded and walked away.

The jail housed a lot of women in very large rooms. There were several cots next to each other, where we all slept. I played the guitar and flirted with a few of the women. After the lights went out, one of them asked me to suck on her breast. It was the oddest place I had ever done that, but I said to myself, "What the hell, I may as well make the best of it."

Someone must've let Jean Claude know I'd been arrested because after a few nights being locked up I received a phone call from him. He told me he would help me get out and wait for me before he went back to France. I breathed a huge sigh of relief.

Three weeks passed before my court date finally arrived. I was happy to hear that Jean Claude made good on his word. When I arrived in court, I was told he would be responsible for me after I was released. I was free to go, but I still had to do some time, so the judge placed me on house arrest for six months. He then looked down at me from his bench.

"You are very lucky that these people are helping you, but they tell me you are very talented. When you leave this courtroom, I don't want you to ever get yourself in this type of situation again."

"Thank you, Your Honor," I said and breathed a sigh of relief.

He released me to a woman named Susan, who was friends with Jean Claude, and after a few months of living with her, Jean Claude came to get me; there was still time before the festival. It was early spring of 1990, and it appeared my life was about to change forever.

# YOU HURT ME

*Never again I want to feel that feeling*
*Never again I want to hurt like that*

# CHAPTER 16

# My First Band

I wasn't the only person Jean Claude had chosen to be a part of the festival; other contests took place while I was in the house with Susan. Because of what happened to me, his colleagues were not happy with me to remain as a participant. However, Jean Claude ignored their wishes and found extra funding to include me in the process. He was determined and obviously believed in me to go to such lengths to get me into the festival. On the way to the airport, because I was not supposed to be among the winners, he had me sit in the back seat with my head down so I would not be spotted by his colleagues in nearby vehicles.

Once we got to the airport, we ran up against another set of problems. The tickets booked were business class seats, and I was dressed in beat-up jeans and an old T-Shirt. I certainly didn't look like I belonged in business class. Jean Claude wore business attire, but the airline attendant made a fuss about me, the two of them jabbering away in French, and the attendant refused to let me board. Jean Claude shouted at the attendant and suspected the refusal to let me board the plane was racially motivated.

"If you don't accept my traveling partner, then you don't accept me," he said, translating for me.

"Bien!" she snapped, and the plane departed without the both of us.

Jean Claude was livid, and not understanding a word of French, I stood clueless, worrying about leaving the United States, leaving my friends and the two dogs that I had grown to love, as Jean Claude scrambled to secure another flight. I learned later that Jean Claude thought I was whining about dolls and not dogs, which later, caused some much-welcomed laughter.

After several hours of delay, we finally landed in France. As we disembarked on the tarmac, I was so excited after we made it down the stairs that I kissed the ground. It had been such a long trip, and to add to the madness, we had a hard time tracking the luggage. After more complaining, they finally let us into a huge room where apparently lost luggage was being stored, and we found it. Without thinking, Jean Claude led us out of an exit door, which took us outside, bypassing customs. We managed to make it to the street, and within minutes he hailed a taxi, and we headed towards his home in the quaint little town of Niort.

In the beginning, I loved living with Jean Claude. He, his wife, and two kids had a lovely one-story house in the countryside of Niort, and the town looked like it came from a storybook. It was not only beautiful but also quiet and serene and situated near a small river with ducks and rowboats that took you deeper into the surrounding nature. Early in the mornings, I took a small boat out and would row myself along the stream while listening to my Walkman and smoking my weed. This was certainly a change of pace for me.

While I lived with them, I did everything I could to show appreciation by helping with household chores like sweeping, doing dishes, and even babysitting. They were so hospitable that I felt like family, except when they spoke in French, and I could not understand what they were saying. Jean Claude taught me a French word or two as I tried to pick up the language, and in turn, I would teach the children English words.

One of the first people I met outside the family was Jean Claude's secretary, Annie. She was a bubbly girl with dark hair and smiled a lot. Despite the language barrier, Annie and I had a lot of laughs and good times, and we became very close. She would often tell me about the difficult time she was having with a guy she was currently dating. There were now nights where I alternated between staying with Jean Claude's family and Annie's apartment.

After a few weeks in France, Jean Claude told me to grab my guitar and harmonica because we were going somewhere, and he had a big surprise when we got there. We arrived at a house nearby, and we headed to the door, where he told me to close my eyes.

I had no idea what was happening but put my hands over my eyes. He walked me through the door, and I could hear a band playing.

"OK, open your eyes."

I opened them to see a full band of six musicians, and then it hit me, they were playing one of my songs.

"This is your band!" Jean Claude said.

Immediately the musicians began to play *Cost of Freedom*. My mouth opened in shock.

"Oh my God! That's my song!"

It was the first time I had heard my song with a full band, a song I'd written as a child. I put my guitar down, grabbed the mic, and began singing and dancing.

"It's the Cost ... of ... Living! The Cost ... of ... Love."

I finished the song and felt overjoyed.

"Thank you, thank you so much!"

Tears began to well up in my eyes, and Jean Claude introduced me to the guitar player,

"This is Joel. He is the best in Niort. This is his home, and he will be your band leader." I shook Joel's hand and hugged him.

"Thank you, man. This is great. Thanks so much," I said

"You are welcome. Everything will be just fine, and you've written some great songs."

Joel then introduced me to the rest of the band, and afterward, we immediately got to work. The band had been practicing my music for weeks, and they were all fantastic, but I knew how the song sounded in my head, and so I would imitate the instruments' sound to each of them and how I wanted it all to be arranged. It worked out brilliantly, and I loved the band, and the band loved me.

None spoke fluent English, but the power of music and communicating with our hands prevailed. I would say things that just didn't translate from English, and they would look at me like they were really trying to get it. When you feel music, it makes you move differently; it makes you smile, or it creates a physical expression. I would shout to them, *"Feel it! Feel it! The music should be in your bones!"*

The band would look at me oddly and shake their heads at each other. Feeling music is something hard to teach or explain, but they got it in the end when Jean Claude translated. We later added backup singers and practiced for three weeks to prepare for the upcoming festival. I enjoyed every part of the process.

One afternoon, while standing in his kitchen, Jean Claude handed me a contract. I looked at it and saw I would be paid more money for the festival than all the gigs throughout my entire time of doing open mic nights.

"Oh wow! All this is for me?"

"Of course. You worked hard for it."

I had been away from home for quite some time now.

"Is it OK that I call my mom?" I asked Jean Claude.

"Of course."

The phone had a strange-sounding ring tone, and we dialed several numbers to get her.

"Hey, Mom, it's me!"

Mom always asked the same questions when I called.

"Marla, where are you? And do you have a job?"

I could hear the concern in her voice.

"I'm in France, Mom."

There was a pause; then, her voice went up an octave.

"What in the world are you doing over there?"

I so wanted to tell her but knew she wouldn't believe me, so I put her mind at ease.

"Mom, I do have a job. I'm working at McDonald's. They made me a manager.

"Well, how did that come about?"

I didn't want to stay on this conversation. There was so much happening so fast, and it was too much to get into.

"Mom, it's a long story. I just wanted to let you know I'm doing okay and hear your voice."

I could tell she was worried, but I think this put her mind at ease.

"Well, at least you called."

I wasn't sure how long I would be in France, but I would tell her all the details later.

"OK, Mom, I'll call you soon."

I began to focus on what I was there for, and it was overwhelming but fun. Between rehearsals with the band and learning the language and culture, there were a lot of things I was doing for the first time, like dancing on stage. I sang with the most passion I could, and at every rehearsal, I instinctively gave the guys instructions to give my music a full sound. We rocked Joel's house every time we got together and had a lot of fun doing it.

We also became friends, hung out after rehearsals, enjoyed good food, and laughed. Joel asked me to call him JoJo, and it just felt right as everything was running smoothly. Finally, 'The Foire Exposition Fair' arrived, and it ran from April 28th to May 6th, 1990, with thousands of people of all ages walking around enjoying the concessions, artistry, and farm animals. I was excited and a bit nervous about performing for such a huge crowd for the first time, but Jean Claude bought me fresh new clothes and a cowboy hat, and I exuded star quality.

I was new to all this attention, but I loved every minute of it. I was booked on two stages at different times of the day, and the festival would be attended by one of the largest crowds that Niort had ever seen. I was awestruck but ready to take the spotlight. I was a newcomer but wanted to handle it like a pro. We were escorted backstage, and before we got started, I ducked into the bathroom and talked to God.

"Lord, I have no idea how you got me here because this is such an amazing opportunity, and I know you are here guiding me. I just want to say thank you. Amen."

As I finished my prayer, I wondered if the French audience would understand an English-speaking artist from America. I walked around backstage for a few minutes, and Jean Claude approached me with a smile on his face. "I got an idea of how we should do your entrance."

"What is it?"

He pointed to the back door and said, "Follow me."

I was right behind him when he opened the door to a guy holding the rope attached to a huge white horse. It was beautiful. I shrieked, "This is going to be wild! I love it!"

The guy helped me get on the horse, and as I sat smiling taking it all in, I was told we were up next within moments. I got on the horse and headed towards the entrance of the performance stage.

"Hold on, boy!"

The stage was flanked on each side with two large audience areas, and a big aisle ran down the middle of the performance area. As I rode toward the front of the stage, the horse was probably calmer than I was. I heard the announcer speak in French, and the only thing I could understand was my name ...

*"Marla Glen!"*

There was a spattering of applause until people spotted me, and as the horse trotted down the aisle, the applause got louder. The horse arrived at the side of the stage and stopped perfectly, allowing me to get off as if we had rehearsed the entire thing. Once I got off the horse, I could see my band, and JoJo had a big grin on his face. I crossed to the mic, and we began playing Cost of Freedom.

Compared to the audiences in the USA, they were extremely polite. They were taking it all in, and some were barely moving their heads. I performed as rehearsed and had a ball on stage. I had arrived in France and was performing songs I had written years earlier, and by the grace of God, it was one of the most incredible feelings I had ever experienced. The band and I performed like pros, and no one ever knew that was my first big performance. The crowd was eerily silent until I finished the songs, then they gave rip-roaring applause that felt like thunder under my feet. When we finished, Jean Claude was waiting for me backstage with a huge hug.

"Did they like it?!" I asked.

He was grinning from ear to ear.

"More than that. You were spectacular!"

# CHAPTER 17

# Revenge in a Clothing Store

The Foire Exposition de Niort performance was outstanding, and afterward, I had several press interviews with radio, television, and newspapers. They all wanted to know who I was. Where did I come from? Was I a big star in the US? I was welcomed with open arms and felt my talents were appreciated.

After a few days, we were back at Jean Claude's house, and he was very busy working on my behalf. After he finished a few phone calls, he asked me, "I got you more work here. Would you like to stay and work for a while, or do you want to go home?"

"Oh, I want to stay!"

"You are very talented, and I will do everything I can to make you a big star."

I reached out my hand to shake his and said, "Let's make it happen!"

I kept practicing with the band while Jean Claude continued to schedule club dates, television and radio interviews, concerts, festivals, and even appearances at the local schools. After the festival, there was never an ongoing contract in place, it was just understood that he was handling everything on my behalf. I was never given any kind of big paycheck; no bank account was set up, but I didn't need much money because I was still living with him. I got paid for the festival, and he was giving me money for items I needed, but things started not to feel right, so I began to ask questions.

"Jean Claude, how much money am I supposed to get from the concerts?" I asked him over breakfast one morning.

"Marla, I am doing what I can to try to make you a star."

I needed more answers than this.

"There seems to be plenty of money coming in. I don't want to live with you and your family anymore. Why can't I get my own place?"

Jean Claude began to get frustrated.

"I can't get you your own place. I need to keep the overhead expenses low. It's much easier if you stay with us."

"But, I don't want to anymore," I said, and he ignored me and walked off.

I was not happy with this situation. Here I was in a foreign country, living with Jean Claude and his family, and the only time he would give me anything was when I begged him for it. I appreciated what Jean Claude was doing, but at 30 years old, I needed my own independence. I remembered how Ms. Simone had problems getting money from her manager, and I decided to give her a call since I knew she had a house in France. I had gotten in touch when I was in New Orleans but never told her about the contest.

"Ms. Simone, hey, it's Marla."

"Where have you been child? I have not heard from you in a while!"

"I'm in France. I've been over here performing, and I did a big festival. Are you here in France?" I could hear her smiling over the phone; it was good to hear her voice.

"No, I'm not there, but how nice you made it over."

This was something she would say to most people when they went abroad.

"So, how are things going over there?" she asked.

I began to downplay the situation, but I knew she heard the worry in my voice.

"Sometimes I'm working; sometimes I'm not. It's okay, but the problem is I don't really know how this business goes, and I think I need some help."

She was quiet for a moment as she gathered her thoughts.

"Do you have anything recorded yet?"

"I have a cassette tape."

"I want you to send that over to Mr. Raymond Gonzalez. He's my manager."

As she continued to talk, I wrote the information down.

"You might have talked to him on the phone a few times while you were living here. Just know dealing with him won't be easy. He will rip you off, but he knows the business very well and will get you work. And you will need to work. However, the man is sneaky. You're just going to have to watch him. The trick is trying to catch him."

Here I was taking instructions from Ms. Simone again but differently. She was steering me regarding my musical career. I was also aware that stars don't normally refer you to their managers, so this was a big deal. But she was extremely blunt about him, so I heeded the warning. She went on to give me his contact details and talking to her was like talking to family; of course, I was going to follow her advice and would record the next few shows so I could send the best songs to Gonzalez.

In the meantime, I began to chat more with Annie about how Jean Claude was handling the business of getting me booked. I also told her about the money.

"Annie, I'm not getting paid. He just gives me money for cigarettes and a few Francs here and there."

"Really?"

She seemed surprised.

"Something is not right. There is an amount he is supposed to pay you. It's a standard fee."

I know that Jean Claude had gone out of his way, but I felt at his mercy. I wanted things to be clear on how the music business operated and, more importantly, if there was a better way we could structure things so he would pay me. I was sick of asking him the same questions repeatedly, and things became awkward and uncomfortable, yet I kept taking the jobs he set up for me, hoping things would change.

I needed to get my cassette tape to Gonzalez, so I finally mailed it off, and it took a few weeks for Gonzalez to get back to me, and he told me he had received the cassette. It sounded like good news at first.

"I listened to it, and it seems you have a couple of good songs on there. The recording was not the best in quality, but I wanted to call to say thanks for sending it. As I said, some songs were okay, but I didn't like most of them."

He was knocking my work, but I wanted to apologize; he was all I had.

"Well, I could get a better tape. I was referred to you by Ms. Simone."

"Yes, I know. That's why I wanted to call you as a courtesy, but I can't do anything to help you."

"Well, okay," was all I managed.

"So, good luck to you."

I muttered some thanks and hung up the phone, wondering if Ms. Simone had spoken to him. I didn't know anyone else in France or in the music business, and despite his rejection, his comments made me want to get a better-quality tape. I told myself not to be discouraged and that if he heard a decent quality recording, he'd like the songs more. I was even more determined to find someone else to help me because things were getting worse with Jean Claude.

He kept repeating the same excuses as to why I wasn't receiving any money for the concerts he had arranged. I again told my concerns to Annie, who also had concerns because things weren't adding up.

"I don't understand why I'm not being paid anything," I said one day while over at her place.

"Something is really wrong, Marla. You may not understand, but I do."

I was glad to know I wasn't the only one suspecting that Jean Claude had been ripping me off. If I was not getting paid any money, surely he should have been able to get me my own place by now? I kept asking him again and again about that, and finally, he found an apartment for me. He told me it was a lovely one-bedroom place not too far from where he lived and close to the water near his house. We entered the building where lush green plants surrounded a quiet courtyard, and I thought how happy I could be there. Jean Claude walked ahead of me, and once we arrived in front of the door, he handed me the key.

"Okay, here you are. It will be some time before I can get more for you."

I opened the door and looked around. There was only a mattress on the floor, no furniture, no refrigerator, nothing.

"There's nothing here. How am I supposed to live here?"

"You wanted your own place, so here it is."

"How much is the rent, and who do I pay it to?"

"You don't have to worry about those things; I will take care of them," he snapped.

"C'mon Jean Claude; I want to know what's going on. You don't tell me anything. I want to pay my own rent. Why do you treat me like a goddamn teenager? Tell me how much I'm making on my concerts and why you think putting me in an apartment with no furniture and just a mattress is okay? *Where is the goddamn money going?*"

"I will put your money aside."

"Aside, where? How many times must we have this conversation?"

Jean Claude got frustrated again, shook his head, and walked off.

I had no idea how much the rent was or who to pay it to, but I made it work. I took whatever I could from Jean Claude and bought a few things to make it feel like home. I still had to make a fuss about things until he delivered answers or things I needed. Being in Niort and not knowing many people or the language made me frustrated and lonely. That changed when JoJo's cat had a litter of kittens. They were so cute and adorable; I played with them for hours, but one, in particular, kept grabbing my leg, and I just fell in love with it. I named the sweet thing Tassy Cat, and we were inseparable. Having her made me feel better about being in a strange town, far away from home.

Jean Claude used his resources to create as much work as he could, but dates were not coming in very often. It seemed as if the more I questioned him, the less I could get hold of him. He would often disappear, and I wasn't sure if he was still booking shows or where I could find him. I found out later that booking tours for talent weren't really what he did for a living; it was just for the Foire de Exposition that he took on the job. Eventually, JoJo took over with getting gigs for the band, but we all pulled together as a team trying to find work.

Things fell further apart when Jean Claude picked me up after a show, and I noticed he was wearing a brand-new outfit. He was very sharp, wearing leather pants and a new shirt and I could tell they were not cheap. I knew he didn't earn enough for such extravagance, so there was only one place he could have gotten the money from. I didn't say anything, but the next day, Annie and I went into an upmarket men's store and said I wanted to try on outfits that I thought would be good for upcoming concerts and shows.

I picked out a few new suits, and when I was done, I told the salesman he could get Jean Claude to pay. He looked at Annie, who shrugged her shoulders, and gave him the number. While I waited for the call to be made and my new clothes to be wrapped, Jean Claude burst through the door like a bee had stung his ass. We had a blazing argument, but I didn't back down, and in the end, he paid.

Once Jean Claude had stormed out of the shop, Annie and I left there giggling. Jean Claude had earned my trust by believing in me, even waiting while I was in jail, but things had changed, and I knew he was only interested in the money I could make for him. The relationship was totally soured, and I was desperate to find a way out. I got lucky when he came over to my apartment to discuss a show and accidentally left his briefcase in my living room.

I called Annie, who was now looking for another job to get away from Jean Claude and told her I needed to get it back to him. Annie came over quickly but surprised me with what she said.

"Marla, he keeps everything in here, and if we open it, we might find the proof we need to show that he is cheating you."

I didn't need to think about that for long; it was a great idea.

"Okay, but what do we do?

She grabbed the papers out of the briefcase, and as she began to go through them, a wide grin spread across her face. She left with the briefcase in hand, and half an hour later, she came back with copies of all the important papers. She then called Jean Claude and told him he had left his briefcase at my apartment. When he showed up, it was as if nothing was moved and Annie was gone. I had the proof I needed that Jean Claude was not paying me properly, and Annie helped me find an attorney to sue him in court.

In January 1991, the paperwork I confiscated won me my day in court, and I was awarded 12,000 Francs, but I never received a dime from Jean Claude. It was noted in the Niort Newspapers and local news, but it wasn't a big story. I later found out that it cost Jean Claude his reputation, his wife divorced him, and he left to spend time in Africa. I was still grateful that he gave me such an opportunity to get started, but I wish he had done things differently. As it turned out, he was only the first to take me for a ride. Ms. Simone had often warned me music was a dangerous business to be in, especially regarding being able to watch the people who were in control of your career, and things were going to get progressively worse.

# CHAPTER 18

# Sandrine

After the hearing early in 1991, Tassy Cat and I moved into a small studio apartment the courts assisted me with obtaining, which was quite lovely. The news about the case was in a small article in the local newspaper, so it could've been easily missed and didn't generate much publicity. However, I was still occasionally featured on a few local television stations, in newspapers, and in other press events, so the band and I picked up where Jean Claude left off.

We continued to get booked for shows throughout the Niort areas and other places in the western region of France, taking gigs from wherever we could. We were determined to keep moving forward and make things work, and most of the gigs we found on our own by talking to club owners of bars, and promoters. I wasn't going to let this setback stop me, but I found it ironic that I was almost drifting again, albeit on a bigger scale. This was a different town in a different country, but I was determined to survive and find a way to achieve the success many people had told me I deserved.

JoJo did most of the organizing because I couldn't speak French fluently enough to handle the details of getting booked. We all did what we could without any one person acting as a manager, and whenever we landed something, we split the money equally. We were a very close-knit group with a great working relationship.

Most of the shows didn't pay much, but we had a lot of fun doing them despite the struggle we experienced to keep the momentum going. After every show, we would hang out, laugh, drink, and just have a good time. Despite the language barriers often causing misunderstanding, we laughed so hard our stomachs hurt. Even when we weren't performing, we would hang out practically every day as I tried out new songs. Despite the ups and downs of the music business, I felt these guys were like family members hanging out, playing music, and having fun.

One winter evening, on the way to a show, the van we were using to get around in broke down, and we pushed the van several miles through the snow to where we were scheduled to perform. Despite the breakdown, we weren't late, and this was typical of the fun times we had that provided wonderful memories. Even though we were getting booked, things were financially getting tighter. I found a studio that was able to copy cassettes with my songs *Believer* and *Cost of Freedom*, and we sold them at our shows. The extra money helped, but once split among all of us, it wasn't very much.

By the next summer, we were still doing what we could to make money with the band when one evening, while performing in Niort, I stopped at a bar and saw a very beautiful brunette. She was fine as wine, and I wanted a sip. She was sitting at the bar alone, and when the band stopped playing, I walked over and took a seat next to her. She smiled and said, "Wow! What a show!"

I looked into her eyes, "Thank you, glad you enjoyed it. Let me buy you a drink."

I waved to the bartender, "Please give the lady another of what she's having."

I could not stop looking at her, as she was so beautiful. She only wore a pair of jeans and a nice top, but with the way she moved, I was attracted to her sexy, feminine frame.

"So, what are you doing here by yourself?" I flirted.

"I'm not here by myself; I'm with you now."

Her quick-witted response threw me off a bit, but I rolled with it and leaned closer.

"Yes, you are, and I'm loving it. What's your name?"

"I'm Sandrine."

"Hi Sandrine. I'm Marla, your new boyfriend."

She giggled, and I knew I had her.

"Your voice is so interesting. You're very talented."

"Thank you. And what do you do?"

"I'm studying to be a chiropractor."

I smiled and said, "Well, why don't you study on me sometime. I'd love for you to crack my back; right after we wake up from a long nap."

This time she laughed out loud, and I joked with her for about thirty minutes before the band was all packed up and ready to go. I simply said goodbye to her but knew something had happened. The next few evenings, I hung out and about in Niort until, while I was walking down the street toward the same bar, I saw her again. We were walking in opposite directions, and without hesitation, I said, "Hey Sandrine, go out with me!"

A big smile crossed her face, and she said, "Sure, why not!"

From that moment on, we really hit it off and started hanging out regularly. Sandrine was as intelligent as she was beautiful, and I couldn't get enough of her because she really intrigued me. We spent a lot of time together and would go to each other's apartments or hang out around town. People would stare, and I wondered if it bothered her.

"You live in this town. Do you care what people say about you dating a stud?"

"No, I don't – they don't know me."

Sandrine's place was much bigger than mine, so I spent most of my time there. We loved each other's company, and the lovemaking was amazing. Eventually, Sandrine introduced me to her mom, and although she was hesitant about telling her dad, I understood. She invited me to dinner at her parents' house, and once I got to really know her dad, our dating didn't seem to be a big issue. After getting to know me, they accepted me with open arms.

After a few months, it was no shock to anyone when Sandrine asked if I wanted to save money and move in with her. It made sense, so of course, I said I would love that. She was a great support, and she began working with JoJo to get concerts organized, but before that happened, I raised my concerns.

"Look, you're my girlfriend, and you don't have to help out. I know you're studying to get your chiropractor's license. I don't want to get in the way of that."

She looked at me with her big, beautiful eyes and perfectly styled hair.

"I want to do this. You're talented, and I know you're a sure thing. I believe in you."

I loved her even more for saying such a thing. I was lucky to have her.

With Jean Claude out of the picture, JoJo was becoming overwhelmed with doubling up as the bandleader, arranging rehearsals, and helping to book gigs. A lot of French conversations flew over my head, and sometimes I didn't understand the language or how things were working out. He eventually called on a musician friend who had great contacts by the name of Phillipe to help with bookings so JoJo could just focus on the music.

Phillipe and Sandrine began working together to get bookings, with Sandrine making sure I got where I needed to be, and Phillipe dealt mostly with promoters. As we got more shows and performed for larger audiences, Sandrine set up a makeshift office in her apartment. I trusted JoJo and Sandrine, which was all that mattered. However, Phillipe brought a different energy to the group, and he rarely spoke much around me, making me uncomfortable until I spoke to him properly. From then on, his management of the bookings seemed to be growing into him organizing the whole band.

# CHAPTER 19

# Enter Mr. Gonzalez

It was now mid-1991, and the Compact Disk (CD) technology was becoming popular. To take advantage, in front of a live audience, we re-recorded the songs on the cassette from *Marla Glen Live* onto a CD. Not long after the recording, Phillipe sent the CD to several record companies in an attempt to get a record deal, and two companies responded favorably. One of the companies was Vogue Records, and it looked like this would be a big deal for all of us.

Phillipe, Sandrine, and I took a trip to Paris and sat down for our first meeting with the head of the record company, a young Frenchman by the name of Fabrice Nataf, who seemed very excited to have us on board. Upon entering the office, I was a bit nervous but definitely excited when Fabrice greeted us with a smile.

The meeting was casual, and I listened as best I could while everyone in the room spoke French around me. I could only pick up on the occasional word I was familiar with.

"So, Marla, how do you like it here in France?" asked Fabrice.

"I love it here. The people are nice, and I'm having a good time performing."

I did not know what questions to ask, but he seemed very interested, so he kept asking me questions.

"I hear you are doing very well at your concerts. You have more songs?"

"I have been writing songs for a long time. From when I was a kid."

Sandrine interjected, "Marla is a great performer, and I have never seen a bad show."

The conversation turned and they began speaking in French again until we got up to leave. There was no contract available to sign, but it seemed everything was going well because they all were smiling, so I could only guess he liked my music. We left the office, and before we reached the exit, they were both smiling. I could tell that it went well, but of course, I asked, "How did it go?"

"It went very well," said Sandrine, taking my hand. "He wants to come to one of the shows."

We had a show in the next few days, so after the meeting, I focused on what I needed to work on to get ready. By now, the concerts hardly stopped, and we were booking bigger and better shows that were getting closer to Paris. About a month or so went by, and while I was going over some music in our apartment in Niort, I received a phone call from Mr. Gonzalez. He was very different this time and seemed more interested,

"Hello, Marla! This is Raymond Gonzalez; how are you, dear?"

I had almost forgotten I had spoken to him.

"I'm fine. Who is this again?"

"Raymond Gonzalez, you were referred to me by Nina."

It came to me that he said he wasn't interested.

"Oh yeah, how are you?" I said noncommittally.

"Listen, I got a chance to see one of your concerts, and I'd like to talk to you about working together."

"But I thought you weren't interested?"

"I have to say I spoke too soon, but the tape you sent me was not the best quality. I guess I've had a change of heart. Come to Paris for a meeting with me, and let's have a conversation."

There was no contract from Vogue Records yet, and Ms. Simone referred him.

"Sure. I'll meet you."

I decided to take this meeting without Sandrine and Phillipe. It might have been different if Gonzalez only spoke French, but I didn't need anyone interpreting with him. Despite her complaining about him, he had worked with Ms. Simone, so I felt confident in talking to him alone. I asked Sandrine to write down the instructions for me to take the train, and I took the ride from Niort to Paris. I wasn't intimidated at all by taking the train, but the idea of reading French to navigate was a challenge. Before I left, I made a phone call to someone else.

After several hours on the train, Gonzalez picked me up at the station. He was a small-framed man with a big smile, and he welcomed me with a hug as if he knew me. He called me by the wrong name when we first met, but I let it go. It was a good feeling to simply be able to have a conversation with someone who was from the US, and I was happy he changed his mind about working together.

We arrived at his apartment, and it was a nice size, elegantly decorated with tasteful Victorian furniture. He introduced me to his wife, a very beautiful French woman. She was much taller than him with long brown hair and did not speak English at all. They had a small baby boy, around two or three. His wife made tea as we sat down to talk.

"So, Marlo, how did you make it to Europe?" I wasn't sure if I could handle him calling me the wrong name all day.

"It's Marla, Mr. Gonzalez. Marla Glen."

"Oh, Marla. Got it!" I kept going with the conversation by telling him the story of my winning the competition in New Orleans.

"And now I understand you've had a conversation with Fabrice Nataf."

I hadn't told Gonzalez, so he must've heard about Fabrice's interest in me. This must have been why Gonzalez changed his mind. I said nothing about it.

"Yes, and the meeting went well. I may be working with him, but I don't know for sure yet."

"I think you will. He likes what you do."

I wanted to ask more questions about him and how he would play a part, but I didn't know what questions to ask him. However, I made it clear what I wanted.

"I want to learn more about the music business."

He leaned back in his chair like a tycoon, lit a cigarette, and crossed his legs.

"You will learn as you go, and I will tell you what I can as we work together. But some things you will have to experience on your own."

When the conversation turned into him telling me how we would work together, it seemed to be a clear sign that things were going well.

"You join me, Marlo ... Marla, and I can make sure you get bigger shows, and I will also arrange tours for you that I will attend."

"What about the people I'm working with already?"

"There is room enough for everyone to work on your behalf."

I was happy to hear he was open to working with us as the team had already established a groove. Clearly, he was very experienced in the music industry, and we could get even more concerts booked with him on board. About half an hour or so into the conversation, there was a knock on the door. Gonzalez looked at the door and said, "I wonder who that is? I'm not expecting anyone."

He crossed to answer the door, and then I heard a voice I knew very well.

"Oh my God, Marla, look who's here!" he said, and moments after, Ms. Simone sauntered in like she owned the place.

"Hello, hello, everyone. I'm *so* glad I could make it here."

Gonzalez was surprised, but she'd told me she might show up when I called her the night before and learned she was in France.

She spoke fluent French, greeting Gonzalez' wife, then took a seat next to me on the couch.

"I have so much going on right now, but I really wanted to be here for you, Marla. I'm sure by now that Raymond has told you enough lies."

I laughed, but Ms. Simone did not. Gonzalez immediately went on the defensive.

"Oh, Nina, I'm being quite honest with Marlo."

Ms. Simone flashed me a look and raised her eyebrows. He corrected himself again.

"I meant Marla, forgive me."

Ms. Simone jumped right to business.

"What have you discussed?" she asked, looking first at me and then at Gonzalez.

"I was telling Marla how I can get larger audiences and—not that his team isn't doing well right now—but I can bring other shows to the table and—"

With a motherly tone and demeanor, she interjected, "He's right, Marla, and this is why I referred him to you. He will get the job done, but you are going to have to watch him. He's tricky."

I didn't know what to say and felt confused as to why I was sitting there if she knew there was a huge downside to the arrangement. It was one thing doing bigger and better shows, but it was another thing to get ripped off, as I had with Jean-Claude.

"There are others, but he is good," she said, adding, "and maybe a little less of a shark than the rest. They are all as bad as each other in this industry."

Gonzalez tried to defend himself.

"Oh Nina, I never ripped you or anybody off and—"

"Bullshit, Raymond. You don't go there with me, today or ever. Now listen ..." With a finger held up, she pointed to me. "... you make sure you don't do anything to hurt this one, you understand me?"

Gonzalez sighed and shook his head as if he'd heard it all before. While her accusations seemed like water off a duck's back to him, Ms. Simone continued to rant.

"Listen, you do not play those games you play with me on this one. You are to protect this one, and I mean that, Raymond, or God's wrath will certainly come down on you. Do you hear me?"

"I don't know what you are talking about. But I will make sure Marla is getting the best I have to offer. You know that, Nina. I plan to call everyone I know across Europe for bookings. Just as I do for you."

Gonzalez was as cool as a cucumber, and his personality reminded me of that first attempt at working with Steven in New Orleans.

As they continued to debate his behavior, I got bored and started to play the guitar I'd brought with me as always. Eventually, the mood in the room changed, and we shared a few laughs. However, no contract was mentioned, nor was there one given, but Gonzalez and I agreed to move forward with working together. I was excited it could lead to better things, but it felt good to have Ms. Simone there to ensure I was okay. She truly felt like my spiritual mother.

Shortly after the meeting with Gonzalez, things began to get chaotic, and the first thing that happened should have been a clue that things were not going to be anything like I expected. I arrived at a rehearsal at a new location, and when I walked into the room, I was stunned to see a completely new band in front of me. With no time to protest and get things sorted out, new band members were learning the songs I was singing, which was very uncomfortable. Gonzalez appeared and told me that Fabrice came to a show, and he decided my band was not strong enough.

"Honey, this is now your band," Gonzalez explained. "You will have better people that will take your show to another level."

"But they were *my* band! Why would Fabrice do this without talking to me?"

Tears welled up in my eyes, not knowing how to deal with this, and Gonzalez tried to explain.

"Look, if he is going to invest in you as an artist, he wants to make sure you are shown in the best light. This happens all the time, and once you get used to these new guys, you will be okay."

There was a concert coming up, so I needed to rehearse. I did the best I could with the new guys, but the changes never stopped. New musicians were coming and going all the time, and none of them spoke very good English, so I had no say about who would join the band or not. Things were frustrating, hectic, and often uncomfortable, but I tried not to show it. On top of band changes, there were times when I didn't know if I was coming or going. Both Phillipe and Gonzalez were booking shows at the same time, leaving me, in some instances, having to be in two places at once!

Whenever I asked Gonzalez about things constantly changing, he would give a half-assed excuse, and I didn't know what to say or do about it. I would ask people around about what was going on, and no one had answers; some of them did not speak any English, and I was struggling to learn French because I never had any time to study and had never been any good at languages in school.

Sometimes things were fun, but more often than not, it was frustrating. I traveled a lot and had a concert or some other booking almost every day. The musicians were good, but they were not my band and didn't give the feel JoJo and the others had developed.

The bookings were coming in from all over Europe, France, Germany, Turkey, Israel, Switzerland, and Austria. I began performing at a lot of the top festivals; I did some television appearances, commercials, private parties, and promotional events. I shared stages with some of the greats, including James Brown, the Temptations, and Paul Simon, to name a few.

While it was a lot of fun on stage, things continued to be crazy and awkward because I felt like there were still so many unanswered questions. With the two teams still in place, things became even more confusing, and some things got dropped because of communication issues, frustrating everyone. It was clear there were a lot of people making decisions without talking to one another.

Gonzalez opened up the markets of Austria, Switzerland, and Germany, and it was clear Phillipe was no match for the seasoned Gonzalez, who did whatever he could to get shows booked. Sandrine was responsible for bringing me to and from Niort, but the four-hour drive from Paris became too much to work into my hectic schedule. Instead, the record company placed me in a cheap, run-down hotel that housed many refugees.

I had been in the recording studio for a few weeks, singing the same songs over and over, and I rarely got enough sleep. I never missed a rehearsal or show, and even though my head was spinning, I knew things would be alright after I signed the contract with Vogue. I had rarely seen Fabrice since the last meeting, but he did show up to a few recording sessions and seemed pleased with how I was doing. Eventually, after a long day of rehearsal, Gonzalez approached me looking excited and told me Fabrice wanted to meet me that night.

After we were done with rehearsals, a town car picked us up and took us to the Vogue offices, where we waited for Fabrice to finish phone calls. After he completed shuffling paperwork, Fabrice picked up a bottle of champagne along with three champagne glasses and his briefcase as he walked out of his offices and headed for the exit. He and Gonzalez spoke a few words in French, and Gonzalez and I quickly followed them out of the door.

"Where are we going?

"He has to take a train," Gonzalez explained, "we will do business there and celebrate on the train. It's fine. Let's go, Marla."

I didn't know exactly what we were celebrating, so I just waited to see what they were going to tell me. Once we got on the train, we made our way to a table in the dining car, and we all took a seat. I sat next to Gonzalez, and Nataf sat across from us. Fabrice pulled out a contract of several pages, all written in French, and began to explain it. The key component was that I was to deliver four albums in eight years and receive monies when I signed the contract. It was late, almost midnight, and my head was spinning. I was elated but also felt I was diving into a hornet's nest.

"Can I get a contract in English?"

Fabrice looked at me. "We don't have the attorneys to do that, but after you sign, you can take it to an attorney to look it over."

I looked at him for several moments and eventually shrugged.

"Where do I sign?"

Gonzalez looked like he'd won the lottery as Fabrice turned to the relevant page, and I signed on the dotted line. I wasn't sure if I was doing the right thing—writing enough decent songs to fill four albums seemed reasonable—but it didn't seem like I had much choice. I felt comfortable enough to sign the contract, but as I looked up, I turned to Gonzalez.

"Are we discussing today how we are going to be working together?"

"I've already begun working for you."

I was not clear on how he was working on my behalf without a contract.

"There's no contract between us? I don't know what you are supposed to be doing, or how I'm supposed to pay you? Fabrice has said I could take his contract to an attorney. Can you help me do that? And can you give me a contract, too?

"Sure, honey, we will get it done. I promise you."

Within a few days, Gonzalez set up a meeting with an attorney who stepped out of his office and greeted us. We took seats opposite him, and I handed him the contract. Gonzalez and the attorney spoke in French for a while, but afterwards, Gonzalez said very little. The attorney went over the contract, reading in silence. After a few minutes, he looked up from the contract and over his glasses.

"This is a very good contract. Publishing and everything else is in your favor."

"Does it say, four years, eight albums?" I asked.

"It does, but just be careful because the man you are with appears not to have your best interest in mind."

How on earth could he know that? Could this attorney have spoken to Ms. Simone, or was his reputation broader? The attorney turned to Gonzalez and pointed his finger in his face.

"If you do anything to manipulate this contract, you will be in a lot of trouble. You better take care of this artist."

Gonzalez did not respond right away; after a pause, he only said, "Of course. C'mon man."

Without understanding the language, I had learned to rely on watching people's expressions, their body language, and listening to their voices and the tone in which the attorney spoke, which assured me that he was being honest and upfront about the contract. However, Gonzalez's body language showed he was stiff and uncomfortable. Was Ms. Simone right about him?

I left hoping I would be okay, but glad to be moving forward knowing that the contract was a good one. However, I was still very much on the fence about dealing with Gonzalez. Yes, he'd helped get me the contract and was getting some great bookings, but would I have money problems again?

# CHAPTER 20

# Catch 22

The relationship with Sandrine had run its course, and she and Phillipe were no longer in the picture. I found out later that Gonzalez paid them off—with my money, no doubt—so he would pick me up and drive me everywhere I needed to be. The record company wanted me closer to Paris, which made sense because of the long commute from Niort. I agreed to the move, and Gonzalez was responsible for finding me an apartment. At first, he wanted me to stay with him for a while, but I said I needed my own place. I wasn't going to repeat my experiences with Jean Claude.

He quickly found me a place near the Gare du Nord, a very busy part of Paris. The building was dark and rundown, and the rooms seemed like an old hotel that had been converted to an apartment building. Inside the unit, there was no kitchen, one window, and the bathroom was extremely tiny. A lot of refugees from Africa and other parts of the world lived in the building, and in and around the area, I witnessed people selling drugs out in the open. This was good and bad, as I didn't have to go far to get my weed, but it didn't feel like the safest place I could live. I had just signed a contract for a major record deal and was living among those on the breadline.

"I know I'm making good money, so I want somewhere better," I said to Gonzalez.

"We have a lot of overheads, Marla. The good times will come, but we have to plough the money back in right now."

I knew he was bullshitting me, but I could do nothing about it.

I wasn't there much because I was busy with concerts, rehearsals, and other musical appointments, but it was still a seedy place to call home, and I was hoping I didn't have to live there long. Me and Tassy Cat simply made the best of things. Sometimes I'd visit the local bars in the area, make a few friends in the building, or hang out at some of the nearby restaurants. It wasn't unusual to see Africans in the area, and I liked the idea of being around black people; while living in Niort, I rarely saw any.

I befriended a neighbor in the building who was originally from Madagascar, who I think was gay, and his name was James. He had a bigger and better apartment, and when I was in town, he would invite me over and cook great dishes native to his country. It was rare to get a home-cooked meal, so I enjoyed it and welcomed his hospitality. James was soft-spoken but loved to talk, and we became good friends. When I was on the road, he would look after Tassy Cat.

Many of the people I met in the area didn't speak English very well, nor did we share the same cultural backgrounds, even though many of the black people looked like those I had grown up with. One afternoon, while walking down the street where I lived, I saw an African guy staring at me. I, too, was staring at him. He smiled, and I smiled. We stopped in front of each other, and with a thick African accent, he said, "What are you smiling for?"

I was mesmerized at how dark his skin was; it had a blue hue. I had never seen anyone that dark before.

"What are you smiling for?" I asked back.

We laughed and began to walk down the street while chatting;

he seemed pretty nice. I felt comfortable enough to ask, "You know where I can get some weed?"

I put my fingers up to mouth and blew to be clear he knew what I was talking about. He understood perfectly.

"Oh, the good stuff."

I laughed, and he looked around conspicuously.

"I cannot do it here, my brother."

I said, "Well, I live right there."

Once inside my apartment, he pulled out a bag of weed and rolled a couple.

"Where are you from?" he asked.

"I'm from America; where are you from?"

"Congo."

"I'm from Chicago, and you from the Congo," I said, and we laughed again.

"What's it like over there?" I asked.

"Some people are poor; some are rich."

"Hell, that's just like it is in America."

We laughed and sat talking about the differences and similarities in our cultures. In mid-sentence, he grabbed my head, pulled it slowly toward him, and began examining my scalp, separating my hair as if searching for bugs. He was feeling the texture of my hair. Impulsively I pulled my head back.

"Hey man, it's just hair; get your hands off my head."

"Is that your hair?"

I laughed and said, "Hell yeah, man. Is that yours?"

We both laughed hysterically as we continued to smoke. The weed he had was good, too, and being in his company for a while, with someone genuine, someone who didn't seem to want to exploit me, was such a refreshing change.

The next day, I was scheduled to be with Gonzalez. I couldn't navigate Paris or the music industry on my own, so he took me everywhere, especially when handling business or organizing concerts. Gonzalez handled all the paperwork, interviews, photo shoots, and after-concert events. The benefit of this was I was in his car with him when I made another breakthrough.

"Marla, they just said your name on the radio."

I listened closer.

"They did?"

Seconds later, *Believer* was blaring from his car speakers, and a huge smile came over my face before screaming, *"Aw man! This is so cool!"*

I was so excited to hear my name and music on the radio that it made me feel like all the hard work I had put in so far was a dream come true. It also reminded me of home, when everyone on the block would listen to WVON 1450, the most popular R&B radio station in Chicago when I was growing up. We had a radio in the kitchen and even in the bathroom.

I remember when my childhood friends, Larry and Leroy Ball, landed jobs at an early age with Smokey Robinson, Earth, Wind & Fire, and other artists, and whenever one of the songs came on the radio they were playing on, all the neighborhood kids who were listening would be sitting on the porch and we'd shout, "That's Larry on that bass! That's Leroy playing that keyboard!"

It was such an exciting moment, hearing my song being played, but underneath this newfound fame, I was not happy. I was frustrated and upset because while Gonzalez was booking plenty of concerts, I would only get money sporadically. I still hadn't signed a contract with him, and he was working hard on my behalf, but I didn't know the details of what he was doing or how much money he was bringing in. When I asked him he'd tell me I didn't need to bother about that side of things, I needed to concentrate on my act and more songwriting.

While the shows were not as big, and we would split the money, it was much easier when I worked with JoJo, Sandrine, and Phillipe. Dealing with Gonzalez was such a different situation, and he was rarely forthcoming with any information. With Sandrine and Phillipe no longer around, most of my questions went unanswered. If I did get an answer, it would no doubt change the next day.

I was getting paid a few francs after a show. Gonzalez would hand me large amounts of cash in envelopes. With this being a new level of business, I knew this wasn't how things should have been handled. One day after a show, he came into my dressing room, and I rattled off a bunch of questions I had asked him before.

"How do I know this is the right amount I'm supposed to be getting?" "What about my taxes? I know this isn't right." "If I'm getting this much, how much are you keeping?"

Gonzalez looked at me, unaffected, and said, "Look honey, I'm doing it this way because if there were any problems, it would fall on me and not you."

Every fiber of my being felt like he was lying, but I didn't know what to do about it. I had mentioned what was happening to a few musicians, and I could tell they didn't want to get involved. I finally pulled a guy who spoke English quite well aside.

"Look man, I know this guy is ripping me off, but I don't know what to do."

He looked at me for a moment and then shook his head.

"Marla, I can't say anything, or I'll get fired."

I felt as if they saw me as an artist who was getting famous and getting paid, so I must have been in a good place in my life. It wasn't the case; I was dealing with things minute by minute, one day at a time, praying and hoping things would make sense. The details about the music business were very unclear, and the language barrier didn't help, given I still didn't have the time or the aptitude to learn it properly.

Even after my time with Ms. Simone and Bo Pop, I didn't know much about the music industry and its dealings, and everyone around me knew this as well. The most I knew was from Ms. Simone, and the most she said was how everyone got ripped off! If they did, how come they had fancy cars and houses, and I lived in virtual poverty?

I could see the record company was promoting me well; by now, I was on MTV and other television shows in France, Germany, Switzerland, and Austria. I was doing all that, seemingly living the life of a music star, but when I wasn't on stage or in the studio, I would sit and watch television in that shitty studio apartment.

I would see myself singing and wonder how much money I got from those videos being on TV. I began to see my picture on large advertisements throughout Paris, and on every newsstand, I passed by, I'd see me on the cover of a magazine or a newspaper article, sometimes on multiple covers at the same time. By now, people began to recognize me wherever I went. I wore suits and hats on stage, but when I wasn't performing, I would dress in jeans and T-Shirts, so I thought I was remaining incognito. They still recognized me, and I wouldn't hesitate to take photographs with fans or provide autographs. It was a very humbling experience, and I treated fans the way I wanted to be treated if I were one of them, but I could not help thinking about what might have been going on behind my back.

Even when meeting fans, I did not consider myself a star; in my mind, Ms. Simone was a star. At the time, I was working as a performer trying to figure this music thing out. I'd stop by newsstands and purchase magazines and newspaper articles with my face on it, and I had no clue about what the articles were saying. Since I was smiling on the cover of a magazine, I assumed everything they wrote was good. The idea of having my picture on huge posters and doing concerts all over Europe, being in commercials and television shows, posing for pictures while walking throughout Paris, not knowing when or if I'd get another envelope of cash was a crazy, mind-boggling existence.

There were times when I had important questions, and Gonzalez wouldn't even answer my call. If I ran out of money occasionally, I'd have to beg him to give me money for food or simple toiletries. I felt stuck, so I did the same thing I did to Jean Claude, but I tried to deal with it another way. Instead of asking for money, I began to spend money at different vendors, and I'd bill the record company or mostly Gonzalez' production company.

One time, I ordered a limousine and kept it for an entire week, and another, I stayed at a five-star hotel, where I knew the staff and gave them the information to send the charges to Gonzalez. One afternoon, I walked into a branch of Boss and bought three suits with matching accessories. When Gonzalez found out, he called me in a fury.

"But you're not giving me any money for clothes, so what am I supposed to do?" I said when I could break into his ranting. He slammed the phone down, and I smiled for the rest of the day. It was just like it had been with Jean Claude, and I felt like this was my own form of retaliation. It was my way of getting back a fraction of what I knew was owed to me, but without a contract, I was helpless. Without Gonzalez, I'd not get the kind of work he could find me, for which I wouldn't get paid. I didn't know what to do, but I was living my own Catch 22. I was damned with and damned without him.

# CHAPTER 21

# More Unanswered Questions

Gonzalez and I continued to have a tense relationship, but he was mostly the only person I had contact with regarding my career. He would often be friendly around other people, but when we were alone, he was rude and abrupt. We would get into arguments, especially when I suspected he was lying, which was often. No matter what question I'd ask, he'd have an excuse, and I had no choice but to believe him because I was so naïve to how the music business was run. There were also times I'd call Vogue Records and complain, but they would always take Gonzalez' side, and it became a losing battle trying to get real answers.

There were even times band members seemed not very friendly, and I was sure they were laughing behind my back. I may not have known the language, but you can tell when people are laughing at you and not with you. Gonzalez was responsible for paying the band, and it was clear he would have conversations with them without me knowing about it. One evening after a show, I was in my hotel suite when Gonzalez came running into my room, frantically telling me the band might say some things but, no matter what they said, he told me I should ignore them.

I would discover in time that the band was threatened that they might be fired if they spoke to me about anything, but one musician shared that he witnessed Gonzalez signing checks made out to me over to himself. I knew if I asked him, he would deny it, so I tried to pay more attention. I later walked into a promoter's office where Gonzalez was talking and clearly handling some sort of business. This time I saw him with checks, signing my name on them. The checks were made out to me, and I tried to look at the amount but could not see it. I still threw a fit.

*"What the hell are you doing? Are those made out to me?"*

Gonzalez stared at me for a second, then said, "Look, I need to do this for you."

"I want to sign my own damn checks. You have this all wrong! I get paid and give you your portion, whatever that is."

I looked up at the promoters, who seemed to look away as Gonzalez got up and walked out of the office with the briefcase and checks. I followed him.

"How much do I get out of those?"

"I need to pay other people first."

"Other people, like who?"

He kept walking, trying to get away from me.

"I need to pay your taxes and the musicians, but there are other people, Marla."

I kept asking because I needed answers.

"How much are my taxes, Gonzalez? What kind of taxes am I paying? How much is left? Why don't I get a paycheck? You only give me cash."

"I'll tell you later, honey," he said and left the building.

Later never came. I had been asking these questions no matter where we were, and he would have different excuses. He would give me envelopes of money, French Francs or German Marks, and I didn't know how much they were worth in relation to American money. It seemed like it was quite a bit, but I'm sure I should have been expecting a *lot* more.

"How do I know I'm not supposed to get more than this?" I often asked.

"Just take the money, Marla. You need it."

"How much is the band being paid?"

"I took care of the band."

Sometimes he would give me bullshit answers; sometimes he would not answer at all. One evening when we were driving to a rehearsal, I asked him to show me the contracts from the promoters. The next day he handed me an envelope, and I opened it, thinking I was finally getting some real answers. First thing I saw was a header on the top of the page signifying his production company. These weren't the contracts, he'd just typed some numbers on a page, and the bulk of the profits was going to him.

"Aw man! What are you doing?"

"What, Marla?" he responded innocently.

I didn't know what to do. I thought of the times Ms. Simone warned me to be careful, and now I truly understood what she meant. There were so many unanswered questions. Why was he doing this, and why wouldn't the record company jump in and do something on my behalf? I figured Gonzalez must have been paying them more—out of what was mine—than were actually owed to keep quiet. There must be a way I could get him to tell me the truth, but it seemed as elusive as knowing how to build a rocket.

Months went by, and concert after concert was sold out. The shows were good, and beyond not getting paid properly, I was beginning to see the fruits of my labor; so many people loved my music, and to see them singing along to my songs thoroughly warmed my heart. Yet, I was still living in a dark room with no kitchen.

Finally, after yet another 'no response' from Gonzalez, I decided to call the record company and got Nataf on the phone.

"Hey, I know I'm making enough money for you to get me out of this fucking ghetto! Please do it now, or the next time I have to do an interview I'm going to tell them what Vogue Records is really like!"

"Okay Marla, I'll see what I can do, but this won't happen overnight."

My threats seemed to have worked, but as I waited until it was time for me to move, I came back to the small apartment so tired after a concert one night that I fell asleep with my clothes on. I began to dream about the desert and rain and felt sweat pouring down my forehead. I heard a crackling noise as I suddenly began coughing, and when I opened my eyes, the entire ceiling was on fire. I panicked, looking around for Tassy Cat, who was cowering in the bathroom. I grabbed Tassy and my guitar, ran out of the apartment, and rushed out of the building. Several people were behind me, and while outside, I could hear the fire department coming.

The firemen put out the fire, and within a few hours, we could go back in to retrieve our things, but we could not stay. It was a mess, water was everywhere, and the smoke was still hovering. One of the firemen approached a few of us as we stood outside, the fireman spoke in French, and a neighbor translated.

"Who was on the second floor?"

"I was," I said, and he gave me a strange look and then got specific about exactly where my apartment was.

"The gas line running through your unit was tampered with, looks like it was deliberately set."

I could not believe what I was hearing. I could have died in that fire, but I never found out what happened.

Gonzalez showed up shortly afterward, and I had him wait so I could get a few things out of the apartment; then he took me to The

Grand Hotel for a few days. No one ever found out how the fire got started, but I'm glad that Tassy Cat, myself, and my old guitar escaped.

Workwise, things were still on the upswing, the concerts were coming in like crazy, and the fans seemed to be happy and growing in numbers. Other opportunities came up, and I received offers for TV shows, clothing sponsorships, and commercials. Nataf must have convinced Gonzalez to do something acceptable, and the new place that Gonzalez eventually secured for me was a spacious three-bedroom flat on the famous Parisian street, Boulevard St. Martin. Located over a theatre, the windows went from the floor to the ceiling, and I could see Le Tour Eiffel in the distance. It was so much nicer, and I bought a few things to make it feel more like home. But getting a new place came with new questions.

"How much is the rent at my new place?" I asked when Gonzalez had picked me up for a rehearsal one day.

"Don't worry about it; I'm taking care of it," was his stock reply.

"Well, can't I pay my own rent? How much is it?"

"Marla, you don't need to worry about those things." Another repeated answer.

"Well, can you tell me how I would go about paying it?"

"Sure, I'll tell you, but not now," he said as he handed me an envelope with a small amount of cash.

"Mr. Gonzalez, can I please get enough to at least buy some curtains?"

He looked at me, and as his eyes returned to the road, he said, "You don't need curtains."

I had never been in a place that didn't have curtains and having them would have made the place feel more like home. It was just another thing further frustrating me, and I became even more vocal about how things were being mishandled. I was still asking how the money was being handled and dealing with other issues I had no clue about, but my questions were not being answered.

# CHAPTER 22

# Old Friend

I was glad to hear from Ms. Simone from time to time, and when she was in Paris, she came to visit if she could. We now had a lot in common, being represented by Gonzalez. One afternoon she rang the bell excessively, about ten times before I could make it to the door, having been in the bathroom.

"Oh, good! You're here," she said when I opened it and she marched right in. All I could do was laugh.

"Yes! Ms. Simone, I'm here, come on in," I said to an empty space before I closed the door.

"Do you have some tea?" she asked as she sat on the sofa. It was just like being back in California.

"How are things going?" she asked as we settled down with our drinks.

I didn't want to give details because I didn't want to complain to her, knowing she had her own problems.

"It's going alright, Ms. Simone. I'm getting a lot of work, but there's a lot of things I don't know."

"That's how it is in the beginning. But from what I hear, you are coming along nicely."

"Have you talked to him today?" I looked at her, wiggled my nose then chuckled.

"Gonzalez? No, not today." She looked up at me and returned the laugh.

"Oh my goodness, how did you know I was talking about him?"

"I don't know. It's just the expression you made that made me think of him."

We laughed until we were crying, and it just felt like the old times until she asked me again how things were. This time she looked more serious rather than just making conversation.

"Well, Gonzalez is doing a lot, but I haven't even signed a contract, and I have no idea what he's doing."

A knowing look flashed across her face.

"Tell me about it. He's certainly one to watch," she said as she shook her head.

We sat in silence for several minutes, sipping tea and staring at the blank apartment walls. The teacups we drank out of chinked in their saucer, with the occasional heavy sigh from each of us. I knew Ms. Simone knew exactly what I was going through, but I also knew she couldn't do anything to help. If I got rid of him, I wouldn't have any work, and anyone who replaced him could be as bad. Or even worse.

I would never know exactly all she had experienced, but now the phone calls where she had me delivering messages about her money all made sense. Just like her, I wanted answers. I could feel her pain and frustration with the music industry. I wanted answers, but I knew there were none. I swear there were times, I could hear her voice in my head saying, "You are going to have to watch him." That was such an understatement.

Eventually, we began making small talk about how long she would be in Paris, and I reminded her she was more than welcome to come visit at any time. I even gave her keys to my new place, but she never used them, probably because she liked ringing the bell several times until I'd answer.

She did indeed stop in a few times and even slept on my sofa after we sat up, drank wine, and talked all night. Our roles didn't change. I still cooked her food and made sure she had what she needed, just like in Los Angeles. If she needed me to make a phone call, run an errand, I helped her with whatever she asked.

In many of our conversations, though, she would ask me if everything was alright and seemed genuinely concerned, but I did not want to bombard her with my problems or the numerous questions I had. It was just not the type of relationship we had. On one of her visits, she told me she had purchased a home in Bouc Bel Air a little north of Marseille and wanted my help with some things.

"Sure, I'll travel down to help you, Ms. Simone," was the natural, unbidden response.

A few weeks later, with a break in concert bookings, I took a train to the south, and in the house in Bouc Bel Aire, she was still getting the place together. She still needed me to do a few chores, run errands, cook, clean, wash dishes, and even cut the grass. In some respects, I was becoming a star like her, but I never uttered a word of protest. This was Ms. Simone, and I'd always do whatever she asked me.

One evening, we were watching television, and an interview I had done a few weeks earlier popped up on screen, and she was so excited.

"Well, look what we have here; let's watch how this goes."

"Oh, Ms. Simone, do we have to? I was there; I've seen it already," I said, moving to get up.

"Sit still, child. Don't make a fuss."

I watched the person interviewing me ask a few opening questions, and all seemed to be going well, then I was asked if I'd done drugs before. I didn't see a reason to lie, it was a part of my past, and it was who I was, but I didn't go into details, especially about the crack. I also didn't mention my ongoing smoking of dope.

"Sure, when I was a teenager, I did some purple microdot and other things."

Ms. Simone shook her head as if it was disastrous, and I could tell she was frustrated with how the interview turned out. I felt embarrassed, and after the interview, I stood up and said, "What? It was the truth!"

Ms. Simone stood up and hugged me and said, "You poor, poor fool."

I accepted the hug, but when we released each other, I went into the guest bedroom and cried. Maybe I should not have told the interviewer that, but I was not accustomed to lying, and I had a lot of pride in knowing I got myself clean before I came to Europe. I thought she might understand because she once told me stories about her heroin addiction she had kicked.

I still felt like I let her down, and with her being the mother figure in my life at the time, I didn't want to do that. I had earned her respect, and I didn't want to lose that. I was grateful to have her as a friend and confidant, but it was heartbreaking to know that maybe I let her down.

After being in the room for a while, Ms. Simone came in and said, "Hey, grab your harmonica; let's play together."

I sensed it was her way of making me feel better. It did. She sat at her piano, and we both played, making up a song as we went along, acting silly and laughing in between the music. It was nice to laugh with her again, and afterward I mowed her lawn and helped tend to her garden in the back of her house. Just like old times, only in another country. In some respects, I wished I could have gone back to those old days.

# CHAPTER 23

# Going Gold

After a few weeks of being back in Paris, I was watching television one afternoon when I heard a knock on the door. I wasn't expecting anyone, it was late in the afternoon, and when I opened the door, a case of champagne and a large thin box was on the hallway floor. The note attached to the champagne only said "Congratulations!" and it was not signed by anyone. I opened the box, and there was a gold record in a frame, stating that my first album had reached gold status.

I wanted to be excited and probably would have been if I felt I had a better understanding and handle on things. I called the record company, but I could not get Nataf on the phone, so I called Gonzalez, who finally answered after a couple of attempts.

"I got this gold record thing at my door."

"Oh, hey honey, congratulations. *This is Marla Glen* went gold."

I didn't really know how to feel. I was still constantly short of money. I hardly had any furniture in the apartment, and now I'd sold enough copies of the album to go gold. The whole thing just left me confused. I had no idea it meant I'd sold over 500,000 copies.

"Well, what does that mean? What does that get me?"

"What do you mean?"

"I don't know what it means, and you just leave it at my door like this? I got this gold album, but there's no party? No celebration?"

I could hear Gonzalez talking to someone in the background.

"We will do it later, honey. I have to go, honey. I'll call you tomorrow."

That was that. As usual, he cut me off rather than answer my questions. I was alone in my apartment with very little money in my pocket, no one to celebrate with, and no food. I wanted to feel excited, but I felt alone, and there was no one around I trusted to share the success with, and I continued to feel that I was being robbed and taken advantage of. In my bones, I could feel there was something wrong.

I woke up the next morning, and as I got out of bed and strolled over to the window, all I could think was that I had a gold album but no curtains. I was looking for answers, so I took the gold album box and hopped on the train south to Ms. Simone's house. When I got there, she opened the door, and her jaw dropped.

"Marla, I wasn't expecting you. Come on in."

I entered sluggishly and sighed.

"Ms. Simone, they left this at my door. So, what does it mean?"

I pulled the heavy frame out of the box. Ms. Simone looked at it, then she looked at it and looked at me, her eyes wide like a kid on Christmas morning.

"*It means you get more money! Did you get the money?*" she shouted.

"What money?"

Her eyebrows rose, and with her eyes wide open, she said, "A lot of money."

I stared at her in frustration, not knowing what to say, and she stared right back. I was being suckered on every turn, and there was no way to turn it around. I was in deep, and I knew I was gullible and naïve, but it made me mad as hell. If there was money to be had from that album going gold, I knew I was probably not going to see any of it. I managed to make small talk, and we had dinner before I left the next morning, even more frustrated, and still not knowing what to do about anything.

When I got back, I decided to go out and look for new musicians. I had lost the band I began with, but I needed some people I could trust to help me get through the next few albums required to fulfill my contract. The ever-changing musicians Gonzalez kept turning up with were not good enough.

There was a local club named *Front Page Club*, so I went to listen and check out local talent. When I arrived, there was an amazing band on stage that was really jamming. The keyboard player was exceptional, and he was playing with a great deal of passion. After the set was over, I approached him.

"Hey man, you were really jamming up there."

"Thank you. I only had four hours to learn that song!"

I couldn't believe it. He showed no signs of being unfamiliar with the music.

"Hey man, that's amazing. You must be good then. My name is Marla Glen." I extended my hand, and he reached out his.

"Michele Crosio, yeah, I recognized you."

I smiled and felt relieved that if I could end up working with this guy, I had a little bit of control over my destiny. We sat down and talked about music and the evening went by fast, we exchanged numbers, and I felt a lot more excited when I left than I had getting the gold album. I hadn't even told him about it.

Crosio came to my place, and we began to forge a friendship and started playing together in the studio. He was really talented, and he totally got me as a musician. Much like JoJo, Crosio had a great ear for music, and after a few weeks, we bonded as musicians and friends. I felt comfortable enough to tell him how I wanted to work with him.

"So, I want to bring you on as a band leader, which means I have to introduce you to Gonzalez and the people from the record company."

"Okay. That's fine."

I continued looking him dead in the eyes.

"But I need you to promise me that you will not sign with them as it relates to my music. There is a lot of stuff going on that I just don't know about, and I need you on my side."

"I understand where you're coming from," he said, nodding his head.

I liked the idea of being close to my band leader and did not want things to be taken over like the record company. They had managed to let JoJo and the guys go, but I didn't want that to happen again. I felt like I had no control, and this was my way of feeling like I had something to do with managing my own career.

"Gonzalez acts like my manager, but I never signed anything with him," I told Crosio. "He's always up to something, and I need you to understand that. I want us to work together as a team too, and I won't sign anything."

The next call I made to Gonzalez.

"I have a new band leader."

"No, no, no, Marla! What are you doing? The band leader we have is fine."

"The band leaders you guys are choosing are not working for me. I want someone I pick. So, I have chosen someone else, and that's it."

Gonzalez was not happy, but I felt I needed to do this. Crosio met Gonzalez, and it was a rocky start because Gonzalez had an attitude about me bringing him onboard. I just ignored Gonzalez because it seemed like no matter who I was around, he would act the same way. Crosio did a great job, and ultimately, he and Gonzalez got along, and he brought on other musicians to the band as well. I was happy we were working nicely together and excited about working on studio music with him.

Crosio had music equipment at his small apartment in Paris when we began working on tracks. I would take the train over to his apartment, and I had to climb about eight flights of stairs to get to his apartment door. Eventually, Vogue records bought me my own equipment so Crosio could work in my apartment instead of his, and they got me exactly what he had. My place had more space, so this worked out nicely. We recorded a lot of songs between both apartments. Then I got a sense that Crosio and Gonzalez became closer.

When it came time to master the songs, I was no longer invited to participate in the process, so I called Crosio.

"Michele, where are you mastering the songs?"

He responded hesitantly, "I'm not sure yet, Marla."

I didn't believe him.

"You have to know something; Gonzalez likes to cause confusion. These are *my* songs, and I need to be there. I don't know why it's a problem in me knowing."

"I don't know; you have to ask Gonzalez."

I did just that. By now, I'd dropped the 'Mr.'

"Look, Gonzalez, why can't I be in the studio?"

"You don't need to be there, Marla."

I did not understand this. Frustrated, I began to shout.

"*Why not? it's my goddamn music!*"

"Just trust me; we have it handled."

I slammed the phone down, madder than a cow on fire.

They persisted with mastering the songs without me, and I was not happy about it. No matter how much I insisted on being there, I was never invited or told where they were. I never met any of the musicians Crosio was bringing on board to do the studio work, and

I was not happy about that either. I hated working that way, and Crosio knew it.

Then I began to notice that Crosio was working with other Vogue artists, and there were newspaper articles featuring him and how he was hired to work with me. I found out that he had signed a contract with Vogue Records, and that was exactly what I didn't want him to do. We began to talk less, and when we were in the same room, tensions were high. Even at the shows, we kept our distance from each other. In an argument after one of the shows, I asked him, "Why are you doing this to me?"

Crosio answered quickly, "You're being punished!"

He then walked off, crossed to Gonzalez, who was across the room, and they headed towards a flight of stairs. I was so mad that I could spit hot coals. I saw a pole nearby in the backstage area, rushed to pick it up, grabbed it, and then I charged him. Immediately, bodyguards jumped in, and several people grabbed me before I could get to him.

"*What the hell do you mean I'm being punished?!*"

Crosio stood shocked.

"*Tell me! Tell me what the fuck you're talking about?!*"

I felt like I wanted to slam his body to the ground and punch him in the face. I'd had enough; all the unanswered questions, the issues with Gonzalez, and not being a part of how my music was being mastered caused me to feel like I was ready to snap at any moment. I was beyond being tired of it all, and it was time for things to change. But how?

# CHAPTER 24

# The Mystery Chocolate

After telling the musicians about the gold record, one of them suggested I should have gotten a hundred thousand dollars. He had certainly been in the music business longer than I had, so I believed him. Everything began to weigh even more heavily on my mind as the record company continued to push the album, and it remained at the top of the charts, and concerts continued to come pouring in.

With the gold record, it seemed like the record company was seeking other opportunities for exposure. They tried to secure a concert date with one of the hottest acts in the music industry at the time, Whitney Houston. It was the mid 90's, and Fabrice Nataf informed me he had spoken to someone at Houston's offices to see if I could secure concert dates opening for the popular singer. I was excited to hear this, and I wanted it as well.

I got a call from Nataf and was told they'd send a car for me at 6pm for a call. Gonzalez came by before a town car arrived, and we both rode to the office. We arrived and sat in Nataf's office, and he placed the call on speaker. The phone rang in that strange tone because we were abroad, and a man's voice answered.

"Hello, Houston office."

"Hey, this is Fabrice Nataf from Vogue Records; we had a call scheduled."

There was a delay, and Fabrice filled the void in the air.

"I'm here with Marla and the road manager, and I have you on speaker. I just wanted to see if Ms. Houston got a chance to listen to Marla's CD, *This is Marla Glen* that I sent over."

The man on the phone responded, and I could hear him shuffling papers."

"If you don't mind, I'm going to ask you to take me off speaker." Fabrice picked up the phone. "Hold on a sec."

There was silence, and Gonzalez and I sat in anticipation, wanting things to go well. I had a smile on my face, thinking I could be on tour with Whitney. It would certainly boost sales for Vogue, and I would be honored. So many thoughts ran through my mind in that moment of silence. I envisioned myself telling Whitney how I first saw her at that rooftop party in Chicago. I was a fan, and she was fine as hell. Nataf's head dropped, and shortly after, he hung up the phone. Gonzalez said, "Well, how did it go?"

"Do you want me to tell you the truth?"

I quickly chimed in, "Yes, of course."

"He said, Ms. Houston listened to Marla's CD in her hotel room, and she said quote, "I don't want that bitch opening on my concert.""

My mouthed dropped, and the breath I was holding released. The words were sharp and stinging. I was shocked and devastated as I sat there, wondering why she would say such a thing. Nataf just sat behind his desk, equally as surprised, yet he did not look up at me. Perhaps he was embarrassed because he shook his head and sort of laughed it off.

I said, "Aw man, that's messed up."

"I did not know she was going to say that."

There were no other words, but I was not going to let this affect me; I had work to do with or without touring with someone as rude as Houston. I knew how hard I worked to have good shows, and just because someone wanted to be mean and cruel wasn't going to stop me from doing what I needed to do for my career.

Other opportunities began opening up, such as radio and television interviews, special appearances, concert dates, and I began hearing my songs on the radio more and in the MTV rotation of videos. My career began to climb to new heights, and things were getting busier all the time. This was exciting, but it was frustrating because as things continued moving in new directions, I became even more fed-up with Gonzalez and his antics. I became more vocal, and less patient.

He gave me the news I got an offer to perform in Turkey and Israel. He and I took a flight over, and we were treated very well. Turkey was absolutely beautiful; the sky was so close that when I looked up, it felt like I could almost touch the clouds. But even though I was in a beautiful country, I still felt uncomfortable with Gonzalez.

"What's going on with the money from this concert?"

"I have everything taken care of. Like I always do."

"That's the problem, you always do things without my consent, and I know it's not right what you are doing. Taking all the money for yourself and giving me a few Francs."

"Well, this time I'm going to give you all your money, and you can then tell me what to do."

I looked at him, knowing he was up to something, but I had no idea what it was.

We moved on, and performing in Israel was a joy, everything went well, and when I sang *Cost of Freedom* and other songs from the *This is Marla Glen* album, the crowd responded wonderfully, and people there were joining in like back in France. After the concert, we took a shuttle bus back to the hotel, and I grabbed a seat at the bar to unwind. While sitting there sipping a beer, I watched Gonzalez talking to a tall guy with a beard. I believe he might have been one of the concert promoters. Gonzalez finished his conversation and came to sit next to me at the bar. He was holding the briefcase he usually carried on the trips we took for my performances.

"Look, I'm going to give you your money, and I want you to be careful."

I looked at him, "What do you mean, be careful?"

"I'm just saying, honey, it is a lot of money, and I want you to be careful."

"Just give me the money and stop trying to scare me into something."

"I'll give it to you. But, let me walk you up to your room to do it."

"Okay, fine."

I finished my beer and hopped off the barstool as Gonzalez summoned the promoter over. I had no idea why we needed this guy to go with us, but I started walking, and they followed. Once in the room, Gonzalez gave me an odd look.

"Marla, you have to try the chocolates here. They put one on your pillow, and Israel is known for their amazing chocolates."

"Yeah, but ... I'm not much of a chocolate person."

The promoter said, "It's very, very good. Much better than American chocolate."

"Really? I'll eat it later."

Gonzalez chimed in, "Oh, Marla, go ahead and try it."

"I promise you, it's really good," the promoter insisted,

What the hell was all this? Just to shut them up, I picked up the chocolate, opened the wrapper, and ate it.

"Okay, so it's tasty."

I really just wanted them out of my room so I could rest. I noticed Gonzalez had a smirk on his face.

"I'll try mine when I get to my room. So, here you go."

He stood directly in front of me, turning his back to the promoter, reached in his briefcase, and pulled out a white envelope full of cash. Gonzalez said, "This is your money from the show. Make sure you keep it safe."

I took the envelope and looked at him.

"Okay, see you in the morning."

"Okay, good night."

Gonzalez nodded to the promoter, they left the room, and I locked the door behind them. Once alone, I counted it, and there were ten thousand US dollars. There was no safe in the room, so I chose a bottom drawer to try to hide the envelope. I then placed some clothes on top of the envelope and shut the drawer tight. Maybe Gonzalez was going to play fair now. I was thinking, maybe I complained enough for him to do the right thing. I took a shower and laid down to relax, quickly drifting off into a deep sleep.

It was the middle of the night when I could hear something rumbling in my room. I don't know what time it was, but I kept hearing these noises. I tried to move, but I couldn't. I felt paralyzed. The noises were loud now, the opening and closing of doors and dresser drawers. I tried to open my eyes completely but couldn't, and I could now tell I had been drugged. My mind was working, but my body wasn't, and it was the scariest of feelings.

I could see figures moving in the moonlight coming in through the window, and whoever was in the room was dressed in all white, like they were wearing a long white coat, similar to a doctor's coat, and white gloves. Even though I was incapacitated, I could tell the person was going through every drawer in my room. I couldn't see the person's face, but I could hear drawers opening and closing, clearly hearing them going through the closet. They were tossing things around in the room, then, after a few more minutes, the figured disappeared, and I was left alone.

All I could do was lay in bed, and it wasn't until hours later that the sluggish feeling subsided. The sun was coming up when I could move, and I slowly got myself out of bed to put water on my face. There were clothes on the floor from the closet, my belongings had been disrupted, drawers slightly opened, and the money in the envelope was gone. I sat on the side of the bed and cried before going downstairs to the front desk.

"Someone came into my room last night. They stole money from me, and I need you to call the police."

The woman at the front desk looked shocked.

"Oh my God, are you okay?"

"No, I'm not. I feel awful. I don't know what happened to me, but I could not get up. They were in my room while I was sleeping. Thank God I woke up."

She picked up the phone to call her manager. On my instruction, she also called Gonzalez, who arrived at the front desk within a moment's notice. As if he'd been waiting for the call, he acted surprised when I told him what happened and seemed genuinely concerned, but I knew it was an act. He and the promoter had been like B-movie actors in their attempts to get me to eat the drugged chocolate, but it would, of course, be my word against theirs, so, as usual, I felt like I didn't have anything I could use to get my money back.

A plainclothes police officer showed up and took a report, saying he would do further investigation. I left Tel Aviv without the money, and beyond my obvious suspicions over the chocolate, I thought I recognized the police officer as having been in the bar the night before but now without his uniform. Again, it was all very suspicious, but I had no evidence beyond my suppositions.

This wasn't the only time something happened to my concert money, but it was the first time I felt like my life was compromised in the process. Gonzalez had claimed on other occasions that he had been robbed after a concert. One time he entered my hotel room disheveled, saying two guys followed him and took all the money. I found it suspicious because they never took his briefcase, only the money. He would tell me we had insurance, so I'd get the money back from the insurance company. He may have gotten money back, but I didn't get anything after those incidents, and Tel Aviv would not be the first time I was personally robbed. It wasn't only money.

Several weeks after the show in Israel, I learned from someone at the Vogue offices that I had won an award. Delighted, I asked about going to pick it up, only to be told that Gonzalez and Crosio had been already, apparently saying I was sick! As usual, my anger at Gonzalez was water off a duck's back, and no matter how loud I shouted or ranted about something, Gonzalez would often laugh in my face. It sometimes felt as if the more I yelled about something, the more he seemed to like it. I learned later that sometimes he intentionally pushed my buttons because he thought I performed better when I was angry.

My frustrations were sometimes revealed during interviews, or in public. I don't know if he instigated situations in front of reporters to get good interviews or if we were truly just at odds. One time after a concert, during an interview with several reporters, Gonzalez and I were arguing about several things. The reporter noticed and said, "You two argue like you are husband and wife."

Without missing a beat, I turned to the reporter and responded, "Yes, you're right because he fucks me all the time."

The reporter chuckled and began to write,

Gonzalez quickly turned to him and said, "Don't print that. It's not funny."

The reporter gave him a look, and we continued with the interview. Later I saw Gonzalez pull the guy to the side and hand him a few bills to keep things out of the press.

# CHAPTER 25

# Mom Learns the Truth

Things had been moving so quickly, and the months had flown by because my schedule was so hectic. I had a couple days off and finally took a moment to call my mom. It had been a while since we had spoken, and so much had happened since I last spoke to her. After a couple of rings, she picked up the phone, and I was happy just to hear her voice.

"Mom! It's me."

I could hear her smiling, and it made me feel good in the moment.

"Marla?! Where are you? I have not heard from you. How are you?"

"Mom, I'm fine; so much has been happening."

"Well, what are you doing now? Are you still working at McDonald's?"

I didn't know how to tell her everything.

"Mom, well. Yes, I'm still working there."

She suspected something.

"Well, tell me exactly what it is you do? Is it hard?"

She was so into it; I just felt like I needed to keep it going.

"Mom, it's not too hard. I got a promotion, so now, I go from location to location to check on other managers, and I talk to some of the employees and make sure they ... mop up and stuff. That's kinda it."

She hesitated, and I couldn't keep it going. I needed to tell her. I took a breath and blurted out.

"Okay, Mom, I don't work at McDonald's. I'm going to tell you the truth. I'm actually a singer, and I got a hit record. I've had concerts in France, Germany, and other places, and I've been touring and singing songs I've written—"

She interrupted, in disbelief and said, "Marla, stop making up these lies. I can't believe you are lying to me! Stop!"

I had a feeling she would say this. I had to try to get her to believe me.

"Mom! I'm not lying. C'mon. Aw, man. I am a singer, and this guy is ripping me off, and I got a gold record ..." I took a breath. "Mom, I know you are good with numbers. I need you to believe me, and I really need your help ... There's this guy—"

She stopped me again.

"Marla, stop! When you are ready to tell me the truth, then you call me back."

She hung up the phone, and it left me speechless. I should have told her the truth from the beginning, but I didn't know how things would go. My mother always told me to handle my business on my own and try not to bring my parents into it. I always respected that advice.

A couple of months after that phone call, my mother called back. The first thing she said was, "Marla, I am so sorry!"

"Mom? Sorry for what?"

"About not believing you are in Europe as a singer. I saw your video on MTV, and I just couldn't believe it was you. I'm just so surprised."

I could hear my mother's voice crack and could tell she was about to cry.

"It's okay, Mom. I should've told you from the beginning."

"Tell me what's going on? Is it going well?"

I wanted to tell her everything, but there was so much.

"Mom, I'm going through a lot, and I'm sorry, but this is not a good story to tell. But I'm okay."

"What do you mean? Is there something I can do?"

It would have been nice to have her come to Europe,

"Mom, I'm being ripped off. If you could come here, I know together we could find a way to make them stop."

She hesitated, "I'd have to get on a plane?"

I knew my mom was afraid of flying, but I had to try to convince her.

"Mom, flying isn't so bad. After you take off, you can barely tell you are on a plane. C'mon Mom. I really could use you here. You are so good with numbers; you worked in a bank before, and I know you would help if you were here."

She was silent for a moment, and I could hear her sigh.

"Mom?"

There was a bit of a pause, but she finally answered, "Marla, let me think about this. I just don't know."

She was clearly uncomfortable with even the thought of getting on a plane. I tried to change the subject.

"Mom, I just want to thank you for everything. You're such a good mom."

"Oh, Marla."

This was a conversation we never really had before.

"I mean it, I had a really good childhood, and I miss you. And remember when you said that when we grow up, me and Tuggy will have to pay you back for all the diapers and the milk you bought? I want to send you some money for buying all the things I got when I was growing up. I want to pay you back."

She laughed. "You are so silly. I was just kidding. Moms are supposed to say those things."

"I want to do it anyway."

We talked a bit about the rest of the family, and then I ended the phone call.

"I'm going to go 'cause I know this call is costing you a lot of money. I'll be in touch again soon, Mom. Okay?"

"Okay, look, you hang in there, a'right?"

"I will."

We hung up the phone, and I felt much better after talking to her, but it made me miss my family even more.

# CHAPTER 26

# Gonzalez Goes Too Far

Things got busy again, and most of my time was rehearsals, studio work, and concerts. I needed a break, and just a few days weren't going to be enough, so I shut myself away at home. One afternoon, Gonzalez popped in unexpectedly and told me he wanted to show me something. I threw on some shoes, and we headed out. While we were walking, he was very talkative, and amid the conversation, he mentioned, as if talking about the weather, that I made my first million. This is the conversation I was waiting to have. I immediately began asking tons of questions.

"Well, where is it? Where is the proof? Are you putting the money in a bank somewhere?"

He wasn't providing answers quickly enough for me. We kept walking throughout Paris, and it was the middle of the day, and people were milling about. It took us about twenty minutes before he stopped in front of a gated concrete flat. He opened the door, and we followed a short walkway, entering into a 2-bedroom loft-style house. Dust was everywhere, and beams were being drilled into the ceiling.

"What do you think of this place?"

"It looks like it's not finished yet."

We walked around, and it had two large bedrooms and a basement.

"Once this place is done, it will be really nice," he said. "Do you want to live here with me and the family?"

"Why would I want to live with you and your wife and kid? Can't you just give me my money so I can buy my own place?"

He ignored the question and kept looking around.

"This is where the kitchen is going to be; the appliances will be over there."

He pointed, and I knew he had heard me, but I said it louder.

"You're not giving me answers."

Gonzalez walked through the place, not saying a word.

"I want to pick my own place," I said.

"I'm not sure how this will work, but we will figure it out."

I knew he was bullshitting me, and it was really pissing me off.

"Well, if you are planning on getting this, then it's probably with my money. I'm telling you now, just give me my money so I can find my own place."

Gonzalez stopped walking around and headed towards the front door.

"Well, honey, I think we are done here."

He headed out the door, and I followed him, not knowing what to do. Talking to him was worse than talking to a brick wall. We walked back mostly in silence, and I went to my apartment and prayed that somehow this whole thing would work out in my favor. I tried to remain positive and be grateful for being a working artist with a gold record and amazing fans. However, there were times when I could not deal with the many issues I was having with Gonzalez. I could not keep up with all the problems that were occurring.

I continued working, but the pressure was building. Gonzalez had far too much control over my life, my finances, and no matter how many times I called to complain to Vogue Records, they did nothing to stop him. At one point, they completely stopped taking my calls. I would call Vogue and ask them to find me an attorney, but they never helped, and the pressure of it all was getting to me, and people were beginning to notice.

I lost all respect for this man but refused to give up trying to find out how I could legitimately get my money from him. But I could not stop performing because it was the only way I was able to eat and continue to survive. I did all I could to take it in my stride, but it was driving me under.

After one of the concerts, I noticed the band members were acting odd. We had been laughing and joking when we had rehearsals, but after a few shows, many of them stopped talking to me. I spoke to my guitar player, who assured me everything was okay but quickly walked off.

It wasn't just the band members, it was also DJs, reporters, or other professional people we encountered who would shy away from talking to me or be completely evasive. I would walk into a room where everyone was talking, and they would just stop. No one said anything to me. They seemed cold and afraid to speak. One night, one of the musicians agreed to have a beer with me.

"Why is everyone acting so weird?"

"Gonzalez said that you are on drugs, and you have a really bad temper. He told us not to talk to you."

"That son of a bitch! Why is he telling people that?"

"I heard you yelling at him."

"Because he has my money, and he won't give it to me! That's why I was yelling. It has nothing to do with drugs."

The next time I saw Gonzalez, I said, "What are you telling people? I need you to stop with the lies."

He pretended he had no idea what I was talking about, but I refused to be silent anymore. I needed to call him out on his shit, and

I was beginning not to care what people thought about me yelling at him. It was clear a lot of the band members knew something when one evening I was ranting on the bus about not having any money. I sat away from everyone when one of the background singers came and sat next to me.

"I believe your manager, Gonzalez, is stealing from you."

I hated when people called him my manager because I never signed a contract.

"He's not my manager, but why are you saying this?

She leaned closer to whisper, "He has given us all extra money, not to say anything to you."

I was glad she told me, but I was shocked as well. I sat in disbelief.

"Why is he doing that? I can't believe this."

When the bus stopped, and we arrived at the concert, Gonzalez got on the bus, and I immediately approached him,

"Gonzalez, why are you giving the band more money than you need to? What are you doing behind my back? How much are they really being paid?"

Gonzalez stood perplexed, but I needed it to be clear. I pranced through the aisle of the bus and made an announcement:

"Listen up, everybody; this man is not my manager. He is my booking agent. I did not sign anything with him, so he works for me, just like you do. So, I could fire you all if I wanted to and start over. Do not listen to him!"

I'm sure this confused everyone, and the band appeared not to know who to devote their loyalty to. I needed people to know things, and hopefully someone would help me. In front of everyone, I turned to Gonzalez and yelled at him.

*"When are you going to make that fucking contract between us so I can know what you're doing and how much money I've made?"*

Gonzalez looked livid but tried to avoid the conversation in front of everyone by responding, "This is not the time or place."

By now, I did not care.

"*Gonzalez, I have no clue what you are doing, but I know I'm being fucked out of everything!*"

"*If you don't stop asking me questions, I will leave you out there with the wolves to eat you up!*" he yelled, and I shouted right back in his face.

"*You're fired!*"

After the show, I fired all the musicians as well. I'd had enough.

# CHAPTER 27

# The Truth Emerges

I knew I had to keep my bandleader, Michele Crosio because he knew all the arrangements, and I could not manage everything on my own given the levels at which I was now performing and the prices being paid for tickets. Building everything up again from scratch was not going to be easy, but we worked days and nights making sure we had the right people to form a whole new band. Several concerts were lined up, and we needed to be prepared. Gonzalez had received the first half of the payment, and there was no getting that back, but Crosio and I made it work with only the remaining portion of show fees. After I paid Crosio, I kept what was left.

Those were times that Crosio seemed to be on my side. Like the time he took me to register my songs. He told me we were going to the Sacem office to register songs, but he didn't explain the process. Once we arrived, he filled out paperwork and handed it to the person behind the counter. I just stood around and watched as he talked to them in French in a lengthy conversation. Everyone but me in the office spoke French. I kept asking, "What did she say? What is she saying?"

They'd laugh and keep speaking in their language. He might translate two or three words, and I'd say...

"But y'all talked for almost a half hour."

Michele continued to handle the paperwork, not saying much to me.

He finally finished, "Okay, it's done."

We left the office and went our separate ways. After a while, I finally put two and two together and realized this was the office I would pick up my royalty checks. I went to the Sacem office twice more after this visit, and picked up one check for ten thousand francs, and on a second visit I picked up a check for about five thousand francs.

There was a section in the building where they would allow you to cash your check on the spot, and I did that each time. Finally, I felt like I was getting money for my work.

The last time I went to the Sacem office, I walked in hopeful, showed my identification, and I managed to say in French, "Do you have a check for me?"

The woman looked at her computer and said, "I have nothing for you."

"Are you sure?"

She said with a stern look, "Your manager, Raymond Gonzalez picked up your money."

I was shocked. I shouted, "He's not my manager. I don't have a contract with him!"

"She said, "Do not raise your voice in here."

I got closer, "What do you mean? That's my money!"

She backed up a little. "I can't help you. Sit down and shut up!"

I'm not going to sit down. You gave my money away to a man who is not my manager!

"If you don't leave, I will call the police."

I stormed out of the office. Boiling hot. I felt like I was always one step behind the bastards in a game where the chips were stacked against me. And I continued to have problems with Gonzalez.

Gonzalez was fired, and he was still affecting my livelihood. Concerts were coming, and rehearsals were scheduled. I walked into the rehearsal studio and overheard Crosio talking to Gonzalez in a rear corridor. Gonzalez appeared to be giving him detailed instructions on ensuring things were going smoothly. I was livid, and both of them soon knew it! I didn't want Gonzalez anywhere near me, talking to the band, or involved in any way. I now remembered the Israel award fiasco and began to doubt Crosio, wondering if Gonzalez had been influencing Crosio to do things behind my back for some time.

Not long after I realized Gonzalez was still seeking to run things, we began to have more trouble with shows, and without knowing how to fix things, I ended up having to hire Gonzalez again. I had no other choice and no one else to turn to, but during this time, I discovered how low this man could go.

We were supposed to go over scheduling and details for upcoming shows, and I went over to Gonzalez' loft. It was the same place he walked me through when it was still being updated. His wife let me in, and I had planned to wait for him to return. His wife seemed upset and using both French and English explained what was bothering her.

"You must know this, Marla, I have heard you having arguments on the phone, but he's not a nice man. He can be very evil sometimes."

"I know; he really gets to me. I don't know how you do it, living with someone like that."

"I get by, but since you are here, and we have a chance to talk, there is something I must share with you. It is very, very, important you know this.

I nodded, listening intently.

"He bought this house using your money, and it is under the name of Maria Glen. I don't know how he did this, but I know this for sure. But you can never tell him that I was the one who told you."

I gasped and sat speechless. Finally, I said, "I knew he was doing things like this; I just cannot prove it."

We sat and stared at each other for a moment, but I needed to get up and leave because of the rage I felt swelling up inside me. I didn't know how to keep this woman's secret and get what was stolen from me at the same time. She said a few words afterwards, and I was so angry I could not even listen anymore. I got up to leave. As I headed toward the door, she said, "Wait, here."

I turned around, and she had a few pieces of mail in her hands; she handed them to me, and I folded them up and put them in my pocket as I continued out the door. As I walked home with tears streaming down my face, I was mad as hell, and it felt like someone had ripped my heart out of my chest and stomped on it. I had just left the house that he lived in, and I worked for. It was one of the worst feelings I had ever had in my entire life, but I refused to let Gonzalez break me. That motherfucker, all I could think was Ms. Simone was right.

When I got home and opened the mail, it appeared to be some sort of tax papers, in the name of Maria Glen. The tax bill had been paid. I had only gotten bits of mail at my apartment before and now it made sense; he was having all important and official documents sent to that house.

Continuing to be damned with him and damned without him, I carried on working with Gonzalez, over the next three years or so. Several times I fired him again and hired him back, and the cycle didn't stop, but the frustration levels got even deeper. This was the same thing that Ms. Simone did, and it's hard to explain to anyone the cycle of dysfunction that you can't escape. He booked lots of concerts throughout France, Switzerland, Germany, and Austria, and while I cannot always name what specific venues he booked me at, I had many experiences that left me with mixed emotions or things that I couldn't explain or understand.

Most of the time, I could tell Gonzalez was behind unexplained incidents and things that just didn't make sense. If he had been involved, things just seemed to go against me, like the time I had with Ms. Simone's daughter Lisa, who had also become a singer. Gonzalez booked a concert in Geneva and shared with me that Lisa Simone and I were on the same bill. The venue was small, but that didn't matter. I was excited to meet Lisa. I felt that since we had her mom in common, we had a lot to talk about. Without even meeting her, I felt a sisterly kinship to her because of the years I spent working for Ms. Simone.

Once we arrived, and I got settled in my dressing room, I asked Gonzalez to see if he could make sure we had a proper introduction, and he was delighted to do so. He left to talk with her, and about an hour or so passed, and when he returned, he was flustered. I could tell something was wrong.

"What did she say?" I asked.

"She doesn't want to meet you."

"Did you tell her that I was close to her mother? We have so much in common; I really want to meet her. I used to talk to her on the phone. She's like a sister to me."

"Honey, I can't explain it. She just said no."

"Why would she say that? I feel like we could be friends; I don't understand this."

Gonzalez seemed like he was confused himself, so I let it go. Before the concert, I was headed to sound check when I got a glimpse of Lisa pass by me in a stairwell. She had her head up high, in a regal-like posture, and she was wearing a fur coat. She walked right past me and didn't even look in my direction. I was close enough for her to acknowledge me, but after what Gonzalez said, I dare not approach her. It appeared to me that she was desperately trying to emulate her mother.

This was something I had heard from Ms. Simone herself, who wanted Lisa to be anything other than a singer. Nothing would have made her happier to know that Lisa escaped all the frustrations of chasing down money from promoters, dealing with shady managers, and contracts that didn't really have your best interests.

I felt a loss that day when Lisa didn't respond to me well. I wondered if it had something to do with my being a stud because I felt that sometimes being into women made some people uncomfortable, and I respect that. No matter what it was, I was certainly not going to force my friendship on her. I performed and left without trying again, but I was really disappointed that I didn't get a chance to meet her. I wish things would have turned out differently, but they didn't and I moved on.

Things got the lowest ever when I was told I got into tax trouble. I didn't know anything about filing taxes in another country and didn't even know how much money I was making. I hadn't received any paychecks; I had no paperwork for my concerts. Gonzalez handled everything I did. I didn't even know who my rent was being paid to. Whenever I approached Gonzalez with a question about money issues, he would tell me it was none of my business! Later, I found out I wasn't in tax trouble, and because Gonzalez did everything for me, he also did my taxes, but I never received a copy of them.

It got to a point where all I could do was laugh at the situation because that stopped me from losing my sanity. I felt like I was being taken for a fucked-up ride on a broken ferris wheel and simply wanted to jump off. I was tired of the deceitfulness, the thievery, the disrespect, the arguments, the lies, and shouting. I began to cry a lot, I ate less, and I was barely sleeping. I was bitter, and nothing made sense. Yet, the success and the hits kept on coming. The first album went two times gold and twice platinum, plus the second album went platinum—a total of over five million copies sold—yet with each award milestone, the money envelopes Gonzalez gave me were getting smaller and smaller. Then something changed.

I began to notice my music was not playing as much on the radio anymore, nor were there as many videos playing on television. I began receiving letters about unpaid bills at the same time Gonzalez became harder to get hold of. I was at my wits' end. I needed answers, and I would not let up on the questions. We were at an airport, headed back to Paris, and we had another huge fight. I was relentless, determined to get answers, as we walked down the long corridor headed toward the plane.

"Where is my money from me going gold and platinum? There is no way that I get another platinum album and there's no money to show for it. I could have a whole orchestra backing me and still make a ton more money, so tell me! Tell me where my money is! I know it is a *whole* lot more than what you are giving me in those goddamn envelopes!"

Gonzalez kept walking. I'm sure he was sick and tired of hearing the questions, just as I was sick and tired of asking them. I persisted, and then I got more information than I could ever have expected.

*"I know you are ripping me off; you need to stop doing it."*

We were just about to get in line to board when he stopped, looked me dead in the eyes, and yelled back at me.

*"You're damned right! I went around your head so fast you didn't know what happened. I stole your money, and it's gonna take you a long time for you to figure out how I did it ... honey!"*

This was the truth that shook me to my core.

*"Fuck you, Gonzalez! You're fired again, and one day, I will find out how you did it!"*

As we boarded the flight, people stared at us both, and all I could do was go to my seat, which was behind his, and sit in silence. Tears would not stop flowing from my eyes, nor would my mind stop spinning. But I refused to let him break me.

# CHAPTER 28

# Goodbye Europe

Of course, I had known what he said was true, but to hear the words and for him to actually have the balls to say it was the ultimate slap in the face. I wanted to get out of my seat, grab him, and beat the living shit out of him. I'd been naive to think everything would eventually turn out okay and that I'd get what was mine. For sure, I'd probably buried my head in the sand, but it's not in my nature to believe people wouldn't act in the respectable way I would. I had always expected other people to behave toward me as I would them.

It was a long flight, and so many things kept running through my mind as the tears continued to stream down my face. I remembered the days when I begged him for money to get food and cigarettes and the several times, he claimed concert money was stolen. There were times when the record company ignored me when I asked them to find me an attorney and the recent conversation with his wife admitting he bought their house with my money. I wondered how many people knew what he was doing, and Fabrice Nataf certainly knew or suspected it.

Did the promoters know? The reporters even? I remembered after a concert, a promoter approached me, patted me on the back, and thanked me for the boat he purchased. He then walked away with a smirk on his face. Like a kaleidoscope of memories, hundreds of little incidents crossed my mind as the plane headed back home to Paris. How could I have stopped this? What kind of monster would do such a thing? There was a horrible feeling in the pit of my stomach, and with every breath I took, I felt like I was going to lose my mind.

Back in my apartment, I continued to cry for several days. I couldn't eat or sleep for not knowing what to do. I needed to find a way to get the hell out of Europe, but concerts were coming up, and I certainly needed the money. My mind was spinning, and I remembered overhearing Ms. Simone saying once, "If I knew then, what I know now, I would have jumped out of the window." I now knew what she meant by that. I desperately wanted to call her but feared all I'd get was, "I told you it would happen."

There was no one I could trust, but I needed someone to help navigate things. In the end, I called my childhood friend from Chicago, Leroy Ball, who knew quite a bit about the music industry and was well connected. Through the tears, I told him what I was going through and that I had fired Gonzalez. Leroy wanted to help, and he referred me to his brother Larry, who couldn't come at the time, but he connected me with a music manager he knew by the name of Earl Bryant, who had worked with Smokey Robinson and other celebrity artists.

I called Mr. Bryant and told him everything. He understood my situation with Gonzalez and the record company and agreed to help. It was going to take him a couple weeks or so before he would be able to arrive in France, and I still had concerts lined up, so I had to do them without the help of Gonzalez. It was hard for me not to share with the audience what I was going through and get the money from promoters who weren't used to paying the artist. But I did it, and I paid the musicians and kept the rest to live off of. I'd decided I would go back to Los Angeles and find a way to start over.

I began clearing out my apartment; I didn't have a lot of furniture, but what I did have was good quality. My friend and weed supplier Frank came over to my place, and I knew I was going to need it, so I purchased a big plastic baggie full of weed. We sat and smoked a joint before I left, and he told me his wife was pregnant. That one spark of normality seemed alien in my world at that time.

Before I left, I gave Frank all my furniture, and I purchased a bassinet and other pieces of baby furniture for his unborn child. He was so thankful when he came to pick things up, and it warmed my heart because I knew he could use it. After he'd gone, the only things left were a few odds and ends, my TV, and my studio equipment. I needed the equipment to keep working and so I planned to have it shipped to the U.S.

With an empty apartment and not much else to do, I sat on the floor and watched a bit of television, noticing that my music videos were out of rotation on MTV. Seeing them removed was odd, and I wondered what was happening, so I went to the record company, and Nataf was sitting in his office when I showed up.

"Fabrice, do you guys have anything to do with my music not being played on MTV?"

"It probably has something to do with you being sold."

"Sold? What does that mean?"

"We sold you to Germany. You're under them now."

"What the hell does that mean?

"You'll have to ask Gonzalez," he said standing up. "Now I have a meeting to go to. Bye Marla."

And that was that. I had no idea what he meant by "sold," but it felt like slavery, with me being some nigger on the auction block. A few days later, having convinced myself not to go anywhere near Gonzalez, I telephoned for more information and to ask again where the money was for going gold, and I was told Fabrice had left the company. No one had the decency to tell me, and I still didn't understand about being sold. I guessed I'd have to go to Germany to figure out what he was talking about, but maybe Earl Bryant could help.

He finally made it to France, arriving just in time to help me with a few concerts. Before we went out on the road, I explained to him how Gonzalez had handled things and told him that I wanted us to work close together because I didn't want to go through the same thing again. Mr. Bryant assured me he was ready to step in and help.

"You know, I've looked after quite a few artists in the States, and we will make sure you get treated right here, Marla. When I manage people, I make sure they get what they should, and I—"

I stopped him mid-sentence.

"I'm not looking for a manager; I just need you to help me with these concerts and find out where my money is going from the record sales; I've been told I've been sold to someone in Germany, but I've no idea who. I'll pay you a commission, but I don't want a manager."

I was firm with him because I didn't want to fall into a trap again. Mr. Bryant hesitated, but then nodded in agreement. As far as I was concerned, we were clear on things. There was no talk of signing anything with him, and because he came recommended by Larry, I felt things would be okay. I was tired, and it was good to have someone to help me with all my problems.

The following morning after the last concert I had booked, I called the limo company and asked them to send a car to pick me up, and we swung by to get Mr. Bryant from the Grand Hotel and headed to Vogue. As we approached the meeting room, the hallways were filled with large posters of myself and other artists. Mr. Bryant had explained what had probably happened, that they'd sold the rights to my music, but I needed to be released from the record company, and I was hoping we could get it settled. However, deep down, I expected it would be some of the same old bullshit excuses I heard from Gonzalez.

We sat in a conference room with a gentleman I had never seen before, who explained that Fabrice had been transferred to London because of some trouble he had gotten into in France. I was disappointed that he didn't have the decency to let me know he was leaving or tell me who would handle things after he left. Earl Bryant began talking to the executive telling them what had been going on. Why didn't this guy know already? I should not have to explain things to them; they needed to be explaining things to me. The executive was as cool as a cucumber while listening to Bryant, and he finally nodded before speaking.

"We want Marla to be happy as well, so how can we help you?"

I couldn't sit silent.

"Fabrice told me that at the end of the contract I could get a piece of paper getting my rights back, and I want that now. Fabrice said I'd been sold to Germany—I've no idea what that means—but I presume I will have nothing more to do with Vogue."

The executive looked perplexed.

"There is no such paper."

Bryant tried to take over the meeting.

"As Marla's manager, I want to make sure there are no contractual obligations here."

I looked at him but didn't want to cuss him out right there. I talked over him.

"I don't know why you guys won't just give me my rights back. I have given you gold and platinum albums, you have made enough money from me, and I want out now. You can put out a 'best of' and that will be three albums, but I've done the years, and I'm not recording another thing for you!"

The guy was calm. "I'm just saying, there is no such paper that says that."

I stood up, and Bryant tried to interject, but I could not take it anymore.

*"You guys know this is wrong! I'm sick of you fucking me over! I did my eight years, and I want my rights back, and I want them now!"*

I stormed out of the office, and as I walked down that long hallway in a fit of rage, I needed to smoke a cigarette. Bryant stayed in the office for a long time after I left, then he came out without any paperwork. I asked, "Where is the paper?"

"I'll work on them later. I'll get it done for you. In the meantime, let's get you home."

Before the limo dropped him off, we talked about going back to the US.

My mind was still going a million miles per hour, thinking about how things had begun. I didn't want to leave France without talking to my first bandleader, Joe Joe. I had not talked to him for a while, and I began to realize that between Gonzalez and Vogue, all kinds of things were still happening behind my back, but I wanted to make things right between us. I called Joe Joe.

"Hey, it's Marla. Look man, I want you to come to Paris to talk about things. I don't know what happened, and things are changing. Can you come see me?"

He agreed, and within two days, we were meeting at the record company.

"Look, man, I never wanted to lose you guys; you were a good band. They fired you all behind my back. I didn't authorize that. I looked up one day and had a whole new band."

Joe Joe was the kindest man I had ever worked with. He simply said, "It's okay, Marla; it was a bit much to keep coming so far for work anyway. I'm just glad you are okay."

Even though he was understanding, I was still pissed off.

"I want you to go with me to get these posters."

I don't think he quite understood what I was asking, but he agreed to go inside with me. As soon as we entered the building, the lobby had a guard's desk and a receptionist, and both were on duty. Immediately to the right, a framed poster of myself took up almost the entire wall. I walked in and grabbed it by the bottom. Joe Joe helped me get it off the wall. As the receptionist became flustered, she began speaking in French, making phone calls, and the guard stood shocked. I didn't care. I grabbed the poster by two ends and dragged it out of the office and down the street. Joe Joe shook his head and followed. He said, laughing, "Marla, you are crazy."

"Fuck them; they don't deserve me," I said. And we had a good laugh before he got on the train back to Niort.

As it was near time for me to leave, the only items left in the apartment were my studio equipment. I called Michele Crosio and asked about him sending it over to the U.S. for me.

"Can you work out something with Gonzalez and get it to me? I'll send you the address once I get there."

"No problem, I will make sure you get it," he replied.

We said our goodbyes, and a couple of days later, Bryant and I were on a plane to Los Angeles.

# CHAPTER 29

# Meltdown

Upon my arrival, Bryant began working for me right away and helped me secure a place in the Marina Del Rey area. It was a lovely one-bedroom apartment with a view of the Marina, and Tassy Cat loved it. Mr. Bryant continued to ask to be my manager, and I made it very clear to him that I did not want that kind of arrangement. I was still pissed off from everything I had gone through with Gonzalez and Vogue, and all I could think about was putting my hands around Gonzalez's neck. His voice kept ringing in my head, and I could not stop thinking about what he said before we got on the plane.

Bryant had already started to act like he didn't hear me, and the last thing I needed was another person trying to tell me what I needed while ripping me off. He asked yet again about being my manager, and I said, "I don't want a manager. It's road manager or nothing. I might eventually consider you as my manager, but not until I feel comfortable with you as a road manager."

I didn't want to have this conversation with him, but he kept bringing it up. It was clear, he was hungry and obviously saw that I had something to offer him. He knew I could be successful in the US as I had been in Europe.

A few days after moving to Marina Del Rey, I contacted Leroy Ball, and we talked about a few things, including Bryant. While waiting for Leroy and Bryant to get the ball rolling, I bought a RAV4 so I could get around town. I then reached out to Tuggy and called my dad, who talked about flying out from Chicago. I tried to relax, but I knew there was work to be done. I tried to connect with musicians because I knew I would need a band if I played in the US.

I also tried to connect with attorneys to find out what I could do about being ripped off. It was hard to get anybody to call me back or take me seriously, but after a few days, an attorney finally called me back. He sounded interested at first, but when he knew I didn't have any physical evidence, he said he didn't think he could take the case on. I was so frustrated I just hung up the phone. I couldn't think about it right then.

I needed to try to get some things going while I was in California, and I found a club where I performed using a CD for backing music. After performing to a small crowd, the guy gave me a check for one hundred and twenty dollars. Clearly, I wouldn't be able to sustain myself in LA, and I had to figure out some things. I knew I needed to go back to Europe, but I didn't want to go, not after what I had been through.

Weeks were passing, and I had not heard from Leroy or Earl Bryant, and there were still days I was feeling like my world was crumbling around me. While I waited to have a meeting to discuss details of how we were going to work together, I drove around the city searching for musicians.

My dad flew in to visit, and we really had a good time catching up. Dad smoked his cigarettes as I sat and rolled me a joint, and after, we drank a few beers and went to grab a bite to eat in the area. I told my dad what was going on with my career and tried to get some advice. With no experience in the music industry, he simply could not help me.

One afternoon while he was there and we were watching television, there was a knock on the door. I opened it to find Bryant standing there with an envelope in his hand. I introduced him to my dad and told him to take a seat. Instead, he opened the envelope, took out what looked like a contract, and plopped it down on the coffee table in front of me.

"Here, I need you to sign this."

I looked at him and saw Gonzalez and Nataf.

"I'm not signing shit," I said.

He stood firmly planted, staring at me. "If I'm going to do the work, I should be paid."

"I don't even know what is going on. I have not heard from any of you guys, and I need to know something."

"Look, I can book a tour for you, but to move forward, I need a contract in place."

I didn't budge as I listened to him.

"Mr. Bryant, you don't need a contract to go ahead and book tours for me."

"Marla, you need more than that."

My dad sat and listened as the conversation continued, and he nodded at me to keep going as I had been.

"I told you I do not want a manager! I'm done with them. I don't know you well enough to trust you, and I'm not doing it. I've had enough with people trying to manage me. Just do the tours, and we can all make money."

He then tried to talk over me, and the conversation escalated into an argument until he finally said, "If you don't sign this contract, you will be in a lot of trouble."

I matched the volume of his voice and said, "I heard that all before, and I'm still not signing it."

Bryant quickly picked up the unsigned contract and slithered out the door. Before it closed behind him, I heard him mumble, "That's okay, I'll find another way to do it."

I turned to my dad.

"You see what I'm going through?"

Dad nodded and said, "Yeah, that was crazy."

I shook my head and sat back down, my stress level was at an all-time high again, but the next day, my head was spinning even more when I got a phone call from the record company.

"Marla, you need to get back to Europe."

"No, I'm not going. I've been with Vogue for eight years now, and I don't have anything to show for it. Tell me why I need to come back?

"You still have another album to deliver."

"I don't care. I did my eight years, and I'm not doing any more! Fuck you, and if you want another album, make a 'best of' and give me my rights back! I'm done!"

My mind was made up. I really needed to try to get things going while I was in California because I did not want to go back.

A few weeks later, my equipment arrived. However, when I opened the crate, it was not my equipment; it was the older gear that belonged to Michele Crosio. I could not believe he did that. All the equipment was old and some of it didn't even work. I was pissed and the tears started again, but I could not give up on myself. I had to keep moving forward. When could I finally get a break and find someone I could trust not to stab me in the back?

A few days later, I got a call from Leroy; he wanted me to meet him at his apartment in Hollywood. It was good to see him, and I shared all that had been going on. He said he would help me in whatever way he could to secure concert dates. Leroy certainly knew much more than I did about the business and agreed to find a way to pick up where Gonzalez left off. Larry Ball and Mr. Bryant helped set up a band for me to go in the studio to record, "It's A Man's World" and "We have all the time in the World" by Louis Armstrong. I also recorded, "Just as I am" with blues guitarist Luther Allison.

Leroy shared with me that he was able to secure dates in Europe, and since he was a great guitar player, I assumed he would be in my band as well.

"So, are you going to tour with me?"

"No, I have gigs here I'm booked on."

"So, how is this going to work?" I asked.

"We are just going to get you set up in the cities that you toured before and a few others, and you will fly back to play."

"Well, how do you know who to contact? Is Gonzalez involved?"

"No, he's not."

There was a pause.

"I have my own contacts. Besides, you fired him, why would I work with him?"

"I need a lawyer. I can't just let them rip me off and not do anything. I know I'm going to have to fight, but I need someone."

"I'll see what I can do. In the meantime, let's get your tour going."

I left Larry and went back to my apartment. Earl Bryant had left me a voice message, asking me to join him for lunch. It was a sunny afternoon, and after he picked me up, we made small talk until we arrived at the restaurant. It was a nice day, and we sat at a lovely table outside. The moment we sat down, it all went to hell, and all I'd been trying to deal with exploded into a seismic meltdown.

"Look Marla, why is it that you don't want a manager?"

He barely finished the word manager, and the rage inside of me popped out, and I could not contain myself.

*"You don't understand what I went through. Those motherfuckers ripped*

*me off, and they are saying that I'm not going to find out. Well, I'm gonna prove them wrong!*

"Marla, listen ..."

I began shouting at the top of my lungs, and tears began streaming down my face.

*"Don't fucking Marla me! The so-called manager fucked me. The record company didn't do shit about it. I don't know where the fuck my money is, and I can't do this shit no more!"*

# CHAPTER 30

# Hospitalized

I continued to rant until I just stopped talking and continued sobbing so uncontrollably that I could hardly catch my breath. Bryant walked me back to the car, and I heard him say, "Look, you need to see someone. This is not normal."

By now, I was panting, unable to catch my breath.

"There is something else going on here, Marla. Do you want to go talk to a professional?"

I just surrendered. At this point, all I could do was nod yes.

He took me home, and the next day, he drove me to an office in a busy neighborhood where I was seen right away by a woman who sat behind a desk in a nicely decorated office. She asked me a bunch of questions, and I told her as much as I could as more tears flowed. It was a good talk with someone who didn't need anything from me, but by the time I'd finished the whole sordid tale, I felt drained and exhausted. When the session was over, she called Mr. Bryant into her office.

"I know you were concerned about Marla's mental stability, but Marla is fine. What is very apparent, though, is that there has been a lot of mental stress and trauma that Marla has been bottling up."

"Okay, thank you. You don't want to admit her to the hospital?" Bryant asked.

"I'm going to prescribe some sedatives," she said and gave me some pills.

We walked back to the car. I was still crying and shouting.

"He's gonna pay. I'm getting every dime back."

Bryant drove off only to take me to a different facility where the freeway signs said Pasadena. We got out of the car, and Mr. Bryant had a private conversation with the receptionist. Within moments of being in there, a tall nurse approached me.

"Marla, will you come with me, please? We are going to examine you for a few days."

I turned to Mr. Bryant and asked, "What is going on?"

"They just want to run some tests."

I was livid. One doctor already told me I was okay, and I didn't know where I was. Why did I only have people in my life who wanted to control me for their own benefit? I began to rant ...

*"There's nothing wrong with me. Other than people not listening to me and stealing my money, I'm fine! I'm tired of people doing shit to me and getting away with it. Gonzalez stole my money, then told me to my face he did it! I didn't have a contract with him, and the record company knew what he was doing! How do I have gold and platinum albums and no money to show for it?"*

As I continued to shout, two other nurses came out, grabbed me, and strapped me down on a small rolling bed.

*"I was ripped off. I'm not the one who needs to be locked up somewhere."*

They stuck a needle in my arm, and the last thing I remember saying was that somebody should call my dad and tell him where I was. A nurse took the number down, and straight after that, I passed out.

When I woke up, I was in a large bed, in a small private room, steps from a green garden visible from my window. It was a small bungalow-style room and only steps away from another room. I could not see the person in the adjacent room, but I could hear him.

"I didn't kill Tupac. I swear it wasn't me! I know who did, but it wasn't me."

A nurse came and closed his door, and the sound of his muffled voice was still resonating as I fell asleep again. I woke up once more when a doctor came in.

"It appears people are concerned with your mental well-being. After we run a series of tests, we will evaluate what is going on with you."

It transpired that Bryant thought I'd been taking serious drugs, and they took blood from my arm almost every day—this facility was a drug rehabilitation center. Thankfully, my dad was there when the doctor entered the room once more.

"There are no signs of heavy drugs, just marijuana, and Marla mostly needs rest and is dehydrated, suffering from fatigue and exhaustion."

My dad had a smile on his face, "Well, that's good."

Other family members arrived to visit, and I stayed for a few days and rested. It was some of the best sleep I had in a long time, but after about four days, I got restless and wanted to sleep in my own bed. One night I went to the front desk and found no one was there monitoring the entrance, so I called a taxi from the front payphone. The moment I got back to Marina Del Rey, I cooked myself a good meal, smoked a joint, and went back to sleep. I had some decisions to make, and since I wasn't making money in the U.S., I decided that I had to go back to Europe.

# DESTINY (To Get Up Again)

Every time I touch the ground
I find strength
To get up again
To get up again
I find my strength to get up again

# CHAPTER 31

# By the Grace of God and Fans

It shows I still wasn't thinking straight because when I got back to Paris, I didn't have anywhere to go and only enough money to feed myself and Tassy Cat. Ms. Simone did not live close enough for me to crash at her place, nor did I dare bother her with what was going on with me. She had her own problems. What was most important was that I try to make contact with people who could get me some more shows, so I could find a place to live and put some money in my pocket.

I went to a few restaurants near the old apartment, and occasionally, I would get offered a free meal by people who knew me. I was grateful for that. There were still a few posters of me around Paris, and it was weird to see them, knowing my life was in shambles. While wandering the city, in jeans and a T-shirt, looking slightly disheveled, I'd still occasionally get stopped by fans.

"Are you Marla Glen?"

Usually, I remained calm, but with an undertone of desperation, I responded, "Yes, it's me."

I'd sign whatever they offered for an autograph, and after a bit of small talk, I started to admit I didn't have a place to stay.

"Do you have room; can I crash at your place for a few days until I get some things figured out?"

It was an awkward moment for us both, and some fans didn't even take me seriously. Ultimately, I'd find someone to help me for a few days, and then the cycle would begin again.

No matter what the situation, I'd take them up on their offer until an opportunity to make money presented itself. I joined family gatherings or the occasional parties at their houses until I felt I was overstaying my welcome. When I wasn't staying with fans, I would sleep in the park or walk the streets of Paris. I was too well known to play in the streets of Paris, so I kept connecting with musicians and promoters until I could book a few gigs. Some of the people I met through Gonzalez, some on my own. I would take any show I could, to make the best of things, and occasionally booked a small hotel room here or there. I knew enough to make it work, so I just kept pushing forward. It wasn't easy, but it was for my survival.

I was truly grateful for people's generosity, and they helped me through some very difficult times. However, it was becoming more and more apparent that I needed some consistency. After saving money, I rented a sleeper camper so I could just crash in the same place every night and not worry where to lay my head for a while.

Meanwhile, the admission that Fabrice said to me kept ringing in my head—that he "sold me to Germany." People had also been telling me that my music was doing very well there, so it was time to drift on from Paris. I extended the camper rental and hired someone to drive me to Germany since I didn't have a European driver's license. The last thing I needed was to get in trouble from driving without one.

The driver I hired was Jean, someone I met hanging out. As we headed out in the camper early one morning, I sat and looked over the city's landscape, not knowing if I would ever go back to Paris. We stopped to grab a bite to eat, and he asked, "Do you know anyone in Germany?"

"I met a photographer at a concert by the name of Peter; he's the only person I know there."

"Will you contact him?"

"No. I'll figure out how to make things work on my own."

We finished up our meal and headed back on the road. Our first stop was Koln; it looked like a vibrant city. He parked the camper in an unassuming neighborhood, then I paid him for his services and gave him money to get back to France. It was the middle of the day when I began roaming around Koln. I hung out at some of the local bars, began making friends with musicians, and eventually put together a band.

There was so much to see in Germany, and just as I had drifted from different locations back home chasing open mic nights, I did the same throughout Germany, chasing gigs and performing opportunities. I went from Koln to Dusseldorf, to Duisburg, back again to Koln, and other small towns in between, traveling by bus. I was in survival mode, yet still emotionally dealing with all that happened in France.

I continued to tell anyone who would listen and began asking for legal help. I thought I would have a big problem with the language, but almost every German person I met spoke a good amount of English. I was grateful for it because German was a tough language to learn. The first German words I ever learned from Peter, the photographer at one of my shows, was to ask for a cigarette, and I picked up other phrases that helped me recognize bathroom signs, order beer, and one word I considered very important was 'Anwalt'—the word for lawyer.

Justice was all I could think about, and whenever I found an office with the word on a sign outside, I would enter and talk to the attorney hoping they could help me. Because I won my court case with Jean Claude, I felt surely there was a way to win a case with Gonzalez and

Vogue. I was sure I'd been cheated out of thousands, if not millions, from the record sales, bonuses from going Gold and Platinum, concerts, merchandising, and other opportunities. There was no doubt in my mind that the record company knew what was going on with Gonzalez and Fabrice, although nobody said a thing. But every lawyer said the same thing, that I lacked evidence, and I was responsible for taxes and other things, and there was nothing they could present in court in Germany to prove what happened in France.

I constantly tried to get over it all, but there were still days I would just cry when I started to think about what had gone on over the last few years, from being institutionalized by Earl Bryant to being ripped off by Gonzalez. From then on, I refused to let music industry snakes like Gonzalez and Bryant run my life or career. I was determined to get to a place where I was around people that would help me get things done correctly.

I kept looking for gigs because my survival depended on it, and long gone were the days when I could apply for a job at a fast-food restaurant, but that sure was easier. I eventually turned in the camper, and much like I did in Paris, I would run into a fan or two that would recognize me. Some hotel managers allowed me to stay for free or a small cost until I could finally afford my first apartment in Dusseldorf.

I learned the transportation system for taking a bus or a train, but to save money, I walked so much my feet would constantly hurt. I was securing a few large concerts, but when I didn't have shows, I would approach small bars in Karlsruhe, and they would hire me to do playback shows where I sang live to a backing track. Sometimes fans would see me at some of the smaller shows and hire me to do private parties and special events. These acts of kindness helped me through those most difficult times, and I recognized that only these fans and God's grace kept me afloat.

After a small gig, I was talking to a few musicians, telling them what I missed from back home. When we spoke about eating, someone told me there was a traditional soul food restaurant in Koln, about half an hour south on the train. I didn't believe them at first, but I found the address and went to see for myself. I walked in and met the owner, a woman named Brenda. I began calling her Miss B, a small framed African American woman who was bold and authentic. She had an amazing smile and her glowing personality immediately reminded me of many people I missed from home, especially my mom.

"Hey, how you doing? You own this place?" I asked as we struck up a conversation.

She smiled and replied, "I sure do!"

"Well, good! Let me see a menu."

She handed me a menu with food on there that I had not had in years. There were chitterlings, greens, black-eyed peas, and cornbread. I blurted out, "I want some cornbread!"

She laughed and in true black girl fashion, cocked her head to the side.

"Well, now, you've come to the right place!"

"Where are you from?" I asked.

"Florida, baby!"

With a smile, I said, "Then I know this food is gonna be good!"

We kept chatting as I ate her delicious food and discovered we had so much in common. We both were singers and being from the U.S. in Germany was a bit of a culture shock, but we took a lot of pride in what we were doing. She felt like a member of my family. Not only was she cool, but her cooking was damn good. Just looking over the menu made me miss being at home. I recognized so many food items that I could hardly contain myself. That was another thing we had in common—food! Miss B liked to cook, and I liked to eat!

We talked about how she came to live in Germany, and in between, I listened to her as she spoke German to her staff and other customers. It appeared as if she had mastered the language extremely well, and I was impressed with her even more. I learned her place was well known, and she had served food to some of the world's top entertainers, who never hesitated to stop in her restaurant when they came through Germany.

Her former customers included such icons like James Brown, Michael Jackson, Kool and the Gang, George Clinton, and many other black celebrities. I was delighted when she said she liked my music, and just like me, all those artists came to her restaurant, wanting that taste of good ol' down-home cooking like we have back in the States. There was no one like Miss B in Germany at the time, and I frequented her restaurant a lot. Ultimately, we forged a deep friendship and ended up being roommates for a while. I loved her spirit, and we became close like family when we lived together.

Many people thought we were lovers, but we were not. I think because we were both black, and I was a stud, people thought we were a couple. It was simply that she and I shared some of the same issues and experiences that came with being singers who lived away from home. With that alone, we understood and encouraged each other. I shared with her what I had gone through, and she could totally relate, as she had her own stories to tell. She continued to remind me of my worth and value in the music industry, which I understood, but I just didn't want to be exploited anymore as I had been. Miss B also helped me secure a few gigs. However, she had her own problems to navigate, so we supported each other in our journeys for the duration of our friendship.

# CHAPTER 32

# More Bad News

Miss B introduced me to an artist by the name of Tollman, and he hung around a lot. Tollman became a great friend, and he helped me and Miss B secure a house in the countryside outside the city of Cologne that Miss B and I moved into. The place was a good size, and a black guy who was also a musician by the name of Brian lived with us as well. We all had a lot of fun. Tollman would send a car for me to hang out at his house where he hosted exhibitions for his art, and sometimes it even led to me getting gigs. While wandering the neighborhood, I came across another Anwalt. When I entered the office, I was greeted by a tall bearded German guy with a big smile who sat behind a large desk, with stacks of paperwork everywhere.

"What can I do for you?"

"My name is Marla Glen, and I need a lawyer to help me with getting my money back."

He immediately took out a pencil and pad and said, "Nice to meet you, Marla. Tell me what is going on?"

I ran down the situation I had with Gonzalez and Vogue and told him what I had been through while trying to hold back tears.

"So, can anything be done?" I asked when I'd finished.

He looked me dead in the eyes.

"I think you definitely have a case."

A sense of relief flooded my body, and I then asked with bated breath, "What can you do?

"I can help you get your money back."

I was anxious and ready. I opened my backpack and pulled out 22 thousand marks, which I had saved a little at a time for this very moment. I refused to accept that nothing could be done, and now I'd found someone.

"How much is this going to cost?"

"I'll let you know on our next visit."

"I don't know how much it's going to take to get justice, but this is a start," I said, handing the money over.

He looked at me, his eyes wide.

"Oh my. Well, thank you. I'll begin working right away. Give me a few days to do some research, and we can talk again next week."

I left the office feeling a sense of accomplishment and without getting a receipt. It had been about two years since my world blew up with Gonzalez's admission of guilt, and I felt that maybe justice was now just around the corner.

I went back to the house to try to relax, but I could not escape the flood of thoughts about the past. I was getting settled in front of the TV when the phone rang.

"Hey, Baby!"

It was easy to recognize my dad's voice. It was always deeper than mine.

"Hey, Dad, what you doing?"

It was like I could hear him smiling on the other end of the phone.

"Not much. Went fishing last week, but I need something else to do."

"Dad, why don't you come out here to visit?"

He didn't hesitate, "I'll come out."

Unlike my mom, my dad loved to travel. I guess his early days of being a bellman on trains that traveled all across the US had a lot to do with that.

"Dad, when can you come? I'll get you a ticket."

He quickly said, "Whenever you book it, I'll be there."

I really wanted him to come.

While my dad was directly responsible for introducing me to music as a young child, he had never seen me perform in front of an audience, and I couldn't wait to make that happen. I booked his ticket and immediately got excited because I had not really had anyone from the family come out to stay with me. When my dad arrived, a friend took me to pick him up from the airport, and when I saw him in a crowd of people at the luggage area, I spotted him right away.

"*Dad!*" I yelled, rushed toward him, and we shared a big hug. We were so excited to see each other.

Once we got to my place, I cooked for him, and we chatted about what he was up to and a lot about Chicago, the family, and music. It was a wonderful reunion talking about old times when I was growing up. After a couple of days, Dad took some time to himself and ventured off on his own to visit Frankfurt, where he was stationed while in the Army. I had forgotten that he served in the military before he met Mom, and he had a lot of history in Germany.

In the evenings, Miss B, Brian, my dad and I, sat and talked for hours, and it really made me miss home, but I knew I couldn't go back. I was on a mission to get my money, and I could not look back. While dad was visiting, the lawyer called and requested that I return to the office. It was great news, and I was happy that my dad was there during this time because I could use the support. We walked into his office, and I'm pretty sure he was surprised to see that I was not alone. I introduced him to my dad, before we both took a seat in front of his large mahogany desk. He pulled a stack of papers out of a large folder and placed them at the center of his desk. He then looked over his spectacles and said, "So, I know what you told me, and I made some phone calls."

I sat on the edge of my seat, waiting for what felt like an eternity. "Okay, and ...?"

He began flipping through the paperwork.

"Well, based on my research, you owe money."

My mouth dropped, and my temperature was raised with adrenaline.

"To whom?"

"For insolvency and a few other things ..."

"What the hell is that?"

"It's like taxes in the U.S."

I could only look at him in disbelief.

"And it's a lot of money."

I was furious.

"I don't owe that! Why would I owe that when all I did was my job but never got paid? I don't know anything about that! Why?"

My dad sat in silence, shaking his head as the attorney read a few items from the papers on his desk.

"It looks like none of the taxes from the money you received was paid?"

"I knew nothing about that. Nothing! Are you sure that's right?"

"Yes, it all has your name on it."

I shook my head and stood up.

"No! This is not right! It's not! I don't owe anything; the people who ripped me off owe that money."

"That's not what it says here."

"*I don't care what that says! Why do I owe money is the question, be-cause the people responsible for handling my business were ripping me off. I won't accept this. I won't! I can't accept this. I need to report this to someone! Newspapers, the courts, somebody needs to know.,Äù*

The attorney tried to calm me down, but I could not accept it. The shouting became louder, and I realized he had talked to people who fed him the lies I had been fed.

"I am not accepting this bullshit. I don't even believe it. Here I am doing my job, and now they are saying I owe? This is crazy!

"At some point, you are going to have to pay this," he said, and I began to pace,

"No, it's bullshit. And I can't deal with this. Do you know they ripped me off and did this to me? I was asking about my taxes, and no one would tell me. I don't know what you're talking about, and it's clear they are the ones responsible for this!!"

The lawyer became frustrated, cut me off, and pointed at me like I was a child.

"Look, you need to shut up and sit down."

His telling me to shut up in front of my dad really made me mad.

"You don't tell me to shut up." I immediately turned to dad and said, "C'mon, Dad, let's go. Dad got up, and we quickly walked out of the office and down the street. After a few moments of silence, Dad said, "It's gonna be okay, baby."

"No, it's not. And he's wrong, and he knows he's wrong, and he's also got my money. Whoever that lawyer talked to, he believed them, and not me! I paid this man to be my lawyer, not theirs!"

# CHAPTER 33

# Out on My Own

I never got my money back but refused to stop looking for attorneys who would work for me. I knew with God there was always a way, and I refused to quit trying to find the right person to help me get my money back and find some justice. It was during these times in which I could not help remembering some of the conversations I had with Ms. Simone that I saw her in France.

"Ms. Simone, I think God will find a way to get me my justice," I said.

Stern and firm, she responded, "So, you want to go the long way, huh?"

Maybe Ms. Simone was right, and me putting my faith in God was the long way because growing up my mother told me many times, "Marla, you have the patience of Job." At the time, I didn't exactly know why mom would say that about me, but I was beginning to realize she was right.

After a couple of weeks, dad headed back to the U.S., and I realized as much as I wanted him to jump in and help me with this fight, he couldn't; I was on my own. The concerts were picking up, but after my dad's visit, I began to think more about home. I could not give up on getting shows or seeking justice, but I missed my family being around. I called my brother Tuggy and asked him to come out to help me with upcoming concerts.

"Hey, big head. What are you doing?" I asked.

He laughed when he heard my voice.

"Headed to work, and you the one with the big head."

"How much they pay you on that job?"

"Not as much I want."

"Why don't you quit and come work for me. My concerts are picking up, and I could use your help."

"Cool. When you want me to come?" he replied immediately, and I was delighted.

I booked him a flight and hired him as a bodyguard. Tuggy started right away, and even though we fussed a bit like siblings do, we had some good times. It was Tuggy's birthday and knowing that Tuggy likes cameras, one of the first things I did was buy him a video camera. He loved it! He videotaped almost every concert during his visit, and his recordings included sound checks, backstage gatherings, meetings, and sometimes, he wandered off around the venues. Tuggy was having a lot of fun, and I was enjoying his visit, but I needed more than the help of my brother.

As the concerts were coming in, it was clear that I could not handle the money and being a performer; it was just too much to deal with as an artist. Earl Bryant had been contacting me, telling me repeatedly how I needed someone like him, so I asked him to come out to help with the tour. I was desperate, but I didn't really know who to turn to, and there was no way I was going back to Gonzalez. The moment Bryant arrived, he seemed different, arrogant, and pushy, leading to us getting into arguments about how he should handle the business.

Instead of helping, he made things even more difficult and kept insisting that he wanted to work with me as a manager, and I was not having it. Working with him made me remember what Gonzalez always told me: that I had to ask for what I wanted. After several arguments with Bryant, one in particular really got to me when we were both at a bar. The owner approached us and introduced himself as George, and I noticed he had a set up for a band to play for his patrons. We chatted as I began thinking it was a nice place to hold a playback concert, and I liked George's energy.

"How many people does this place hold?" I asked as Bryant simply nursed his drink.

"If I position the chairs right, about 60."

"Oh, that's great. I'd love to perform here sometime."

George smiled, and I knew I sealed the deal.

"Let's make it happen," I said, and Bryant still stayed quiet.

Once I'd finished talking with George, it dawned on me that I booked a show as Bryant was standing in front of me, doing nothing but drinking. I also realized that I didn't need him. As George left to head over to the other side of the club, I turned to Bryant.

"Man, why do I even need you?"

He shook his head and got snippy with me.

"What are you talking about, Marla?"

"I should not be the person talking to club owners, you should, and you didn't say a word."

He took a sip of his drink before he turned to me.

"Do it your damn self then."

I got in his face and shouted, "I just did! You're fired!"

Within a few days, Bryant went back to the States, and I was happy that he did. I still needed someone to handle this influx of concerts that were coming in regularly. It was very strange. I had no idea who was booking them, but I knew I could not turn them down. I called them the 'Ghost Concerts'.

During this time, I had been in touch with Larry Ball, who introduced me to an attorney named Ira, who came out to help. We talked about finding a way to take Gonzalez to court, and I was excited to finally have an attorney to help me find a way to reveal how Gonzalez might've ripped me off. Quite soon, though, Ira was more concerned with being on the tours, getting free cigars, and finding sponsors. I felt very uncomfortable with his presence as he walked around the house I was renting with his shirt off, revealing a mountain of chest hairs.

It soon became clear that Ira was not actually doing anything to go after Gonzalez, and just like with Bryant, we got into arguments. Ira left Europe just as quicky as he came, but I soon found that it was Larry and Ira who were booking my concerts. This came as a complete surprise to me because I only knew Larry as a guitar player, and he and Ira were partners, with Larry booking concerts from the U.S. I had no idea what percentages they were being paid or how they managed to pull it off from working abroad. I could only guess that maybe Gonzalez was behind all that was going on without my knowledge.

In later conversations, Larry claimed he never spoke to Gonzalez, but I found it odd, and it still upset me. I never signed a contract with Larry but felt he had soured our friendship. After what I went through with Vogue Records and Gonzalez, I was hesitant to sign anything at all unless it was something clear and uncomplicated. I was surprised to hear how they handled things regarding my career without involving me, and I never wished to work with them again.

I was on a mission to find out what the hell Fabrice Nataf meant by saying I was sold to Germany and was now with GEMA, the German music rights management company. I didn't know how they operated or what they bought me for. It just didn't make sense to me, and it kind of made me feel like a slave. As much as I loved performing and songwriting, the music business kept me in shackles, always guessing how to figure things out.

Even though more concerts were coming in, it was hard to know what was the right amount, because Gonzalez gave me several variations of what I was getting paid, or why I wasn't getting paid at all. During this time, I felt as if I needed to begin rebuilding relationships with promoters who I worked for across Europe. I didn't know what lies Gonzalez had been telling people, but many promoters treated me as if I would not be able to do their shows. I have never intentionally canceled a concert. I have gotten phone calls from promoters telling me they booked me, but it was later discovered that shady individuals claiming to be my manager swindled promoters out of their deposit money. They were musicians familiar with the process of booking talent. Those incidents were completely out of my control, and I explained to promoters that I never knew about the booked concerts. When I got phone calls like that, it really made me upset.

At the same time, I was constantly trying to learn a new language, understand cultural differences, and find people I could trust. I was always trying to figure things out, and I continued to replay in my mind that day at the airport when Gonzalez admitted he ripped me off. On any given day, I would still be so fed up that I would just break out in tears. Somedays, I'd just pick up the phone and call Gonzalez to cuss him out. Never once did he ignore my calls, which usually went like this.

"Gonzalez, It's Marla Glen."

"Hey honey, how are things going?"

"I'm fine. When are you going to pay me my money back?"

"C'mon, Marla, let's have a real conversation."

"Just pay me what you stole from me, Gonzalez."

"Honey, I don't know what you're talking about."

"Of course you do; just give me a couple of the houses you bought with my money."

No matter what I'd say, he'd change the subject, laugh it off, or slyly insult me.

"Marla, I tried to help you, remember? You ran off. I probably was the only person on your side. You were not easy to manage."

Eventually, he would propose that we work together again.

"You know, Marla, I may have some gigs for you. Let's meet and talk about working together again."

"If I ever work with you again, it will be on my terms, not yours, because I know what you've done to me."

As I write now, a day does not go by without me thinking about the events at the airport with Gonzalez. Now, of course, I know how naive I was in dealing with him and Vogue Records, yet I kept hoping that they'd come to their senses and eventually find a way to make things right by me. That may be a bit naive in and of itself, but it didn't stop me from thinking it. I just wanted them to treat me as they would others, as they would want to be treated themselves. I kept thinking tomorrow would be better, but that never happened.

I believe that with God, all things are possible, which helped me know what to look for when handling business on my own. Overall, my instincts were usually right about certain people and situations, and basically, there was no one in my life who I was dealing with who I could trust.

# CHAPTER 34

# Tragic Loss

Early one morning, I was flipping through the television channels when I got a phone call from Tuggy, who had gone back to the U.S. He sounded winded.

"Hey, what you doing?" he asked.

"Watching TV. What you doing? And, why you sound so odd?"

There was a brief silence, then Tuggy said, "Mom had a heart attack."

He had my full attention, and I sat up on the sofa.

"Well, how is she?"

He sighed before he spoke, "Not good. She's still with us, but things don't look good."

At that moment, a kaleidoscope of childhood memories went through my mind, and without hesitation, I said, "Let me book a flight; I'll call you back to tell you when I can get there."

I sat still in silence for a minute to digest it all, and I prayed for my mother. All I could think about was how much she meant to me. Tuggy was living in California, and he could not get away to go see Mommy, and after I talked it over with the team I had in place, I couldn't leave either. I had no choice but to continue the tour I was on. I was extremely busy and felt bad that I couldn't go. I never shared much with anyone regarding my mother because knowing how much she loved me was one of the few joys of living that I kept to myself. I tried to call, but things were so hectic I could only call once in a while. After a few days, I eventually found she needed triple bypass surgery.

I arranged to see her after the procedure, and Tuggy and I managed to visit her simultaneously. By the time we got there, she was on the road to recovery, and the three of us could sit together and talk for hours. Tuggy was mostly quiet, and sometimes he would go outside and roam about our old neighborhood. With Tuggy gone briefly here and there, Mommy shared things with me she had never told me before, and she gave me a letter telling me what her wishes were if anything happened to her. She made light of the situation, but I knew she was worried about her health. We laughed a lot, reminisced, and we prayed.

I had a very different relationship with her than Tuggy did. Mom had tended to mollycoddle Tuggy more. After a couple of weeks, she seemed much stronger, and I went back to Germany to resume my already booked concerts. Tuggy stayed in Chicago for a while, but after a few months, I sent him the funds to come join me on tour to work as my bodyguard again. Mom was doing much better, and I made sure I stayed in touch a bit more.

Almost a year later, I had been living at the Crown Royal Hotel in Koln, and money was tight. Tuggy had been coming back and forth to help me on shows, and he was with me at the hotel during this time, helping out as security. I wasn't performing that particular week, but I had an upcoming concert in Koln. I usually sat at the bar with the bartender just chatting, and on this particular night, the Temptations, Maceo from James Brown's band, the Supremes, and other acts from my childhood were also staying in the hotel. They were performing at a nearby festival. Growing up, I loved these groups, and it was exciting to have a drink at the same bar with some of them.

I saw one of the members of the Temptations, I could not recall his name, but I recognized his face.

"Hey man, are you with the Temptations?"

"Yeah, how you doing?"

"Oh, man! I'm great; I grew up listening to you guys! I'm from Chicago."

"Really, how did you end up all the way out here?"

Before I had a chance to answer, the bartender answered his phone, and I overheard him say, " Ja, Marla ist hier. Einen Moment."

He handed me the phone, and a female's voice said, "Is this Marla Glen?"

"Yeah, that's me."

A woman with a soft-spoken voice paused for a brief second before she spoke again.

"I'm sorry to tell you this, but your mother has passed away."

I said, "Okay, thank you."

I handed the phone back to the bartender, and the next thing I remember was waking up in my hotel bed, unsure how I got there.

"Marla? You're awake?"

I looked up to see one of the guys from the Temptations.

"Yes. My mother died."

"We know. You fainted. Are you alright?"

I wasn't okay. I was in shock. After I passed out, I found out that one of the members of the Temptations and someone from James Brown's band carried me up to my room.

Full of emotion, Tuggy and I hopped on a flight to Chicago, and it was the longest plane ride I had ever taken. When we arrived, our dad picked us up from the airport. He grabbed my suitcase and tossed it in the back seat before he hugged me. "Hey Baby, you have a good flight?"

I responded, "Yeah, have you seen Mommy?"

"I only stayed for a minute. I couldn't bear to watch her lying there like that."

"Well, what's going on? The woman who called said she passed."

I could tell that Dad was sad.

"She's in a coma, and she's not responding. Her brain activity is nonexistent, so she's not far from being gone."

We quickly headed to Mercy Hospital, and we barely said much. Even though my mother and father were divorced, they talked often. Their marriage didn't last a lifetime, but their friendship was still strong. He stopped in front of the hospital and said, "She's in room 342."

I sat for a second and sighed before I said, "Dad, you're not coming up with us?"

"No. Her husband is there, and I don't want to cause any problems, you know?"

"Yeah, I get it. Okay, I'll call you later."

I could tell my dad was heartbroken; he had a look on his face I had never seen before.

"Okay, baby. Call me."

We jumped out of the car and headed toward the front desk. It was evening, but the hospital was bright and smelled of disinfectant. I was exhausted from the long flight, but it didn't really matter; my body was running on adrenaline. I took the elevator up to the third floor and found the room. As I walked down the hallway, Tuggy told me to go in first, so we could each have a private moment with her. I hugged him briefly before entering the room.

As I walked in, I saw my mother lying unresponsive in the hospital bed. She was connected to machines, tubes coming out of her body, and an oxygen mask on her face. I rubbed her forehead, and I let her know I was there, "Hey, Mommy, it's Marla."

After a second, I saw a slight twitch in her hand. I took another sigh before I continued to speak.

"Mommy, we all want you to get better. We love you and want you to rest so we can see you laughing again."

My mother did not move, and all I could do was lower my head in prayer. I prayed for God's will because I knew that my mother had a great relationship with God, and things were out of my hands. It was still not easy to see her like that. I felt like I had to be strong for Tuggy because he was really more of a mama's boy than I was. As I stood over her, I could only think of the many conversations we had when I was growing up.

"If I am ever in the hospital, and end up being a burden to someone, don't hesitate to let me go. And don't cremate me, bury me whole."

My mother was very independent and clear on what she wanted for her life. She never wanted to be a burden on anyone.

Moments later, her husband Calvin walked into the room. He spoke, but he seemed unaffected by what was going on. With a firm voice, he said, "Marla, you made it."

I looked at him. He was drinking coffee and spoke like it was a regular day at the office.

"Yeah, I made it."

I hated seeing Mommy like that, but I left her side and went into the hallway, Calvin followed. Tuggy and Calvin and I stood there for seconds in silence before a nurse approached us.

"You must be Marla and Armando."

I responded, "Yes, that's our mother in there."

"We were waiting on you. Your mother's condition is probably not going to improve. She doesn't have a lot of brain activity. Someone needs to make a decision."

Tuggy and Calvin looked at me.

"Mommy was very clear when she told us. She doesn't want to be in a position where someone has to take care of her. She said if it ever came to that, we should let her go."

Tuggy responded, "Yeah, she said that."

"Mommy said, don't be crying over my good clothes, let me go."

At the time Mommy said this, we had laughed because we knew how she loved her clothes. However, now faced with the actual situation, this was not an easy decision. I turned to the nurse and said solemnly, "We are just going to let her go."

The nurse nodded and said, "Okay. I'll let the doctor know."

Tuggy and Calvin went in to say their goodbyes, and then it was my turn to see my mother alive for the last time. I took one last look at her, picked up her hand, and prayed for her soul. Mommy passed on December 3$^{rd}$, 1998, at six o'clock in the morning, and when it was all over, we all left the hospital, and Tuggy and I went to Dad's house. Tuggy seemed to be handling things well, and that put my mind at ease.

That next evening, I made it over to see Calvin and walked into the house I grew up in, knowing my mother wouldn't ever be there again. When he opened the door, a flood of memories came rushing back, including the time Mom and I laughed about Tuggy eating all the spaghetti she made for dinner, not knowing we hadn't eaten, and the time my mother asked me about the first time I had a date with a girl, and the kisses my dad used to steal from my mom during Christmastime.

I felt awkward talking to Calvin. He was not warm, and when he spoke, the tone of his voice was as if he was handling a business transaction. I followed him to the backyard, and we stood and talked.

"Marla, I'm glad you came to see your mother because I wanted to run some things by you." The more he spoke, the more awkward I felt. Calvin didn't look directly at me; instead, he held his head down or looked elsewhere.

"I think that you should cremate your mother's body."

I couldn't believe he could say that when my mother's body probably wasn't even cold yet.

"No. My mother didn't want that."

Calvin seemed so unaffected. I didn't want to be rude, but because my mother left final decisions up to me, and I knew what her wishes were, I was firm. She had shared how she wanted to go all her life. I didn't really understand why he wanted to go against her wishes. I felt that Calvin was trying to cover something up, and I was not having it. I refused to listen to him, and his biggest concerns were about details around money and the house. I felt like I had to do what was best for her before I went back to Germany. I insisted she be buried with white roses and other flowers I knew she loved. I picked out a pearl casket and made most of the arrangements for her homegoing service.

The funeral was held at Gatlin's Chapel and attended by several friends and family members. She was a young, 57-year-old vibrant, amazing woman, and I will always miss her. She was the best mom ever. I know that I would absolutely not be who I am without her guidance and loving spirit. She taught me so much about life and independence, and I was lucky to have her as a mother. My only wish was that I had hoped she was able to get over her fear of flying so that she could have come to see me perform.

Tuggy and I flew back to Germany, and I was back on stage within one day of attending her funeral. I never got a chance to cry, only reflect. My mourning came out in the form of a song that my heart led me to write for her a few months later, entitled *White Roses for My Mother.*

# CHAPTER 35

# Trouble in Switzerland

One night, Tuggy and I took a train from Germany to Switzerland to prepare for a concert. I got up early that morning and rushed out wearing an oversized shirt and some old jeans, looking like some random black dude from the south side of Chicago. I always enjoyed taking the train while in Europe; it's such a relaxing ride watching the countryside watch go by. I was dead tired and fell asleep, because we left so early. When the train braked and jolted, I woke up and realized I desperately needed the toilet.

I was on my way to the train's toilet when the conductor announced our stop was coming up quickly, and people began to crowd around the doorway. I realized I would miss the stop if I used the toilet on the train. So, when the doors opened, I quickly hopped off and ran to the bathroom. Tuggy was straggling behind me, and I shouted to him, "I gotta pee! Wait for me!"

I began pulling coins out of my pocket, still on the move. While squirming, I quickly tried to put the German coins in the Swiss machine, but they kept falling out. I didn't have any Swiss money, and my bladder couldn't wait another moment. Frustrated and desperate, I jumped the turnstile and rushed towards the men's bathroom, but that was locked. Then I saw the women's bathroom was open, so I went in there. If I didn't, surely there would be a mess to clean up. The attendant ran in after me and began banging on the door, speaking Swiss-German while I was using it.

"Was machst du da drinnen? Was machst du da drinnen?"

I couldn't understand what she was saying; I was just going to deal with it when I finished.

"I'm sorry, I really have to go. I'll be out in a minute!"

She was persistent in knocking, and the stall was moving, Bang! Bang! Bang! Bang! She was annoyed by me being in the stall, and she got louder, *"Ich habe dich gesehen, du hast nicht bezahlt. Herauskommen!"*

"I'll be out in a minute. I really have to go!"

The room went quiet, and finally relieved, I finished and washed my hands, but when I stepped out of the bathroom, I saw the police had arrived. There were two male officers and one female officer. I tried to explain the situation and had barely finished what I was saying when the female cop grabbed me by the hair and dragged me toward the wall outside the restroom.

"What is your problem? Don't you understand the rules?"

I tried to explain again. "You don't have to push me."

The female officer and I were staring each other down. She did not take her eyes off me, and nor did I take mine off her.

Tuggy saw what was happening and walked up.

"Hey, what's going on?"

One of the male officers responded, "He did not pay. He can't do that. It's against the law."

Tuggy tried to explain.

"Look, we don't have any problem paying. We have the money."

The female cop was standing in my face. We did not stop looking at each other for several minutes.

"You can't just do what you want to do here."

"What are you talking about?! I just wanted to use the bathroom. You don't have to be rude."

I tried to walk away from her, but she grabbed me, and we ended up in a tussle, and she hit me in the eye. I was shouting for her to get off me as she wrestled me to the ground and grabbed me by the hair. I kept trying to get her hands off me, but she was dragging me, and it hurt.

"Let me go! What are you doing?!"

The other two officers had their hands on their guns. Tuggy was shouting, "*What's the problem? I said we can pay the money!*"

Things were now completely out of hand, and the officers were not listening; they all moved in on me and put me in handcuffs. I was mad as hell.

"Where is the human decency?! You arrest someone because they had to use the bathroom? And you don't even try to listen to me?!"

The officers grabbed me, picked me up, and tried to get me into the cell at the train station. They didn't do this without a fight, and as I tried to stop them, I was hit with pepper spray! I screamed, and my eyes hurt like hell. I could not believe what was happening. I had a show in a few hours and was sure I would not make it because they then put me in a cell at the police station.

I sat in that cell, my eye was swelling up, and my arm hurt terribly. Eventually, Janz, my road manager, turned up after Tuggy got hold of him, and he sorted it all out. After a couple of hours, I was released, still not knowing what I did wrong and sure things could have been handled differently. Yes, I did jump the turnstile, but I did not want to pee on myself, and I felt they should have understood that.

Later that evening, I took the stage in a fireman's suit, wearing it because I needed something to get me into a better headspace. I had met a few firefighters that day and they were very accommodating by allowing me to borrow a suit. So, I went on stage with my eyes still a little puffy and a sling on my arm. I explained things to the audience, "I had a rough day. Almost got arrested for having to pee! But I made it."

I gave my performance and received a standing ovation.

# CHAPTER 36

# Following the Money

Every so often, when hanging out with my band, or people in the music industry, conversations about the music business, publishing rights, and getting paid would inevitably come up. By now, it was the latter part of 1999, and I was still uneasy about my career and how things unfolded with Vogue, Gonzalez, and others. On top of that, I felt I still didn't know enough about how things worked. There were some things I had begun to understand about publishing rights, GEMA, the German rights management organization, and other details about the music business, but it wasn't clear enough for me to know how to get back the money I was still owed from being ripped off in France.

Every time I'd find out more information, it made me more upset. One particular night after a concert, I was sitting with the band at a restaurant, and we began to talk about publishing rights and the music industry. I had been getting the impression that many of them thought I was very wealthy. This was far from the truth, and the falsehoods of me having money made me uncomfortable and made me think of the past. My brother Tuggy and road manager Janz were there with the band as we talked about what had happened.

Janz came from a family who owned a brewery, and when we went on the road, his dad would donate cases of free beer to the band, and we loved it. He was cool and smart, and I liked hanging around him. One day in a restaurant, I shared with him how I felt about what had happened, and he always seemed genuine in his response and understanding; the band listened on.

"When I was ripped off by my so-called manager, Gonzalez, he didn't care. I think he was signing my publishing rights and getting my money. I never got any checks from publishing."

Janz seemed surprised when I said this.

"Where is he now?"

"He's still in Paris. He still calls me from time to time."

Janz looked at me again, clearly wondering how this could be true.

"I can't believe someone could do that."

"Believe it. That man put me through hell. You would be surprised at some of the things he still says to me."

Janz's mouth dropped.

"You still talk to him?"

"Yeah, I chase him for my money, but it never works. I could call him right now, and he will deny everything."

"Call him. I dare you," Janz said.

He didn't think I'd do it, but I had no issues sharing a conversation about Gonzalez with him. The band looked at me, and I picked up my cell phone.

"I'll call right now."

I picked up the phone and dialed his number, putting the call on speaker. Tuggy sat at the end of the table and started his video camera to record everything. I welcomed it because some of the things that came out of Gonzalez's mouth were hard to explain, and many people didn't believe me when I told them how he treated me. The phone rang on the other end of the line twice, and he picked up.

"Hello?"

"Hey, Mr. Gonzalez, have you decided to pay me my money back yet?"

Gonzalez laughed and said, "Hi Marla, how are you?"

He completely ignored my question, but I kept going.

"Look, I think you manipulated my publishing contracts; where is my money?"

The band members watched in silence.

"I don't have it. Not sure what you are talking about. You're not getting publishing?"

I was not up for his games.

"Well, no, and of course, you know that. Why am I not getting any money? I worked with you for years. Where is my money?"

"Oh, Marla, I did nothing," he lied.

"You did something. You admitted it at the airport."

He tried to change the subject.

"Marla, I have some work for you; when are you coming back to Paris?"

I laughed and shook my head.

"If I come back there, I'm coming with the police, Gonzalez. It's because of you that I'm in tax trouble."

"Well, you should pay your taxes, honey."

"Look, it's taxes on condominiums, houses and cars, and other shit that I've never bought. How is this possible when I never bought those things? I even think you also released an album without my knowledge of it. I saw a bootleg CD that said, Made in the USA. I never did that; who did it?"

Gonzalez remained quiet, so I kept on.

"Oh, you don't know what I'm talking about? Sure, you don't, but when I bust you, I'm going to bust you so hard, and you will regret it. So Gonzalez, where is my money?"

"I have been keeping your money for you and tucking it away since you left."

He was lying to get me back there, and I knew it. It made me so angry that I couldn't take it any longer, and I could feel my blood pressure rising. I handed the phone to Janz.

"Here you talk to him; I can't do this anymore."

After handing the phone to Janz, I walked out of the restaurant to smoke a cigarette.

Janz continued to talk to Gonzalez, listening to him with one hand over his ear to drown out the noise in the restaurant.

Within a few minutes, I walked back in, and Janz shared what Gonzalez said.

"He said you owe him money."

My mouth dropped.

"What?! That's crazy!" The band had a look of disbelief on their faces; some shook their heads.

Janz looked at the phone and said, "He flipped that so easily; I can tell he's a slick one."

"He's sick and manipulating, and he's full of shit."

I turned to Tuggy and said, "We need to take a trip to Paris to see about where my money is."

I could not get that conversation with Gonzalez out of my head. On December 14th, 1999, within a month of that conversation with Gonzalez, I picked up the phone and called Janz to ask him to take me to Paris.

"Hey man, I'm going down to Vogue Records tomorrow; they made an appointment with me. Can you drive?" Without hesitation, Janz responded, "Absolutely."

I had been telling him about all the bullshit that Gonzalez put me through, and he seemed to get it. I needed someone to understand that I was telling the truth about the bastard. Janz also spoke French, so he could translate if I needed him to.

The next afternoon, me, Tuggy and Janz hopped in the car and drove six hours from Koln. Tuggy was in the front seat and occasionally videotaped different sights throughout France's busy streets. From the back seat, I told him to save the battery because I needed him to record the meeting.

"Don't miss a thing, Tuggy." He kept recording and sometimes turning the camera on me as we drove through the streets.

"Don't worry; I have two extra batteries fully charged. If someone even farts, I'll pick it up on this camera." Tuggy always had toilet humor in awkward situations.

As we dodged in and out of traffic, Janz didn't have much to say, but he was driving too fast for my taste.

"Janz, slow down, man. I want to get there in one piece."

Perhaps he wasn't going that fast, and I was just wound up about everything else.

We finally made it to Paris and stayed in the Grand Hotel overnight. It was one of the places I loved to stay when I lived in Paris. The next morning, we zipped through the busy streets toward the city's center, and Janz pulled into the underground parking next to where the Vogue offices were located. As we all went up the elevator, chills ran through my body. There were so many times I stood in an elevator asking Gonzalez questions he would never answer.

We made it to the offices, and this time there was a different sign outside the door. Vogue was now BMG Vogue. The offices still had dim lighting, and the pale paint had not changed from when I was there eight years before; the only thing different was some of the furniture. Oh, and of course, there was no sign of Fabrice Nataf.

As we stood in front of a secretary who was on a call, she mouthed for us to take a seat. I thought she was cute, but I was not really in the mood for flirting.

"They're ready for you now, down the hall and to your left," she said politely once she ended her call. She had a nice smile, but her teeth were a little crooked.

Feeling uneasy and with my stomach churning, I put on my shades as we headed down the long hallway to the small conference room. There were six chairs around the glass table, and within a few minutes, a brunette entered alongside a balding man; each were carrying folders full of paperwork. They introduced themselves as Alice and George; she had a French accent, and his was British. After we shook hands, I introduced Tuggy and Janz, then we all took a seat. I sat closest to the door, next to my guys. The two Vogue people sat opposite like we were lawyers taking a deposition.

Looking like a schoolteacher trying to be trendy, Alice peered over her glasses that seemed too big for her face.

"Marla, I think there is something very bizarre with some titles ..." she began, and I could tell she was nervous.

I quickly interrupted her because it seemed as if she was already looking for excuses.

"Look Alice, there are a lot of bizarre things going on, including Fabrice Nataf's name on one of my songs, claiming he wrote it. I have been calling people, and when I went to Germany to figure out what was going on, I discovered that Gonzalez and Nataf had been telling lies in the press, trying to make me look crazy."

"I don't think they ..."

Alice tried to explain their actions, and that was all I needed to truly get pissed. I interrupted her just as she interrupted me.

"Look, you don't know what they did. I lived it; you weren't there. I was the one in a straitjacket trying to figure out where the hell my money was going."

Alice sat back in her chair as I dug in.

"Listen, I don't know what's going on, but I have been calling and recording conversations with people who won't give me answers. I had Glam Records Company call you guys to try to clear this up, and the answer they received was Marla Glen did not exist in our company, nor was I ever at Vogue. Not to mention, I had gold and platinum records, and I have not received any money from you. *I want to know where my damn money is!*"

Alice smiled uncomfortably and took a breath.

"Okay, this is what I have." She opened her folder, and the first page listed about four or five names. She spoke as clearly as she could and gingerly began to direct her comments to Janz. Tuggy held the camera steady and kept recording. I couldn't keep quiet.

"Look, they were stealing my money, and no one believed me. I have not seen any money from you since 1992. *Where did the money go?*"

George opened his folder and spoke for the first time.

"Well, this was for publishing. The last check we had for you was in the amount of twenty thousand marks. It was sent to Marla Glen Productions, care of Earl Bryant at 385 Lemon Street, Walnut, California."

I was in disbelief and began yelling to the top of my lungs.

*"Earl Bryant!? He was never my manager! That's another man who is ripping me off!"*

As I wiped spittle from my chin with the back of my hand, George tried to further explain and began directing his comments to Janz.

"We must've paid Marla directly because Marla Glen is clearly on the check."

My voice filled the room like a freight train traveling through a narrow tunnel.

*"Bullshit!"*

I took a deep breath and tried to calm down.

"Look, both of you. If you gave that man my money, in care of me, I never received it. So, basically, you gave my money away. *He was not my manager. Do you understand?*"

Janz tried to interject, "Marla, calm down!"

Why was he telling me that when he was on my side?

"Why?! They took my signature out of some computer and forged it. I never signed with that man to represent me, and you gave him my money! I have a goddamn right to be upset!"

Janz jumped in again, "Marla, we are trying to fix it."

"Marla, BMG wasn't sending the money to Mr. Bryant, SACEM was doing it," George said calmly, but at that point, I had had enough.

I had no idea how GEMA, SACEM—the French equivalent of GEMA—or any supposed organizations claiming to take care of the client's royalties worked. I only knew they weren't working for me in this situation because I was never contacted about anything regarding my money.

I stood up in tears and shouted, *"SACEM is wrong too, damn it!"*

I walked out of the office, leaving the door open. If I'd slammed it, it probably would have been hard enough to knock all the pictures off the damn walls.

Nothing came of the meeting, and eventually, me and Tuggy got on each other's nerves as siblings often do. He went back home to California, and I continued to drift throughout Germany, working any gig I could and taking every musical opportunity I could get paid for, for a fraction of what I was sure I was worth.

# CHAPTER 37

# Time For A Change

It was the year 2000, and the new millennium had crept up on me without me securing any kind of recording contract nor finding a way to get all the money back I was cheated out of. I kept moving forward in trying to make things happen in my career because that was the only option I felt I had. I was tired of chasing gigs and opportunities on my own, but managing myself allowed me to understand the business better, and the more I worked, the more my exposure grew, leading to more bookings.

I continued to take whatever gigs I could to keep myself afloat as I drifted around Germany, singing in small clubs using recorded playbacks, where I essentially worked without a band. It was tough because I'd turn around to say something to the band in the middle of the show, and they weren't there. That's how much I was used to having a band. I've never been afraid of hard work, yet I was tired of doing it all alone. Often, I'd get opportunities for writing a few new songs and recording new music with people who helped me put projects together, but it was like starting all over from the beginning, and a lot of the opportunities did not pan out.

Without a record company behind me, I'd spend money out of

my own pocket to try to produce my projects, but it was not easy. The last album I was involved in with the help of a record label was back in 1994. It was my final album for Vogue Records entitled *Our World*, and I didn't feel like the company did much to market it. I had nothing to do with BMG Vogue's release of *The Best of Marla Glen*, but I was happy to be done with them. They had my four albums.

Needless to say, as time passed, it was getting harder to stay financially afloat. Me and Tassy Cat continued to live in small hotels, rented rooms, and other inexpensive places. I hopped from train to train, going from Koln to Dusseldorf and other areas in between for any gig I could get. I needed something to happen, and things had gotten so bad that I didn't have a proper place to stay, but by the grace of God, someone told me about a university residency program for struggling artists. The program was only for three months, but I applied and was fortunate enough to get accepted and during that time, I met Saundra Kaupp in a bar one night.

When I walked in, she stood out like a beautiful ray of sunshine in a grungy alley. I sat across from her and ordered a drink. We exchanged glances, and after an air toast, I decided to walk over to sit next to her.

"So, how you doing this evening?

She smiled after taking a sip of her wine, and said, "I was out visiting my grandmother, and she always makes me happy."

At a closer look, I could tell she was a professional. Her nails were perfectly done, and she didn't have a hair out of place. She looked like new money.

"So, what do you do?"

"I work in banking. Been doing it for over ten years."

"And what do you do?

"I'm a singer. Marla Glen is my name."

She smiled. "Very interesting."

The conversation continued, and we talked a little about music, a lot about life, and I could tell she was an extremely smart woman. I could also tell she didn't know anything about me. Our discussion eventually led to my troubles with being ripped off. By this time, Saundra was probably about the one-thousandth person with whom I shared my story. I never gave up trying to find a way to sue Gonzalez and the record company to get my money back, and with tears in my eyes by the end of the night, she seemed to have the compassion to want to help me.

We exchanged numbers and began to keep in touch. Over the next few months, we chatted a lot. We met a few times for lunch or dinner in Heilbronn. We were still chatting as I was coming to the end of my residency.

"So what are you going to do?"

"Honestly, I don't know."

"Why don't you come stay with me in Heilbronn for a while until you figure it out?"

I was in no position to tell her no, so I said, "Sure, I'd like that."

Right after I left the university program, I moved in with Saundra, and we had already begun having conversations about what I needed to do about getting someone to help me with getting work, and she seemed to be interested in the process. Her one-bedroom apartment was very nice and was located next to a funeral home. I was flattered by her offer to come live with her, but I couldn't tell if this was a flirtatious move or just an act of kindness. I thought she was attractive, but I didn't want to overstep her boundaries.

I continued to tell her about Gonzalez, Earl Bryant, and Vogue records, and I told her of the countless number of attorneys I had paid to help me, but I never got any support from them.

"I know a guy who could definitely help you. He's a great friend

I know personally, and he is very popular in Germany," she said over dinner one evening.

"That's great. When can I meet him?"

"I'll call him tomorrow."

By the end of that week, Saundra and I were sitting in front of an attorney. His office was better than most I had seen, and you could tell he was accomplished. I was anxious to talk to him. When he came out to greet us, he held his hand out to shake mine, and he had a firm grip.

"Marla Glen, I'm very happy to meet you. I love your music."

I was happy to know he knew me and hoped he could help.

"Thank you so much. I appreciate that."

He had a patch over his left eye, and quite honestly, I would not have cared if he had been blind. I was just hoping he could help me. We sat in his office for two hours as I explained my story yet again.

After I finished saying all that I needed to, he asked, "What exactly do you think we can do?"

"Whatever we need to do for me to get justice."

"There may be a way to figure things out, but I'm not sure. Let me do some research."

This time things felt different. I was truly hopeful he could help me, unlike so many others, but I didn't forget the other attorneys who ended up the other side of the fence defending the person I wanted them to sue. I had grown tired of the promises and research people said they were doing, only to come up with nothing that would help me. Saundra and I left the office, and I felt like she was a really good friend.

Not long after that, she and I had a conversation about management.

"I think it's time for you to get help in other ways. I feel confident we can work together," she said one day when we were back in the bar where we met.

Again, for the first time, it felt right, so I agreed. She would be the first one to officially be my manager, with my approval, instead of people assuming the role and working on my behalf without my agreement.

Saundra smiled and said, "I think we can make it work."

"I know we can."

I had been watching her for months, she was professional, smart, and she had an eye for details. I felt that because she was a woman, she could bring a level of sensitivity to the role and be very effective in getting the job done, unlike some of the men I had been working with, who acted like they were bulls in a crystal shop.

Within a few weeks, Saundra quit her job at the bank and became my full-time manager. Her colleagues at the bank even gave her a farewell party to congratulate her on her new role, and everyone was excited about the possibilities. I shared all my contacts with her; she made phone calls and began booking dates. I instructed her on how to handle the contracts, promoters, and other business that came along with management, and she was doing well. Gigs were coming in, I was back on the road with bigger jobs, and things seemed to be moving along nicely until I learned that Saundra had connections with the local Hell's Angels since she was dating one of the members.

# CHAPTER 38

# More of the Same

One day Saundra approached me with a logo that said, SKMg.

"What do you think of this?"

I looked at it, and I could not figure out what it was.

"What is it?"

"My management company, of course."

It bothered me because she never told me she was setting up a company. As a team, I would have liked to discuss it, and I began to feel like she didn't want to run things by me but just run things. That was not what I had in mind when I agreed to have her manage me. Besides, I was her only client. I had a problem because anything done in the company that she started, would directly affect me as an artist. There wasn't anyone else involved; how difficult could it have been for her to say, "Hey Marla, what do you think about this?"

However, she created the company without my input, and it made me uncomfortable, but the concerts continued to roll in. Saundra and her boyfriend rented an office not far from where her apartment was located. I needed more privacy and was used to being on my own, so before they got furniture or equipment, I got a mattress and slept on the office floor. It was private and it was where Saundra began to handle all the business.

Saundra's boyfriend was a member of the Hell's Angels, and the two of them decided to surprise me at the office.

"Hey Marla, we want to show you something. Check this out."

She revealed paperwork where the business entity logo, SKMg was at the top. She asked me to sign it; it was a contract.

"We want to make things official, so I'm going to need you to sign a contract."

I was not going to do that because I had already begun to feel uncomfortable. I said, "Things are working fine, and I am doing my part. Why do we need a contract?"

She shrugged and put the contract back in her bag.

A few weeks later, they had yet another surprise. I was sitting in the office when one of the members of the Hell's Angels pulled out a CD and handed it to me; it was packaged, labeled, and ready to be sold.

"What is this?"

Saundra, with a sense of accomplishment said, "We did a CD!"

I was shocked. The single was labeled, *Dreams*. As I looked it over, it had several credits for people I didn't know at all. I held the CD in my hand, with my mouth hanging open, and she grabbed it from my hand and played it. I listened, and it sounded horrible; the music was arranged all wrong, and it wasn't an arrangement I would have chosen for this song, and my voice didn't sound good at all.

"How did you get this done without me? What studio did you do this in?"

"I got help from Michele Crosio." I looked closely at the back of the CD, and Michele's name was all over it.

"This isn't right. Why would you do this?! And you did this without my permission. I don't know these musicians."

Saundra looked as if she didn't understand.

*"You shouldn't have done this! I don't like it."*

"I don't understand what's wrong with it. It sounds fine."

"Of course it does to you! You're not a musician! This is an old unproduced song that Michele kept when we were working together years ago. He doesn't have my permission to use that. You can't just grab my voice and put it on any record you want to. This song is not even mastered properly."

Saundra looked at the CD, perplexed.

I picked up another one of the CDs and took a closer look. The name Mailo McFarley was one of the musicians listed on the back of the CD cover.

"This guy Mailo was fired from my band years ago. Why would I want him involved in anything that I do? Did you even think about asking me if this was okay?"

Saundra said nothing. She stood quietly as I continued, "You guys even have me thanking people on the back of this CD case, and I don't even have a clue who they are. So, what are you doing with it?"

Saundra looked at me and said, "It's been released."

There was a moment of silence, and all I could do was shake my head.

"This ain't right. I would have never produced that song. How would you like it if I made something you didn't like, put your name on it, and sold it to people? Why would you guys go behind my back and do this? Saundra, Michele has had those recordings for several years. Now you are helping him release songs without my permission? Who else was behind you making this?"

Saundra didn't say anything, but I suspected that Gonzalez had something to do with it. I couldn't prove it, but I could feel it. Yet again, this was the beginning of the end for me. It felt like another complete betrayal, especially since I had absolutely no input in this project. I was so pissed I took to social media and ranted, asking fans not to buy this CD as my voice was basically stolen to do this project, telling them I had nothing to do with it.

I began to complain about sleeping on the office floor, so they eventually helped me secure an apartment not too far from the center of the town of Heilbronn.

I finally had my follow-up interview with the attorney. The first thing he said was, "I have some bad news. Gonzalez was not the only person you needed to worry about. You should also be concerned with Mr. Earl Bryant."

I was astounded when he pulled out a contract I had never seen before. The attorney showed me the signature page. "Is this your signature?"

I didn't need to look at it because I know I never signed anything with Earl Bryant.

But I took a glance and could tell the signature was scribble scrabble, and messy.

"No, it's not. And I've never seen that contract."

"Mr. Bryant has attached his name to your publishing rights."

I immediately got upset and shouted, *"How can he get away with that!? How?"*

Saundra sighed and said, "Calm down, Marla. Maybe something can be done."

The attorney pulled out a blank piece of paper, placed a pen next to it, and said,

"Sign this for me."

I picked up the pen and signed my name. He sat there and watched; then he picked up the contract and the blank paper where I signed my name. He compared the two signatures. It didn't match. They were so completely off it was ridiculous, like a child had tried to copy it.

"How can a man that lives in the U.S. attach himself to my

publishing? I don't understand that. How is this possible? I never signed anything with this man. Nothing. He was only my road manager for a while, and that wasn't much."

"So, you signed nothing with—"

I didn't even need him to finish before I shouted back, *"Nothing! I signed nothing with him!"*

I could not hold back the tears. It was too much to deal with.

"This man was nothing more than a road manager, and I didn't sign any paperwork with him. I hope you can get to the bottom of this. No one has the right to my publishing. No one!"

Tears streamed down my face, and I could barely breathe. He handed me a tissue, and I wiped my face while asking, "Can we do anything about it?"

"Maybe we can ..."

Eventually, I calmed down, and he said, "I want to open up a bank account in your name."

I couldn't believe what he was saying.

"You want to do what?"

"I think we could protect you if we did that."

I shook my head.

"No, this doesn't sound right. Why can't you go after them? They broke the law and forged my name. Why do you need to open an account? You must know something that I don't. I am not going to fall for this again."

He tried to interject and said, "I'm only trying to help you."

*"If you want to help me find a way to deal with the motherfuckers who ripped me off! Don't try this other bullshit. Fuck you! I'm not letting you open up an account in my name. No!"*

I stood up and turned to Saundra, "C'mon let's go!"

As we headed out of his office, Saundra was trying to explain, "You should hear him out and—"

"No! I don't need a slick lawyer who is not going to help me."

I marched down the street to the car, and I didn't say another word all night. I was so shocked and disappointed; I couldn't think straight. As with Bryant, I truly thought this lawyer guy was going to help me. Instead, like all the others, he was only concerned with himself. Deep down, I knew I still had not recovered from hearing people promise one thing, then do something completely different. From the beginning, dealing with Jean Claude to Gonzalez, Earl Bryant, Michele Crosio, and others. The countless lies and the deceit I had experienced continued to take a toll on me. I tried my best to have faith in people, but I could only trust myself and God. I could now add Saundra to that list, even though I thought as sophisticated as she was, she would be the same way outside of her banking job. I should not have assumed she would be a great business partner or completely transparent, and it continued to become apparent that she wasn't going to be.

# CHAPTER 39

# Another Loss

Saundra had promised not to release any more CDs without my involvement, and the money I got from my concerts was paid on time, and it seemed to be the right amount. Despite what she said, I still felt uncomfortable. Her professional banking persona seemed to have changed to a bad girl one in a matter of weeks. It now seemed apparent that the Hell's Angels were financially backing Saundra to help cover the expenses that accompanied handling my career, and she appeared to be living two different lives. One life of the smart professional, the other a free-spirited woman who rolled with the infamous motorcycle gang. I didn't understand how she was pulling off the business side of things, seemingly without the help of anyone who had experience in the music business. Then while in the office one day, as we were going over business, Saundra and her boyfriend said they had another surprise. Shortly thereafter, there was a knock on the office door, and when she opened it, there stood Michele Crosio. Everyone was smiling but me. I tried to fake it as best I could, but I'm sure the look on my face was pure shock.

"Aw, man!"

We reached out to hug each other, and all kinds of things were going through my mind. I'm a forgiving person, but I needed answers. We had a bit of small talk, and eventually, Saundra and her boyfriend left me and Michele alone to talk.

"I need to ask you a question. Why did you sign with Vogue? From the beginning of when we met, I asked you not to do that. But you did it anyway."

"Fabrice asked me to work with other artists besides you. I didn't want to turn down the money."

I felt a certain way because I discovered Michele, and had things been different, we could have been a great team. It's something I've always wanted.

Michele never said he was sorry. He would always twirl a lock in the back of his hair when he was uncomfortable. At this moment, he seemed a little guilty, so I decided to let the past be the past and forgive him again.

"So, since you're here, I guess we could get to work."

Michele smiled. "Ok, let's do it."

I needed to know, so I asked, "Have you talked to Gonzalez?"

He glanced at me and shrugged his shoulders. "Well, no." This made me feel better about connecting with him, and we went to work, and it felt like old times.

Michele and I began working on a demo for a new CD that I titled *Friends*. The name came to me because of Michele coming back into my life after all that had happened. It seemed appropriate at the time. I had already been writing the songs for it, and I was excited to hear it come to life. Michele and I finished the CD, and it was ready to be mastered and produced.

One afternoon, Saundra sent me and one of the assistants, by the name of Anthony, to an office she used as storage space in Hamburg. The office housed CDs of *Friends*, *Marla Glen Live*, and the single

*Dreams.* CDs were everywhere, and as we were picking up boxes to take to a concert, the office phone rang, and Anthony answered it.

I overheard the phone call and recognized the familiar voice on the other end. I quickly said, "Is that Raymond Gonzalez?" He put him on speaker, and he said, "Hey, I have concerts for you, honey." I was shocked and quickly shouted,

*"I am not doing any shows that have anything to do with that man! Nothing! Not one show!"*

Pissed, I stormed out. I was right. Gonzalez was somehow involved in the musical development of the CD single *Dreams* and *Friends*. It was all unraveling and became clear to me that Saundra and the Hell's Angels, through Gonzalez, got in touch with and hired Crosio, and that was how Saundra was handling everything.

The thoughts of my mistrust from working with him in the past and his dishonesty of my equipment were a reminder, and it became too much for me to handle. I ended up firing him for the third time. I had tried but had grown tired of forgiving Michele Crosio.

I went home for a few days to relax and try to figure out how to get out of this situation with Saundra especially knowing she was involving Gonzalez. I stayed in my apartment for a few days and was just calming down from everything when around 3am one morning, my phone rang. I was awakened from a deep sleep, but I figured it must have been important since it was that early. It was a fan who I had been talking to from time to time.

"Hello."

She hesitated before she responded.

"Marla? How are you?"

"I'm fine, but it's early; what's up?"

"Have you watched the news?"

My heart sank. I turned the light on. I didn't know what she was talking about.

"What are you talking about?" I responded,

"Your mother, Nina. She passed."

At first, I was speechless, then I quickly turned on the television.

As I did, the reporter said, "Breaking News, Nina Simone has passed away."

I thanked the woman for telling me and hung up to watch all the different broadcasts. All I could do was sit in silence, shaking my head. I listened to the commentator talk about Ms. Simone's accomplishments, music, and journey. I could not help thinking about how she stormed into my life and helped me in the best ways she knew how. All the times we shared and how we laughed. She was indeed my musical mother. I knew she was in heaven because of the many spiritual conversations we had.

# CHAPTER 40

# Sabrina

The business relationship between Saundra and I continued to sour. It didn't end well. Like most problems I had in the past, I voiced my concern in the media.

In the midst of the chaos between me and Saundra, I was working on hiring a band and backup singers for upcoming concerts. While finding backup singers, I held auditions, for which I met a lot of attractive women, but one in particular, stood out. Sabrina wasn't one of the better singers, but she was still beautiful.

While there was a bit of chemistry happening, it's always been a rule of mine never to date anybody in the band. I don't like mixing business with pleasure. She didn't make the cut to be in the band, but I still remembered her. Weeks after that audition, I'd see her about town in Heilbronn, and we would exchange hellos. One afternoon when we ran into each other, we stopped to chat.

"You didn't make the band, but you made me smile. And being in a band ain't all it's cracked up to be," I told her.

Her dimples were deep, and her smile was welcoming. As we were talking, sparks were flying, and we both enjoyed the small talk. Sabrina's English was surprisingly very good, and it was easy to talk to her. At her feet was this adorable little boy about three years old. He held onto his mother's legs and peeked at me as we talked.

"Hey little man, how you doing today?"

He was shy but cute as ever. I diverted my attention to Sabrina.

"So, can I get your number?" I asked.

She smiled as she pulled out a pen and paper from her purse and wrote it down. As she handed me her number, she said, "I have a question for you too; do you want to get married?"

I thought she was joking but found it flattering, so I instantly replied, "Sure, why not?!"

We both laughed and continued to talk as I walked her home. I was smitten with this woman, and we began dating. We talked about everything, what our lives and future would look like if we were together. I felt as if I finally found someone I could be with for the rest of my life. I was excited about the idea of having a wife and a child and had always thought about being married.

Sabrina was very inquisitive, and she talked a lot about the U.S. She kept asking questions, and one day she said, "I hope we get to go someday. Can we get married there?"

I wanted to be supportive. So I said, "Yes, we can. Let's do it."

A few months passed, and when I got a break from the tour I was working, I flew my by-now fiancée and son to be out to see my family in Chicago. It had been a while since I had been home, so my aunties threw me a party, and all my cousins attended. We all had a great time.

While we were there, we met an attorney, but after a lengthy discussion, a lot of technicalities and attorney fees were needed for our marriage to get approved in the U.S. We were unsuccessful in obtaining a marriage license and decided it was best to get married in Germany.

Sabrina and I were married on July 2, 2004, in the town hall of

Heilbronn, Germany. A couple of nights before the wedding, I flew in from doing a concert in Vienna, and the night after the wedding, I was scheduled to fly out for another show. An official who presided over the services was also an interpreter who spoke English, so I could understand what was happening.

Sabrina's mom and family attended, along with reporters and television crews reporting the glorious occasion. My lovely bride wore a beautiful cream-colored dress and carried a matching frilly parasol along with a yellow bouquet of roses. She was absolutely beautiful. I wore a top hat and coat, along with a matching vest, and it was a proud day for both of us.

Our son, Kareem, also participated in the wedding, and he wore an adorable matching shirt and tie. I took a lot of pride in dressing him and enjoyed it. Our marriage was the first of its kind in Heilbronn. I didn't invite my family; however, we planned to return to the U.S. again as a married couple. Everything went well, and after the wedding, a newspaper reporter approached Sabrina and asked her, "What's better, to be with a man or a woman?"

Sabrina responded, "Marla is not like a woman."

I never understood why people cared what went on in other people's private lives. It's really none of their business.

Before the wedding, Sabrina and I had a lot of conversations about God, primarily because she wanted to learn more about the Lord, and her thirst for that was one of the main reasons I felt so close to her. Loving God was a requirement for me to consider anyone as a wife. Growing up, I loved the times my family would enjoy laughs, family fun, and spiritual conversations. They were some of my fondest memories. I only wanted the same for my new family as well.

At the beginning of our relationship, Sabrina was very interested in discussing the Bible. I read it a lot since it had been a significant source of maintaining my sanity. I have studied and researched the

Bible since childhood, and when I would talk to Sabrina, I'd give her my interpretation. Most times in our discussions, there seemed to be a point of frustration. Ultimately, studying the word became a strain in our relationship because there were many times we did not see eye to eye, and Sabrina, who felt like her questions went unanswered, would often become frustrated. It was the beginning of a rift in our marriage, but we kept going, and at other times, things were okay.

In January 2005, my cousin Stacey called to see if I was available for a visit, and, I was ecstatic to hear from her.

"Hey Cuz, I wanna go to Paris. Can you meet me there?" she said.

"Hell yeah! C'mon Cuz. I have a tour I'm working on, but let me give you the best dates to come over."

I sent her some dates via email, and Stacey booked a flight for the following month. She came along with my three aunties Teka, Carmelita, and DD. It was nice to have the family visit, and I wanted to show them a good time. During this time, I would occasionally travel with bodyguards, so I hired two guards along with a car, and they drove me and Sabrina straight to Paris to where they were staying at "Hôtel de Castiglione."

Once we arrived, I booked a limousine, and we all went to restaurants like the Buddha Bar, shopping, the Tour Eiffel, and traveled about Paris having a ball; we even had dinner with Gonzalez at his home.

Despite all the issues I had with Gonzalez, things were usually civil. Ms. Simone had experienced the same on-off relationship with him, but unlike her, I had not worked with him after things turned sour.

After a few evenings of hanging out with the family, one night, Stacey and I sat and talked in my room until about the crack of dawn. I needed to talk to someone, and because she organized the trip, she seemed pretty savvy about handling things. I fired up a joint, and not only did we talk about old times, but I needed to tell her what was going on, hoping she could help. We sat across from each other, laughing, and when a break came in the conversation, I talked to her all about what I had gone through with Gonzalez. She was the first family member I spoke to about it, apart from my brother and father, whom I'd sworn to secrecy.

A stream of tears began to fall from my eyes, and I couldn't stop them. I began to ramble on, and I could see that Stacey was trying to understand, but it was not easy for me to explain everything. I began talking fast and loud. Stacey kept saying, "Marla, calm down! Just calm down."

I couldn't calm down. I said, "My money is being taken, and it's so much to deal with.

She asked, "What do you need me to do?"

"I need you to call an attorney when you get back to the U.S. Put them in contact with me, and do it right away, please."

She asked, "How do you know your money is being taken?"

"'Cause I'm not getting anything. My royalties, payments for songs I wrote. I can't prove it, so I need some kind of help. I have all these concerts and gold records and stuff, and I have nothing to show for it."

Stacey reached over to the nightstand and handed me a tissue. I couldn't stop the tears. I was so broken.

She responded, "I don't know anything about the music business, but when I get back, I'll ask around and see what I can do."

I wiped my face.

"Thank you, cuz."

Stacey and I stayed in touch, and after a few months, she told me she had reached out to a few of attorneys, but they all said the same thing. No one would talk to me because I was in another country, and they could only handle legal issues that happened in the U.S. I didn't know that's how the law worked, nor did I know how to get out of this situation. I just continued hoping that I'd run across someone who could really help me.

Sabrina and I went back to Germany. When I arrived, there were still problems from the issues I was having with Saundra Kaupp. Working with her and the Hell's Angels left a bad taste in my mouth. I was disappointed after realizing that my theory about having a female manager was as wrong as two left shoes, or maybe it was just working with Saundra. I was ready to move on and needed to find a way to produce my own project. We ended up suing each other, and I was not happy about dealing with it any further, yet I wanted it to be over.

# CHAPTER 41

# Menges

I had to keep working, and I began writing a new album. I had recently been introduced to a music producer name Steingen. I asked around about him, and people said he was a good producer, so I agreed to work with him. Steingen was aware that I didn't have money to complete the album and offered to help me get it done. During this time, Sabrina and I moved into a basement unit in a house where her mother was living in the town of Sinsheim.

The studio where Steingen and I were producing my next CD was in Dusseldorf, which was too far to travel daily, so I rented a furnished apartment in the area to streamline the process of getting it completed. I would also take a few gigs in Koln and other surrounding German towns, and these jobs afforded me the chance to make money to pay for the CD. I was booking these concerts myself. I was determined to find a way to make things work. I had to, in order to keep food on my table, and now I had a wife and a kid to feed, so I had to find a way to make money for the future. I also kept hearing from promoters and people who helped me that I was in some sort of tax trouble, but I didn't know how to deal with that, so I left things alone. One promoter told me once, "You could go to jail if you don't handle your tax issue."

I responded, "Let them take me to jail, then maybe someone will look into it deeper and realize that it's not my fault."

Because of conversations like this and others, there were times when I got mad and would think about the past, which spawned horrible thoughts of harming the people who helped put me in this situation.

I tried to focus on what I could do to make more money and knew that hurting someone was my own destructive thinking. I knew I couldn't hurt anybody; it wasn't God's way. After years of dealing with Gonzalez, I made the conscious decision to put God in front of my thoughts instead of lashing out. Besides, I had been to jail before, and it's a much smaller audience to perform in front of, with no real benefits after a show!

I was in another country and didn't want to do anything crazy enough to get banned from performing. There were several incidents that reminded of the time I lived with Ms. Simone in California. Especially when she would come home yelling and screaming about promoters and other people in the music industry, asking where her money was and how everyone around her was stealing. Despite all her issues, she never stopped trying to find out what happened to the money throughout her career. I think the psychological trauma of it all put her in a bad mental state.

I didn't want to be like Ms. Simone because I felt like the entertainment business wrecked her nerves to the point of needing medication. She constantly dealt with deceptive managers, shady promoters, and other individuals who ripped her off, placing her in precarious situations. I could see the similarities in how she was treated and how some of those same individuals treated me.

Being on the road was not pretty, and several people called Ms.

Simone crazy, but she didn't care because she knew she was right in what she was fighting for, which was justice and transparency. Because of her, I continue to ask for the same things. I simply refuse to give up.

With Saundra Kauup out of the picture, I was on my own again. Left to do my own bookings and manage my own deals, I managed to secure about twenty concerts and used the money to produce a CD that I named, Humanology. I believed in the music and wanted to complete it no matter how long it took. In the beginning, I enjoyed working with Steingen. He was aware I didn't have any money to get it done, and he agreed he would be paid a percentage of sales. He seemed perfectly fine with this arrangement, but he brought his attorney to meet me. It was awkward because we had already talked about everything, and I didn't understand the need for him to do this. Steingen, his attorney, and I met in a restaurant in Koln, and Steingen, made the introductions.

"Marla, this is Otto; he's an attorney. He can help you structure things."

I sat and sighed. "What do we need an attorney for?"

They sat nonchalantly drinking beer, and neither of them answered.

"Look, this is your attorney; I would need my own if we are going to do it this way," I said. "I don't know this person."

Steingen tried to convince me, "Marla, he wants to help. This is not a bad thing."

The attorney pulled out an envelope and placed it on the table. I asked, "Is that the contract?"

Otto nodded. "Yes, it is."

I said, "Can I take a look?"

I opened the contract, and it had some of the longest German words I had ever seen.

"How am I supposed to sign something that I can't read. I can't read German. I can barely have a basic conversation."

"Well, we are in Germany. It has to be in German," the attorney said.

I shook my head. "I'm not signing it."

Steingen tried again.

"How are we supposed to do this?"

"Steingen, can we just stick to our original deal?"

The meeting was awkward and ended with no resolution. I didn't sign anything, and we all left frustrated. Nevertheless, we kept working on the CD, but at times it was uncomfortable.

Work was coming in, and I was dealing with a couple of small promoters, but I tried not to turn any work down. I wanted money to finish the album and support my family. I would take any gig available. A gospel album was even in the works, but things were not feeling spiritual because I was all over the place, doing a lot of things.

In the midst of all this, I received a call from a guy named Menges, who wanted to work with me. It wasn't clear where he came from, but he seemed to be savvy in his conversations pertaining to the music industry, and he said he could work on my behalf. I agreed to meet him at a restaurant. When we met, I shared details about the process of working on *Humanology* with Steingen. Menges talked to me a lot about music, and eventually I introduced him to Steingen. Menges saw what we were doing and wanted to be a part of it. Initially, I wasn't sure about working with him. He just came out of the blue, but he had a lot of ideas and promises. Everything he said, I had heard before.

Things weren't moving, and money wasn't coming fast enough. The marriage seemed to be in flames, this time because Sabrina and I were getting into a lot of arguments because she would not stay out of my business. It was 2006, and I remember pulling together a few euros to grab a beer to go have a drink at a neighborhood bar. While I was there, I heard the disc jockey speak in German, then announce my name. The voice said, "And now, a song from Marla Glen's new CD..."

A song came on the radio that I had not heard in years. Everyone knew me in the bar, and after the announcement, the bar applauded, and I was confused. I didn't have a new CD, and I wondered who had released this song. I left the bar immediately, and I began searching the internet. I couldn't believe it. Someone released a CD without my permission or me knowing about it. What I found on the internet was a weird CD that popped up on the screen with the cover that was horribly designed, entitled *Dangerous*. The moment I saw it, I was livid. Who would even think to name a CD *Dangerous* with Michael Jackson having had the same title? This was embarrassing and frustrating. The next day I went out to purchase it, and in trying to listen to it, I could barely get through the entire CD. It was a horrible attempt to steal my voice without my permission. I was speechless! I recognized the songs as demos I worked on with Michele Crosio years ago when I lived in France. The CD was horribly mastered and sounded like shit. All I could think was, "*What the Fuck! Not this again?!*" I didn't know what to do. So, I went to the computer and posted on every social media site I could, I posted:

"The songs from this Dangerous album were stolen from me! And I did not know it was out!! The cover is shit, and the arrangements are not mine! I will not be performing any of these songs on my tour!"

The CD had already begun getting bad reviews, and there was no way to stop it except to let the fans know directly from me. Because I worked with Crosio on these demos from the 90's, and he and Gonzalez were always close, I suspected they were in cahoots in producing it behind my back. Nothing else made sense to me. I was so tired by this point that I did nothing else to investigate it further; I needed to keep moving forward with my life and making new music. I hated that after several years of being on my own, I let Crosio back in my life. This was done recently with him in touch with Saundra. I suspect my wife had something to do with him showing up at her office that day, but I can't prove it. When I asked my wife about Michael contacting Saundra, she claimed she knew nothing, but I always felt she did. It was a betrayal that weighed heavy on me.

Finally, after three years, the ordeal was over with Saundra, and the case ended up in court, and the website Stimme.de reported in an online article dated February 2007 that I asked her for 55,499 euros and monies from concerts in 2003 and 2002. Saundra filed a counterclaim. The verdict was that neither of us owed the other any funds. I wasn't even in court when it happened, and I found all the details from the newspaper.

In the latter part of 2007, I had been thinking about how I arrived in Europe and wanted to get back to day one. I called Joel my very first band leader and organized a small show in Niort, France. We reconnected and played in a local club that held about 200 people and played our old songs. Being in Niort just felt like home. I always adored that little town, and the nostalgia of it all made me smile. Joe Joe was able to assemble a few other members of the band, and it just felt right. We had conversations about what happened in the beginning, and I really wanted my first band back but realized that it wasn't going to work. After the gig, I headed back to Germany, and it hit me that as much as I loved that time in my life, I had to leave this chapter of my life in the past and keep on the grind.

When I returned to Germany, I had to focus on completing "*Humanology*," and studio time and background singers were not cheap. I took any gig I could to try to make extra funds and worked all concerts that contacted me. Menges had offered to invest money into completing the CD, but initially, I refused.

"I don't want your money. When people invest, things become messy and too much to keep track of."

Menges didn't back off, and days and even weeks later, he kept asking how he could help. I explained my mistrust of managers, and Menges insisted he didn't operate like other people.

"You can completely trust me, Marla."

Where had I heard those words before? I felt uneasy about him, but I was coming to the end of a list of concert dates, and I really needed the cash.

Ultimately, we met again, and when he approached, I had a few bills piling up, so I decided to listen. I met Menges at a restaurant; we were talking about the CD, and in the midst of the conversation, he pulled out a huge stack of Euros.

"I want to invest twenty thousand dollars into it," he said.

This time, I took the 20k Euros from Menges, and we agreed he would get his money back from upcoming concerts that he would book. He was very anxious, and he agreed to help in whatever way I needed him to. The money was timely because I had sunk a lot into studio time, paying the rent for the apartment I rented, and other expenses related to the album.

Suddenly, I stopped hearing from Steingen, and it seemed as if he dropped off the face of the earth. When we began, I was in the studio with him, helping with the mix, sometimes from sun up to sun down. I worked diligently with each song to make sure it was mastered properly. Every single note needed to be perfect. It's the artist's right to be a part of their own creation. We still had songs to finish, and I wanted *"Humanology"* complete, yet I couldn't reach him. I would call him every day, leaving voicemail messages asking him, "Steingen, when are we going to finish? I need to be there."

No matter how many times I would call, he would not get back to me. Although I recognized this pattern before, all I could think was, "What the fuck have I gotten into with this guy?" Then months afterward, he began emailing me asking me to sign a contract I could not understand.

"Steingen, I can't sign this contract. You need to put it in English."

He did not do that. I asked several times, but he only told me bits and pieces of what the contract said, and it appeared that it was all in his favor.

Sometime in 2008, Menges called one day and said he had been talking to people about concerts. I was hesitant, but I had been booking myself, and it's hard to both book gigs and work as the artist. Doing it all had been weighing on me, so I finally decided to work with him, plus I did want to find a way to get him the 20k that I borrowed. I made a point to be firm and told him, "If you get me a concert, I need to see all the original contracts and anything else involved with securing the date for the show."

He responded, "Marla, you can trust me. I promise you; you can."

Menges began to work on getting concerts. He put together the "*Humanology Tour*" to promote a CD that wasn't even finished yet. It was a hot mess. Steingen promised that we would finish mixing the songs, and a couple of times, we had false starts on releasing the CD. At one point, he said it was ready for release, but then it wasn't. I continued to ask Steingen if I could go to the studio and see what was needed to finish the album. He either ignored me, changed the subject, or insisted it was fine.

In the meantime, Menges and I forged a working relationship on this tour, and he was keeping me informed about the concerts, but he wasn't showing me contracts. I kept asking, but he avoided the questions, and things were hectic. Between the concerts, festivals, rehearsals, interviews, conversations about taxes, and dealing with my wife, I was beginning to get anxious. I'm pretty sure there are interviews out there where you could tell I was annoyed and bothered by some of the questions a few reporters were asking me. All while this was going on, I was trying to do what I could to make my marriage work. My wife had been traveling with me as a background singer, and if I had a weekend concert, we would also bring our son. It was a lot to deal with while on tour. Sabrina barely got along with the other background singers, and I could tell that it was awkward for everyone involved. Things were overwhelming, but I kept pushing through.

By the beginning of 2009, Menges had several tours lined up, and it was time to work. We were busy and began touring Austria, Germany, and Switzerland. It was the tour areas that Gonzalez had established and lost when he lost me as an artist. But things were messy with Menges and became even worse with my wife.

# CHAPTER 42

# The End and More
# of the Same

My wife continued to interject herself into the business part of my life, which I explicitly told her not to. One evening at home, Sabrina began talking in German on the phone, and there were a few words that I was able to pick up. "Konzert," "Reisen" and money was mentioned." I also heard a familiar voice and turning to her, I asked, "Is that Menges you're talking to?"

She nodded, looking right back at me.

"Yes, he had questions about some upcoming shows."

I took the phone, "Menges, don't talk to my wife about business. You need something, you talk to me, you understand?"

Sabrina didn't think it was a problem. "I don't understand why you are upset. I was trying to help."

"I told you once before that these guys will take information and use it against me. Stop getting into my business. I let you be a background singer; why do you need to get involved in anything else?"

This felt like a betrayal. I felt like I was fighting with Menges, Steingen, and now my wife. Sabrina began to argue even more, and things were getting uglier by the day.

Sabrina continued to get more involved. Despite my wishes for her to stay away from the people I was dealing with, she began to have conversations in German about concerts with road managers and other people that I worked with, and because I couldn't pick up on all the German words spoken, I didn't understand what she was saying. This made me anxious, but when she began making decisions without asking me, I got quite upset, leading to further complications within our marriage. It was just as I had suspected it would be. Sabrina being in the band was not good for our relationship.

During one of the many arguments, Sabrina expressed her desire to visit the U.S. again, and this time we went back as husband and wife. While I thought this visit back to the U.S. would help, it did not prevent us from arguing, and once back in Germany, things became rocky again. She seemed fixated on moving to America, and I realized she assumed that because she was married to an American, that it would automatically make her an American citizen. I explained things didn't work that way, and she accused me of wanting to get married to become a German citizen; that was far from the truth.

I love Germany and consider it home, but I did not want to give up my U.S. citizenship because my real home will always be in America, where I still have a lot of family.

During some of our arguments, I also felt that she wanted to spitefully get me kicked out of Germany and sent back to America. This marriage was now a roller coaster of emotions for me, and it became a tangled web of confusion and arguments, along with a lot of yelling and shouting.

By March 2009, after five years, the marriage ended in a very ugly argument after I discovered that while singing background, Sabrina was also receiving other funds from my gigs, and I suspected it was some kind of hush money. Sabrina kept a set of financial books for the music business, and I asked to see them. Shouting that I didn't trust her, all hell broke loose, and we both yelled about her being involved financially. Things got ugly.

"*You need to get out!*" she screamed.

"*I'm not going anywhere; all my stuff is here!*"

Sabrina marched to the closet and began tossing all my suits out onto the street in the snow.

Something in my head told me this was a losing battle, so instead of trying to fight for the marriage, I decided it was best that I leave. I grabbed my Bible and a few other personal items and went outside. After I picked up my clothes, putting them under my arms, I called my friend Peter, the photographer, and he said I could stay with him for a while. It was obviously time for me to drift again.

It was around March of 2009 when I arrived in Baden-Baden, with my arms full of clothes, a few papers, and my Bible. I couldn't believe how things had gone so horribly wrong in my marriage, but I knew it was time to move on. It was best that I leave, so when Peter came to pick me up, it was a relief. The quaint little spa town was like something out of a fairytale. The people I met while I was there were graceful, friendly and chatty. It was a welcome change for me. Peter was an interesting guy, but I didn't want to stay with him too long, so I began looking for my own place. I had money coming in from the concerts Menges was booking, and within a few months, I found something closer to the center of town.

Despite my marriage crumbling, I still had work to do. I decided to embrace the little town of Baden-Baden and find ways to clear my head. Before arriving in town, people kept telling me I was in some kind of German tax situation called Insolvency. I often wondered, how in the hell did they know that? As a U.S. citizen, no one knows your tax status but you; even my band members knew about it. They seemed to know more about my business than I did. I wanted to get it handled, so after getting settled in the small town, I walked into an attorney's office by the name of Griesbaum and explained to him the situation. I knew nothing about Germany's tax laws, but I knew that I could not handle them alone. Greisbaum researched my situation, and discovered that the Insolvency guy I had been dealing with, along with my wife, had attempted to work on my insolvency. I wasn't exactly clear on what they were doing, but on all of the papers Greisbaum had shown to me, none of the signatures weren't mine. Apparently, the two had been working on my behalf. He showed me a piece of paper that had my initials on it, and it was not something I had written. While Griesbaum was working on the tax situation, I had also had him look over the contracts that Steingen had been sending me. Griesbaum began helping me with the contract I had with Steingen, and it appeared that the contract was written in his favor.

I continued performing concerts that Menges booked throughout the remainder of 2009. Knowing I still owed him 20k, he agreed to take it from the bookings. After every so many concerts, I'd ask him if he had been paid his 20 thousand euros back, and at one point, Menges told me that he got his money back. However, in subsequent conversations, he kept insisting he had not been reimbursed and I still owed him. This really pissed me off. From that day forth, I didn't let my eyes off him and his antics because, by now, I was clear he wouldn't be forthcoming. There were other reasons for me mistrusting him as well. Shortly after we began working together, Menges secured a record deal with a small company in Manheim, Germany. In the beginning, I was happy about it and thought maybe Menges was legit, but something felt wrong. I called the company, and a representative told me that Menges received an advance. I called him and asked what the hell was going on. Menges pretended that he had no clue what was going on.

"Menges, where is the money you owe me?" I asked.

"What are you talking about?"

"You know exactly what I'm talking about. You got money from that record deal and didn't tell me?"

Menges got quiet for a moment before he responded, "What?"

"I thought I could trust you! What did you do?"

He began to talk fast.

"Marla the company didn't want to give you money directly because you owe taxes."

"You are putting me in more trouble with taxes because you are taking money in my name. How much was it?"

Menges claimed not to have heard that last question, then ignored it when I repeated, "I wanted to know the amount."

"Look, I have to go," he said.

"I'm preparing for a meeting, and I can't have this conversation with you right now."

He hung up the phone. I never saw a dime from the record deal he brokered. Watching how Menges worked, I realized that he was not doing anything I requested. He didn't show me any of the contracts; instead, he did exactly what Gonzalez did, and typed up a breakdown from his own letterhead, only showing me what he wanted me to see.

I was livid, and despite me shouting at him, Menges continued to make deals with promoters and commitments for upcoming gigs. Damned if I didn't and damned if I did, it was Catch 22 all over again. If I didn't do the concerts, my reputation would dive, and if I did, I'd been giving in to Menges' dishonesty. I needed the money, so I continued to work the concerts but was trying to figure a way out of it all. I often wondered if Gonzalez was behind Menges telling him exactly what to do. He used the same deceptive practices to rip me off. I could not go through this again and be as nice as I was before. But I had no idea what to do.

The stress of dealing with Menges was getting to me, and it was literally becoming a pain in my ass. During this time, I developed a huge painful bump on my butt, and I had no idea what it was. At first, I didn't bother with it, as I thought it would go away, but it was growing.

Menges invested in T-Shirts without my consent or approval—and kept all the profits—but I eventually found a way to get the money he earned from the merchandising and used the money I got from the concerts to finally complete the "*Humanology*" album. One day on the internet, I saw that "*Humanology*" had a release date. This was a complete shock. I called Steingen and asked, "What's going on? How are you releasing the album when I have not finished it yet?"

Without an explanation, he hung up the phone.

I kept calling, and he would not answer.

I didn't understand this because I didn't spend much time in the studio to make it better than the demos I left him with. This was very frustrating, and dealing with Steingen and Menges, by now I could tell they had teamed up, really gave me a sick feeling in my stomach.

Other than with Steingen and Menges, there were many situations when I could not figure out what was going on around me, but I would hear people talking in German, and I'd recognize only some of the words I'd overhear them saying. In some instances, I could tell they were saying how stupid I was, and I would occasionally hear them call me a nigger right while I was standing in the room. They didn't know that I knew what they were saying, but I understood enough to know when I was being disrespected. When this happened, I rarely said anything because all they would do was deny it. When I heard these words, I would often shake my head and simply walk away.

During the time he was booking me, I was totally at odds with Menges. Things were so messy that I didn't know what to expect from one day to the next. After a few concerts where he only paid me less than he was supposed to, I decided to go to my concert, a couple of days in advance, to see one of the promoters. I wanted to talk to them about the contracts and take a look at them myself. When I arrived, one of the concert promoters was very accommodating once I told them how I'd been dealing with Menges.

"Look, I need to see my contracts. The guy I've been dealing with is a liar, and he has not shown me anything."

"Of course, I'll show you. It's yours."

We went into the office, and when he showed me the contract, I was shocked at an addendum that stated: "Marla drinks a lot of whiskey, and she is on heroin. You should be careful not to give the artist alcohol, so they won't fall off the stage."

"This is a damn lie! Why would he say that?"

The promoter looked at me and shrugged.

"So, this isn't true?

*"Hell no, it's not!"*

I was so upset I could have spit fire, but I managed to calm down.

"I may have a beer or two before a show, but I have never in my life done heroin. I will admit I've taken drugs in the past, but I'm not on them now. And I'm not a big fan of whiskey. This isn't right what he wrote. It's just not right!"

The promoter looked at me and asked, "So, you never saw these contracts?"

"No. I haven't'!"

I didn't understand why any promoter would even book me if they believed Menges's lies. Certainly, he needed to gain the trust of the promoters, so they would trust him and not me.

"Look, I'm going to deliver a good show for you. Do not believe this."

"Okay, I believe you."

I went on stage and did just that, and the promoter paid me directly.

Some of the other promoters that Menges booked were not as

accommodating. One of the main ones Menges booked through was a company called, A.S.S. I told him from the beginning that I didn't want to work with this company. I'd come across them during my time with Gonzalez, and they had refused to give me details of the contract. Despite telling Menges I didn't want to work with A.S.S., he booked concerts with them anyway.

# CHAPTER 43

# I'm Done ... Again!

By the Fall of 2010, I was doing a lot of praying and tried everything to remain focused, but it was difficult. Things were moving quickly, and the tour Menges pulled together kept me busy. I had very few friends and was rarely invited anywhere by my band members, but someone invited me to a theatrical play, so I went. I can't even tell you the name of it, but I sat and enjoyed it. Despite not knowing every German word, I could make out what the play was about and followed along. Afterward, I was introduced to one of the actresses; her name was Christine. She was funny, beautiful, and lovely. Christina and I flirted and laughed and eventually exchanged numbers. Despite all that was going on, over the next few months, Christine and I were talking a lot, and I began to court her. I had been out of my marriage with Sabrina for a while now, and it was nice to have someone to lay next to.

I hired a driver to take me to Berlin where she lived, and we had a lovely time. I cooked tacos for her, and we drank wine and talked a lot about our lives. We were both in the entertainment business, so we seemed to have a lot in common and quite a bit to talk about. We shared intimate moments as well as traumas about our experiences while working in the entertainment business. As we bonded, it simply felt like we both needed someone at this moment in our lives. I enjoyed her company, and she seemed to have enjoyed mine. Christine came to a few shows, and it was unspoken, but we were beginning a relationship as I introduced her as my girlfriend. With all the drama I was dealing with, it was welcome to have someone during this time.

In the midst of the problems with Menges, he invited me to his office in Karlsruhe to talk business. I was not happy with the way things were going, but I needed to see what he was up to. I walked into this small office building and Menges was there with another guy supposedly from a record company. Menges and I had discussed me signing a contract, and he said he was going to pay me an additional 17k Euros once I signed. Once I got to the office, he gave me the contract and despite everything I was feeling about my business dealings with him, I scribbled my name on the contract, and asked, "When do I get my seventeen thousand?" Menges responded, "You will have it in a few days." We had concerts coming up, so there was no escaping me.

Despite me not trusting Menges, I continued with the *Humanology* Tour, and I had been performing without the album being finished. There were a lot of starts and stops with it, and it was frustrating. We were down to one of the last few shows on the tour when Menges pulled up with a minivan to pick me up for a concert.

"I have a surprise for you!" he said.

"What is it? I don't like surprises."

He opened the back of the van to place my suitcase there; it was full of labeled and packaged *Humanology* CDs. I looked at them, then looked at Menges, "How did you do that?"

"I made it happen."

"Well, I hope it's good."

"Are you excited about it?"

"No. I'm not excited! You finished it without my input, and I have no idea what you did to get it done."

I couldn't believe that I didn't have anything to do with the finished project. Apparently, Menges connected with Steingen, and the two of them completed the final touches on the album without me. I didn't approve the final master, and when I listened to it on the van's CD player, I felt like it was missing a lot of heart and soul that I would have put into completing it. I felt blindsided and could not continue to listen to it.

"Why does everybody have to do the same shit Gonzalez did. Is it some sort of playbook that y'all use?"

Menges laughed it off.

"You are always accusing people of doing what Gonzalez did."

I didn't think it was funny.

"Because people are always doing what he did. Where is my seventeen thousand euros?"

"This is what I spent it on. Actually, you owe me money."

I shouted to the top of my lungs, "FUCK YOU, MENGES!"

I wanted to cry, but I did not give him the satisfaction of seeing that. As we drove away, I felt so violated and disrespected, and I didn't want to be in business with this man anymore. When I looked at the CD packaging, I noticed, that even the credits were misrepresented. Steingen and Menges even took credit for writing songs that they didn't write, and I later confirmed he registered them with GEMA without my permission. Menges even thanked himself! That's something I would have never done due to our business dealings, and they hijacked my project in every way they could. It was the final straw of working with Menges. By the end of the next concert, we were headed to the van when I told him my decision.

"Look, there's not a lot of concerts left, don't come back. I'm done with you."

He looked surprised.

"What do you mean?"

"You're not doing what I ask of you; you are doing what you want to do. I don't trust you, and I'm done."

Menges turned, "What about the money you owe me?"

"Bullshit! You're getting money from concerts; you got money from the record deal. I don't owe you shit!"

"Marla, that's not true."

"It is, and you know it. You got much more than your twenty thousand back, and as a matter of fact, you owe me money."

"No. Marla, that's not true. You still owe me because I paid some things for the album to get finished, and I had to pay for other things as well. Marla, I made you a star."

That was something that Gonzalez would say, and it pissed me off even more. I now yelled in his face, *"It's bullshit, and you know it! Do not come back to the concerts. I am done with you!"*

I was sick to my stomach because now I was in the same situation again, and I couldn't take it anymore.

It was April 1st, 2011, and it was the final concert Menges booked for me; I was backstage when Menges showed.

I knew he was there trying to get the balance of the concert money from the promoters, but I refused to let that happen. I was sitting at a table, and I shouted to get his attention as soon as he walked through the door.

*"Menges, why the fuck are you here?"*

"Why shouldn't I be here?"

"Because I fired you."

"How can you fire me when you owe me money."

"I don't owe you anything; you got your money back from all the concerts you stole money from me on. You took the advance from the record company."

"What advance?" he asked, and I lost it.

On the table was a stack of drinking glasses, and as Menges

started to approach me, I picked up a glass and tossed it at him. He ducked, and it smashed on the floor in front of him. The band began to look on.

"What the hell are you doing, Marla?"

"I should be asking, what are you doing?'

Menges was smart enough to keep a distance.

"Marla, what's wrong?!"

My voice got louder and louder as I continued to toss glasses at him,

*"Where is the money from the record company, Menges?"*

I tossed another glass.

*"What are you talking about?"* he asked as he jumped back.

*"Menges ... where is my fucking money?!"*

"Marla, it was taken because of the insolvency. I told you that."

I knew he was lying, so I tossed another glass.

"That is my business, and it has nothing to do with the record deal!"

The band didn't move, nor did they stop me. I ran out of glasses, and the only thing nearby was chairs. So, I tossed one of those.

*"Menges, where is my goddamn money?"*

With every item I tossed, Menges continued to deny my claims, but the only answer I wanted to hear was "I'll get you your money," and he never said it. Most band members were there to witness this, and I think the promoters hid somewhere to avoid confrontation. Menges did not go away, so I headed to my dressing room, and he followed me. I did not want to be alone with him, so I took one of the band members with me to listen to the conversation. I had nothing to hide. I opened my dressing room door and took a seat. Menges tried fast-talking, "Marla, I thought we were good. I don't know why you are upset with me. I have helped you, and I am doing everything I can to help you. I love you and your work, you know that."

I sat looking at him.

"Menges, you are a liar. I told you I didn't want to work with A.S.S. Also, you go behind my back and accept a record deal. Why wasn't I in that meeting? How much money did you get, and you finished my fucking album that I invested in. You gave yourself credit for my songs and promised me seventeen thousand that I never got."

He stood there speechless for a few moments.

"But Marla, I pay for so many other things ..."

I didn't want to hear the lies anymore. I stood up, opened the closet, and I began tossing hangers at him.

*"Get out! Get out of my dressing room!"*

Menges finally left, and the band member looked at me.

"This business is crazy," he said.

"Tell me about it."

I got the balance of the money after the show, and I paid the band and kept what was left. Menges was gone. To this day, I don't think Steingen knew that the character in one of my songs on the Humanology CD, entitled "Maddy and Johnny" was about him because he had big thighs. The character Johnny was about my ex-wife because she was always looking for more, and I felt she misunderstood how real life truly is about.

### Maddy & Johnny
Maddy girl was up to no good,
She misunderstood
How life can be good.
Johnny boy was right by her side
With a pocket of lies
With his mother's thighs.
You can figure out the things they're up to
We all know who they are

There's no stopping they don't want to.

They think they're going so far.

Look in the mirror and tell me what do you see

Are you true to yourself?

Look in the mirror and tell me what do you see?

Are you true to me?

Look in the mirror and tell me what do you see?

Are you true to yourself, are you true to me?

Do not take riches from a man you don't know

That you can't see.

The city was their best place to go.

They're trying to hide.

Playing Bonnie & Clyde.

Maddy had one on the way,

So she had to stay,

'Cause she knew her way.

You can figure out the things they're up to.

We all know who they are.

There's no stopping.

And they don't want to.

I think they're going too far.

Look in the mirror and tell me what do you see?

Are you true to yourself?

Look in the mirror and tell me what do you see?

Are you true to me?

Look in the mirror and tell me what do you see?

Are you true to yourself, are you true to me?

Do not take riches from another man.

You will never be free.

Look in the mirror and tell me what do you see?

Are you true to yourself?

Look in the mirror and tell me what do you see?
Are you true to me?
Do not take riches from another man.
You could never be free.

# CHAPTER 44

# Losing My Mind

I was not only physically exhausted; I felt I was losing my mind. I needed to get some help, so in August 2011, I checked myself into the hospital, telling the doctors through my tears that I was exhausted, and they asked a lot of questions. I told them about what I had been experiencing, and I just didn't feel good. The doctors kept asking if I had been taking any drugs, and no matter how many times I said I only smoked weed and drank beer, they kept asking me about cocaine. Upon doing bloodwork, it proved to them that I was telling the truth. I know I looked like a doped-up druggie, but if anyone had been through what I had, I assure you they would look the same. I didn't understand why people kept labeling me a cokehead or heroin-using dope fiend who couldn't seem to get things together when it went against the fact that I delivered to sold-out venues every show, and on stage, I wasn't slurring my words or skipping lyrics. I always had a good time on stage, and the fans seemed to enjoy it. Despite what my detractors might have said, I had to keep God in front of me and the naysayers behind me. The real question was if I was all those bad things, why in the world would promoters like Menges keep calling me asking for bookings. I wasn't even done with all the concerts he booked for me in 2011 before he began asking to book me for 2012. My God, I just wanted him to go away!

The relationship with Christine ended after I left the hospital. After about eight months of dating, we had enough of each other. Like most women I had encountered, she had begun to meddle in my business. Maybe she and the others felt entitled to interject themselves because I didn't speak German fluently. No matter what it was, I found it completely disrespectful for any of them to talk to the people I was working with behind my back.

Christine kept asking, "Why don't you keep working with Menges?"

I couldn't believe it. I looked at her and said, "Why are you in my business? I don't go on stage and say your lines while you're perform-ing, so leave me alone with this nonsense."

I didn't ask her for help, and I made that clear. A few months after we broke up, I received a phone call from my cousin Stacey who had visited briefly while Christine and I were dating. Christine sent the doctors' report to Stacey, who was quite alarmed until she heard from me. I could only assume from the medical records that Menges along with Christine had some sort of report done with the intention of putting me into a medical institution. The report said that I had a mental disorder, and I needed rehab. If I had done as many drugs as people said I'd done, I would have been dead long ago. No one believed me when I told them I had not done drugs. It was annoying to have to listen to such lies. The report Stacey read to me said my bloodwork was remarkable, but I needed to be committed. I wasn't having a nervous breakdown, but I was exhausted, dehydrated, and overworked, and during this time, I was experiencing menopause, for which I had run out of my prescription. The head games I had been dealing with from Menges put me in a bad headspace, and the worst of my symptoms was because I was going through menopause. I didn't have any of the little pink pills prescribed to me, and those pills helped the night sweats, the mood swings, but it didn't stop the bullshit from coming my way, nor did it stop people from stealing from me. I needed my hormones to be stabilized and once that was done, I left the hospital in a taxi. I never understood why you needed to get permission to leave a hospital. If you feel better, do you need someone to tell you that? I had asked the doctor to look at the boil developing on my ass, but he was so focused on asking me if I had done drugs, that he didn't try to help me with that. So, I left.

I continued to spend a good deal of my downtime in Baden-Baden. While hanging out at the local restaurants, I made a lot of friends, rested, and laughed a lot, which was what I needed to relieve the stress. I continued eating at the steakhouse and frequented a bar named Leo's, where I ate some of the best food I've ever had. I felt as if many people in the town recognized that I was going through a tough time, and they gave me words of encouragement or helped when they could. Some of the vendors even fed me for free, and I was extremely grateful, but I was still stressing about finances. To add to that, I was still getting calls from Menges saying I owed him money.

We were constantly arguing, and he refused to go away. He wanted me to continue working with him, but I refused. He had ripped me off long enough, and because of his lack of transparency, there was no way I could continue to work with him while he booked shows. I stopped accepting concert dates from him and realized I was basically on my own. That didn't stop Menges from booking gigs anyway and getting the deposit money without me knowing about it.

I would rather starve than work with Menges, and I was almost doing just that. I called GEMA and began explaining to them that Menges falsified paperwork, saying that he produced *"Humanology"* and stole credit from me. It seemed as if they believed him more than they did me. As the weeks went by, I would get phone calls from promoters who would tell me I was scheduled to do a show, and I would inform them that I wasn't coming because I didn't have a working relationship with Menges anymore. I have no idea how many shows he booked without my permission, and for many of them, I never saw any of the money, but he kept booking them. With all the concert deposits, credits, and merchandising, I'm pretty sure Menges received much more money than I ever borrowed from him, and he is still making money from that album.

# CHAPTER 45

# Hospital Again

After a few months of hustling up a few gigs in neighboring towns, I slowly began to get my life back on track. Peter had parties where I met a lot of amazing people from the town. One woman I met was named Gabi, but we didn't really connect until I was in the center of town and met her again in a local steakhouse. Months had passed, and we became reacquainted again. Gabi sat a few seats away from me, and the moment I sat down, she asked, "Aren't you Marla Glen?"

"Yes, I am."

She reintroduced herself, and because she spoke really good English, we began having great conversations. Gabi and I quickly became friends, and we visited each other often. I would eat at her place, where I met her husband, and when she'd come over to my place, I'd make oxtails, and we had a lot of laughs.

One day she asked, "Are you enjoying Baden-Baden?"

"I would enjoy it a lot more if I weren't going through a divorce."

"Tell me about it. I'm currently going through a rough patch with my husband myself. So, I understand how you feel. I just don't know what to do about it. Love is very stupid sometimes, isn't it?"

I nodded my head, "Hell yeah."

Gabi and I were kindred spirits, and she became like a sister to me. It was helpful to talk about what I was going through. She was kind, insightful, and a great listener, and she shared that she wanted to write books. We had more things in common other than the complications we were having in our marriages, and we began to chat more frequently.

Our conversations covered life, love, human behavior, and other deep and insightful experiences. We connected on a truly human level, and I felt she understood me as I shared my life's journey and the complications I had encountered. Gabi and I had become good friends; she eventually began to work as a taxi driver. So, I hired her whenever I needed a taxi in town, or sometimes we would just hang out, grab a drink and chat through the night. The more we chatted, the closer we got, and I began to trust her. I also hired her to go through all my paperwork involving issues surrounding my tax problems, receipts, and other things. Gabi showed me some of the reasons why I got into the tax situation in the first place, and my wife had signed documents to receive money from GEMA, and I had no knowledge of it.

Gabi made me feel comfortable because she wasn't judgmental; she was transparent, and she listened. So, I felt completely at ease when she asked to write an article about me. It wasn't something I'd normally feel comfortable doing. In the past, there were several articles that I didn't know were being written, but I could not understand them because I could not read whatever language they were written. Previously, when I'd seen the articles I had done an interview for, I just assumed that since they posted a picture of me smiling on the cover, the article was positive. Many times, they weren't positive or even true.

One guy in France started out by saying, "So, I read that your mother was a whore?"

Stunned, I asked, "Where did you hear that from?"

He said with a straight face, "I read it in another article."

Dealing with the media is a part of this job as a singer, but sometimes this is the most frustrating part of the job. There were so many myths printed about me in the past that I began to despise doing interviews. It was reported that my mother threw me out at the age of eight; several articles stated I was Nina Simone's bodyguard, and some even said I was a heroin-addicted diva with a lot of demands. None of those stories were true, but many fans believed the lies, and although I'd explain the truth, some would still say they chose to believe those articles. I remember telling Gonzalez that some of the stories I had heard about me in the press weren't true. Gonzalez responded, "But it sells records. Don't worry about it, honey." This was my life he was talking about, and it hurts to know that people didn't know the truth for the sake of selling records.

# CHAPTER 46

# Mr. Badu

By the end of 2011, after being in Baden-Baden for a couple of years, I decided it was time to move on. The quaint town served me well, but it was much too far from where many of my concerts were being booked. My divorce was final, and while I didn't get any of the divorce paperwork, I could only assume it was over. However, several months had passed, and to my surprise, I got a phone call from Sabrina. I answered the unfamiliar number.

"Hello?"

"Hi, it's Sabrina."

I hesitated before answering, trying to catch the voice.

"Well, Sabrina who? I know a lot of Sabrinas."

She got firm, "It is your wife. Really? I can't believe that you don't recognize my voice! I want to know if I can sing back up again."

Inviting Sabrina to be in my band again was *not* going to happen! It was awkward. We ended the conversation with small talk, and I have not spoken to Sabrina since. It was the end of a chapter for me. I think marriage is a beautiful thing; I just don't think it's for everyone.

The divorce was the least of my problems. I focused on making my living situation better, and working more gigs. I knew there was money out there to be made. While still living in Baden-Baden, I walked into another attorney's office to try to get some help making sense of it all. I hoped having the paperwork that Gabi organized might help me get some justice. I took all the paperwork to the guy, and he agreed to take on my concerns and help with my tax problem.

Once he looked everything over, he confirmed my ex-wife was receiving money from GEMA on my behalf, and she had signed paperwork stating she was my manager. The signature did not match mine, and it still baffles how anyone can get away with signing a name and no one checks to see if the signature is authentic. It had gotten to the point where, when I performed at different venues, some of the promoters would keep a portion of the monies and tell me that it was taken because of my tax problems. However, I had not received any notices, and when official-looking paperwork came in the mail, I could not read it because I do not read the German language. I was stuck between a rock and a hard place.

Baden-Baden was a great town, but I needed to be able to handle business with the attorney and connect with opportunities to help me secure shows. I moved back to Dusseldorf because I was able to secure a small, inexpensive studio apartment in the back of an apartment building. It was a tiny room but big enough for me to relax and figure out my next move musically. I was familiar with the area, and obtaining transportation in the area was perfect for traveling around Germany. Winter was coming, and I had very few shows scheduled in the coming year. This was rare for me, as oftentimes, I have a few dates on the calendar for the following year before year's end.

Although I cut ties with Menges, there was a concert in Switzerland coming up that he booked. Menges had again received all deposit funds, but I needed to get to the concert promoter before he did to make sure I got the balance of the money, which I needed badly. The musicians needed to be paid, so I got to the concert venue a few days early. In the meantime, the boil that was growing on my ass had doubled in size, and I could barely walk without feeling pain. The need to work seemed more important than the need to deal with it. I kept working, took a train to Switzerland, and did my show. I'm not sure if the fans noticed me walking funny; I had a great show, but the pain seemed to get worse.

After the concert, I stayed a few days in Switzerland and considered relocating because it had been a great source of peace for me. Usually, after concerts, I would sign autographs, chat with a few fans, and enjoy a beer or two. There were a few fans backstage who I had recognized from prior concerts, and we sat and talked for a while. I mentioned about possibly moving there, and one fan told me about a place in Lucerne.

She took me to the location, and it was a small concert hall with a room over the arena. I explained to them about the situation with Menges and that I needed a place to stay. After the conversation, the club owner allowed me to stay in the basic room that had a service elevator for access. I continued to look around the area, but few small apartments were available. I remembered another fan I would always see at my Switzerland concerts named Nadia. She told me if I was ever in town, I should look her up. Nadia was easy to remember because whenever I was on stage performing, she would scream as if she was at a Beatles concert!

I managed to contact her, and we met for lunch. We chatted a lot about Switzerland, and she was surprised I knew a lot about its history. Often I would study the culture of a town that I wanted to live in. It allowed me to understand many things about the people and their history. We spent all afternoon talking about the concerts she attended and laughed a great deal. I told her I was considering moving to Switzerland and starting a new band there, and she offered to introduce me to her stepdad. He managed two restaurants, and she thought he might have a place for me to stay or know someone.

We walked a few blocks over to a very nice restaurant with booths and tables where several people sat enjoying meals. It was approaching dinner time, and her stepdad, Mr. Badu, was busy. We had something to eat, and when he joined us, I explained what I wanted to do, and he said he had an available place upstairs. He promised I would like it, and he wasn't wrong.

Nadia left, and Mr. Badu walked me over to a small elevator with barely enough room for two people. When the doors opened again, they led into a spacious two-bedroom apartment overlooking the water, with marble floors and other classy accents. It was one of the most upscale apartments I had seen anywhere. The elevator was private to the apartment, and it made for a special touch. However, a set of stairs let you out in front of the restaurant. The place was paradise. Mr. Badu walked me around and showed me the layout. At the end of my tour, he turned to me and said, "Would you like to have all this?"

It kind of creeped me out a bit because he had an odd grin on his face. It was as if the Devil was showing me all the riches I could have.

"This is very nice."

It was certainly nicer than the place I'd seen earlier, and the restaurant being right below the apartment was truly a bonus. While Mr. Badu was a bit odd, the place was amazing. I looked at him and said, "Well, how much do you want for it?"

He smiled and replied, "Just bring your things here and consider it home."

He didn't have to say anything else, and I moved in as soon as possible.

The restaurant was always bustling with customers, and the staff came to know me, giving me free beers, free meals, and sometimes free bottles of Champagne. When I wasn't at the restaurant, I was out exploring Switzerland and learning about its history. I loved it and was happy to have a proper roof over my head. Despite Mr. Badu acting a little odd from time to time, we would have long conversations about many things. I shared with him how many lawyer's offices I had been to, and he said he would help me.

The lawyer he spoke to wanted to know all the details, and again, I was hopeful. I thought maybe I'd have better luck in Switzerland finding someone to help me. Mr. Badu seemed like he might have other connections, which is always good when dealing with attorneys. I did not want to meet them alone when I was divulging everything, so I asked some of the band members to join us so I could have other people listen in to be clear about what was happening. Mr. Badu was extremely generous, but I had lived in this world long enough to know that nothing in life is given to you for free. Most people want something.

When the band members arrived, Badu closed a restaurant section so we could have some privacy. There was Mr. Badu, my band leader Michael Ruber, a few members of the band, the attorney, and myself. I did not want to be the only witness if things got odd. Everyone had questions, and I could not keep up because they spoke in German very quickly. I could barely sit because the boil on my ass was causing me discomfort.

Then, out of the blue, Mr. Badu pulled out an envelope full of money and tossed it on the table.

"That's ten thousand Swiss Francs," he said.

For a moment, everyone just looked at the money on the table.

"That should take care of any of Marla's old contracts," Badu added.

I felt like I was in a Godfather movie with a savvy gangster.

"What exactly is this for?" asked Michael.

"I'm paying this money to this lawyer, who is now Marla's lawyer, and I want this thing over with. This lawyer can handle it."

None of us knew how Badu and the lawyer would make all my bad contract issues go away, but with ten thousand francs on the table, I was willing to see what would happen. There was more chatter from the group, and again I could not understand a word they were saying. The next day, I received a phone call from Michael Ruber.

"Marla, Mr. Badu showed me a contract, and he is going to want you to sign it."

"Really?"

Michael paused for a moment and said, "Don't sign it. It's not a good contract."

# CHAPTER 47

# The Fight

A few days later, I could barely walk because of the pain from the growth. I asked Badu, who often spouted braggadocios, about a doctor, and this time was no different.

"Would you like to go to Tina Turner's doctor? I know him."

I didn't care who he called, but he seemed to take joy in knowing the guy.

"Sure, why not?"

He made my appointment, and I was at the doctor's office the next day. The doctor looked at the growth as I lay on my stomach in the small room.

"My goodness, that must be uncomfortable."

I responded, "Yeah, it's a pain in the ass."

He didn't laugh, but I thought it was funny,

"This is going to have to be surgically removed. It's about 24 millimeters."

"Well, how big is that? 'Cause I can feel it, but I can't see it."

"It's about the size of an American Quarter."

"How did it get there?" I asked.

He began writing on a notepad.

"It's a tumor. And, more than likely, it has been caused by stress."

I sighed and said, "I believe that."

"We are going to admit you, and you will probably be here for a couple of days."

The surgery was quick, and afterward, all I could do was rest. I was extremely tired, and those days in the hospital were some of the best sleep I'd had in a long time. There's something about hospitals that allow me to sleep better.

\*\*\*

Just before heading to the hospital, I had been informed by a band member that concerts were being advertised we didn't know about. After doing some research, I found out that Menges had booked them without my knowledge. While he'd be happy raking in the deposits, I could not make the dates, and the venues were left out of pocket. I had to find a way to get rid of Menges and his shady ways completely. I'd really had enough when all the stress caused me to get a tumor.

Having sought to rid myself of problems by severing ties with Gonzalez, I had been chasing places to live, dealing with marital problems, shady promoters like Menges, and trying to find lawyers to help me handle it all. It was getting too much to bear, but I gritted my teeth, and while recovering, I looked into who had actually booked the concerts. The company in charge of the upcoming tour was A.S.S. How ironic. When I talked to someone at the touring company, I explained the situation.

"I'm in the hospital. I can't perform, and I'm not going to make it."

The voice on the other end of the phone said, "Marla, you don't have the right to be sick. You need to finish the concert dates."

"I can't do them," I said and put the phone down.

After a few days, Badu took me back to the apartment. The Christmas holidays were approaching, and snow began to fall. As I was recovering, I noticed that Badu had been drinking quite a bit, but who am I to judge? I am married to my marijuana. I still had not signed that contract, nor was I going to, but things began to get uncomfortable. Badu seemed to be a little more intense as the days went on until I entered the tiny elevator to head out one night. Badu knew I would be leaving, and he was already inside. He seemed more intoxicated than normal, and I could smell it all over him. After a moment of silence, he shoved his elbow in my ribs.

"You are going to do what I say."

I hit him right back in the ribs, stuck a finger in his face, and said, "Do not hit me!"

Badu pushed me into the corner of the elevator and said it again, "I said, you are going to do what I say."

Suddenly, he grabbed me around the throat, but I mustered enough strength and could peel his hands from around my neck and wrestle him to the floor.

"You need to leave me alone. I don't want to hurt you," I said.

At that moment, the elevator door opened. As Badu struggled to get up, I pushed him out of the elevator with my foot, so I could get out. We began to tussle again. The elevator was located in the private area of the restaurant in the back, and I tried to head out of a swing door that led to where the customers were located. However, before I made it there, Badu grabbed me and tried to stop me. We both grabbed the door to the restaurant, and while tussling, Badu somehow ended up inside the restaurant blocking me from going past him to exit.

"Let me out!" I screamed as I pushed the door with all my might.

Badu was pushing it too to try and stop me; his face was sandwiched in between the door and the frame. I kept trying to get past him, but I had no choice, I punched Badu in the face, and he fell, allowing me to escape. Once he fell, I opened the door, stepped over him, and as I walked through the restaurant, I shouted, *"I told you I didn't want to fight you!"*

There were customers looking on, and I composed myself and kept walking right out of the restaurant. I was frustrated, and this was the last straw for me dealing with his odd behavior and threats. I abandoned my plans for the evening and went to the other elevator entrance up to the apartment, entered, then locked the door behind me. I sat for a moment trying to compose myself, and all I could think about was that I had to get out of there.

# CHAPTER 48

# Teamwork ... Or Not

I had thought my drifting days were over. The situation had me shell-shocked because never did I expect to get into some sort of physical altercation with Badu. I had to defend myself, and it was time to go. By midnight, I was completely packed, and Michael Ruber and a few other band members, including a guy named Detlev, loaded up a van, and we fled into the darkness. I hated that I had to leave that wonderfully luxurious apartment, but I was happy to be away from the evil presence that surrounded it. Leaving in the middle of the night was my only option. As the van sped along the highway, I was still frustrated as I explained the details of what happened with Badu.

We headed back to Germany, where Chrissy, one of my backup singers for the last few years, owned a building in Koln. Detlev said she had a one-bedroom apartment I could stay at until we figured things out. My life was in their hands at this point; all I could do was say was thank you. Chrissy was always level-headed and positive, and I was grateful to have somewhere to lay my head. I was certainly in no position to turn anything down.

We finally arrived in Koln, and they helped me unload my things into the first-floor unit, a small two-room apartment. The living area was narrow, and it led to the bedroom.

"This place is my office," said Detlev. "You can stay in this main room while you're here and sleep on the sofa."

I looked at the tiny sofa and responded, "Okay."

I didn't have a lot of things, but what I did have, I wanted to keep. A table, a trunk, a few dishes, and all my instruments. Michael Ruber placed my things inside the apartment and turned to me. "You are at least safe."

"Thanks, man. I appreciate it."

The next morning, Chrissy invited me upstairs, and I took the narrow stairway to the 2nd-floor unit that was bright and sunny. My first steps landed me in the kitchen where Chrissy was cooking breakfast.

"You want some eggs?" she asked.

Starved, I responded, "Hell yeah!"

We sat and talked for a bit, and Chrissy said Michael Ruber told her about the contract.

"Yeah, he would have owned everything I did. I think he wanted to eat me alive. I call it the fork and knife contract. That was his logo."

We both laughed as Chrissy finished up breakfast.

"I was wondering how that was going to work out," she said.

"It didn't. I got lucky getting out of there when I did."

"Ja, it is a good thing. There would be no Marla Glen band without Marla Glen."

We laughed again, and then her face got serious. I could tell that she switched to her business hat.

"So, the good thing is that this is probably a blessing in disguise. You are closer to the band, and rehearsals will be easier here."

"Yeah, you're right. So, what will you be charging me for rent here?"

"I talked to Detlev about it, and three hundred euros a month seems fair."

"I can make that happen."

"Great. Also, Detlev is a tour manager. Maybe we can talk about booking the band more. He's nothing like Menges and has been booking our gospel band for years. We can form a team to get you back on the road."

"Chrissy, that sounds great, and if you're comfortable with Detlev, then I'm sure he will be fine."

I was happy to hear they wanted to work with me, and it seemed like it would work out. A couple of hours later, I sat down with Chrissy and Detlev, and I looked them both in the eyes.

"I don't want management."

Chrissy nodded. "Okay. Then how do you want things to go?"

"There doesn't need to be a contract unless it's for touring, but as long as you're not calling yourselves my manager, that should be fine. I basically need to know everything you know if it has to do with me."

Detlev nodded, and they both took notes before waiting for me to carry on.

"Look, just do what you normally do as a tour agent, but if I ask to see a contract, it should not be something under your company name. I want to see the actual contracts from the promoters. Some of these guys I know already, and I can give you names of the ones who usually book me throughout the year. But once I put your names on my website, the calls will come in."

"That's great," Detlev said.

"Yeah, I'll be handling the paperwork. So, you can see it whenever you want," said Chrissy.

All this was music to my ears, and they seemed serious about handling business properly, which made me excited to begin with this new team. Chrissy had been working with Detlev for a while, and since he was a tour agent already, I was comfortable with how things were unfolding. We all had our roles, and I was excited about it.

Things got off to a great start, and it helped to stop Menges from booking concerts without my permission. My website had all the pertinent info updated, and it was an easy transition. Prior to moving into Chrissy's Koln apartment, I had been talking to GEMA, trying to find out where my royalty checks were going. This was not an easy task, but I managed to get them to send them. Sometimes the checks would come in big, sometimes small. No matter how much they were, I needed every dime.

Because of my lack of understanding of business German, it would be a strain to have a conversation with the GEMA representatives to get what I needed. I asked Chrissy and Detlev to help and to see if they could get the checks coming to the apartment. They made the phone calls, and things were turned around in no time, and my royalty checks began being delivered to me. My only issue was not having a key to the mailbox. It was awkward to have to ask for my mail, but it wasn't my place, so I just trusted that I'd get it.

My royalty situation was a fiasco. Several people had contacted GEMA and stated they had written my songs or were responsible for arrangements, and I did not know how to stop these lies. GEMA never contacted me to find out what was true or if they had correct signatures, and when I called their offices, their people were slow to fix the problems. It was always a challenge dealing with GEMA and frustrating because everything was done in German. Several royalty checks were issued in my wife's or musicians' names, and I had no way of controlling the situation.

It was a relief when Detlev and Chrissy agreed to help secure my GEMA royalties. Detlev's girlfriend worked at a bank, and he was able to get me one of my very first bank accounts. Everything was cool until Detlev asked me to sign a contract. I wasn't surprised; both he and Chrissy had been acting oddly,

"For what?" I asked.

"We need to make sure things go smoothly. We are putting in a lot of work.

In my mind, all I could think was, here we go again.

"I don't understand; you're getting paid through commissions. You're getting my royalty checks and merchandising. I thought things were okay?!"

He shook his head, "Marla, it takes a lot of money to deal with everything."

"What's a lot of money? Where is the money going that you're getting?"

I was frustrated because I wanted real answers, but he just stared at me for a moment.

"Detlev, where is the money going?"

He seemed defensive when he said, "You have to eat, pay rent, eat steaks sometimes; we buy your weed."

"Steaks? I can't have a steak? C'mon, what is this really about. I can buy my own weed, man. You don't have to do that."

"We want a contract."

"Okay, give me the contract you want me to sign, and I will look it over."

Within the next few days, I was given a contract, but our team no longer felt like a family business. I never signed Detlev's contract because it stated that all monies go into *his* bank. Without really discussing it, we just kept working as a team. We were all cordial and friendly because we were working together and making money, but it was clear things were coming to an end. I was in the process of producing my next album since *"Humanology"* was a disaster, thanks to Menges.

I was glad to be done with him even though he continued to call and try to book me. I made it clear to Menges and promoters that I had a new team. During this uneasy time, my cousin Stacey came to visit again. She had come to Germany several times before working with me on various projects, helping with writing my bio, with interviews, and other tasks. As a Hollywood writer and director, I also trusted her to help me with music videos and other projects we were tackling.

Even though my career felt like it was moving forward again, I was still not ready to give up on getting justice for the past. So, after several conversations, the team secured a meeting with yet another attorney. Detlev arranged a meeting with a guy in Hamburg, and finally, I felt things were going to be resolved. I still had paperwork that revealed my forged signature on some documentation that could possibly prove I was taken for royalties, credits, and thousands of dollars, perhaps millions. I wanted my day in court; it felt like it was time.

This was probably the 30th attorney's office I had visited since parting ways with Mr. Gonzalez back in 1992. God, and my peace of mind, wouldn't let me give up hope. I have always felt that the righteous will prevail, and justice would somehow be found. As Detlev, myself, and Stacey entered the sterile basic office, I felt humble and anxious. It was always draining to discuss the wrongs of the past, but if that was what it was going take to get my justice, then I would do it without hesitation. I sat in front of the attorney and gave him the papers I had been accumulating for years. He shuffled through them for a minute and asked, "Is this your signature?

I looked at the signature in question, "Nope."

"Did you have a contract with this person?"

I glanced at the paperwork to see Gonzalez' name.

"No. He took over things without my permission and began to threaten me. He took several songs I didn't finish and released them without my permission. He even thanked himself on the back of the albums, and I would have never done that."

"So, you didn't you have a contract with him?

"No. I did have a contract with the record company but never signed with him. He claims I signed, but I didn't. He even bought a house with my money. His wife told me about that. Whenever I saw him, I'd always ask. How is my house you're living in?"

"Is there something that you can do?" Stacey asked. "What's the statute of limitations?"

"Three years if you know who it is, thirty years if you don't."

Thirty years ...?

The attorney turned over a few more papers, and twice more, I told him it wasn't my signature.

"I could get someone to do a comparison to attest these signatures on these documents. However, it can be pricey," the attorney said.

"I don't care. If I have to pay it, I will."

"Okay, I'm going to have to do more research. I will contact you when I have something."

I bowed my head. Finally, someone was going to handle this long road to getting my justice. Tears welled up in my eyes as I stood up and shook his hand.

"Thank you. It's been a long time, and I can't believe it. Thank you so much."

We all stood up, and as we headed out of the office, he placed his hand on my back and said, "Let's get this thing behind you once and for all."

I left the office hopeful with tears of joy as I remembered how Ms. Simone had fought so incredibly hard to find someone to go back and sue for the money taken from her as well; finally, my day was coming, and I could not wait.

I was still living on the first floor of Chrissy's apartment building, but I was ready to go. I was being treated as if I had no value and as if I was a child. I sometimes would wait for the mailman to see if I got any mail, but I wasn't sure if I was getting royalty checks or not. I was well into working on the next album, and while the team and the band helped, there was a lot of tension and mistrust. I could not understand how money was being disseminated, and I was being accused of not being able to understand the music business and how it operated.

Things seemed to be going downhill again, and despite the positive end to the meeting with the attorney, I had been given false hope yet again. Nothing ever materialized or moved forward, and meanwhile, the band was acting strangely in my presence. The drama of it all was exhausting, and I was relieved when my cousin came back to visit again. I asked her to help me with the situation, and Stacey tackled Chrissy.

"Chrissy, can you give a financial accounting of the money that Marla is bringing in and how the funds are being disseminated?"

Without hesitation, she said, "Ironically, I am working on that. I'll have it done before you leave to go back to the U.S."

We all went out to dinner to a trendy restaurant in downtown Koln and had a wonderful time. I'm glad that Stacey came because I just needed someone to come in and look at things from a different perspective. So many times, I had been accused of exaggerating a situation or making up lies that it made me always want to have people around to verify that I was not making shit up.

After dinner, we went back to the apartment, and Stacey and I sat down to talk.

"You guys seem different. What happened since my last visit?" she asked.

"I don't know, they are acting very odd, and when I asked them what's wrong, they tell me I'm eating steaks, and I can't afford it. They are up to something; I can feel it."

"Steaks? What does that have to do with anything?"

We laughed.

"I have no idea. I'm hoping you can talk to them."

"I'll try to find out," she replied.

"All I have is my instincts, and when people start acting weird like they are, then something ain't right. I've been working this road for a while, and the money they are spending makes no sense. Where is it going?"

"I don't know, but we will find out."

Every week for the six weeks that Stacey was in town, Chrissy said she was still working on the reconciliation showing how the money was being distributed. Finally, on the last day of Stacey's visit, the four of us sat down at Chrissy's kitchen table. It was only hours before my cousin was scheduled to return to California, and it felt very awkward. Chrissy passed around a twelve-page list of expenses they supposedly had incurred on my behalf.

"What's this expense here, labeled 'Flat'?"

"That is the rent we are charging for Marla to live downstairs."

"It says twenty-four hundred euros per month. When I first moved in, you said it was three hundred! How did it get from three hundred to twenty-four hundred?"

Detlev chimed in, "Well, we thought you would just stay in one room, but you are using the whole unit."

My cousin and I looked at each other, not knowing what to make of it. Stacey tried to get clarity.

"So, did you tell Marla that you increased the rent?"

"No. We didn't," Chrissy admitted.

There was an awkward moment of silence. Having my cousin there made me feel better because I could not believe what I was hearing. The entire mood of the room changed, and I really didn't want to look at any more numbers.

"I don't need to see anything else. It's all made-up nonsense."

Stacey wanted to continue, she said, "Hold on, Marla. I just have a couple of questions."

She looked at Chrissy and asked, "So, what is the grand total you believe Marla owes you?"

Chrissy flipped the pages of her copy and said, "It's on the back."

Stacey and I turned the countless number of pages to the grand total. I saw Stacey's mouth drop.

"*One hundred thousand euros?!* Marla owes you that much from living here not even two years? How is that possible? You only added up a bunch of numbers and wrote them down. There are no receipts or invoices from anyone; it's just your word against Marla's."

"It's all here and accurate; that's what took me so long," insisted Chrissy. "And things cost. Nothing is free."

I sighed and said, "Stacey, let's go. I can't do this anymore."

She tried to continue, "Chrissy, how do you say Marla owes you this money, and nowhere in this document have you listed the monies that came in from the concerts, merchandising, or anything else."

With a straight face, Chrissy said, "It may be different. I still have receipts somewhere, but I only had time to do the expenses."

We all began talking at the same time. "This is crazy! How is this possible?" was coming from Stacey and myself while Detlev and Chrissy were saying, "These are the numbers, and things aren't free."

I shook my head as Stacey and I got up from the table. Before we made it to the stairway, one of the last things Chrissy uttered was, "You know; I suspect that we will be one of the long line people who Marla said did wrong."

"When you are adding up numbers like you did, looking only at the debit side, then you are probably right."

In the downstairs apartment, we looked at the documents closer to discover both Chrissy and Detlev had over-inflated salaries for themselves, well beyond the industry standard. Chrissy was being paid as the bookkeeper, landlord, and backup singer. Detlev was paid additional monies adding in commissions and other miscellaneous items. What was it about me, that made people think they could get away with it? Where was their moral code?

Moments later, Detlev came downstairs, and Stacey left with him to take her to the airport. I was so messed up from the meeting that I could not go with them to drop her off. I couldn't keep my head from spinning and needed to figure my way out of another fucked up situation. I know I had been naive in the past when it came to some areas of the music business, but simple addition and subtraction is not a hard thing to figure out as it pertained to people getting paid. How could they demand payment without looking at the income they'd already received?

There was no way in hell that I owed them one hundred thousand euros, but I suspected they would make things difficult. I needed transparency, and it was clear that I wouldn't get that from the so-called team members.

# CHAPTER 49

# Bruno

Not long after things had turned sour between us, many of my band members began acting strangely. They were argumentative and disrespectful, but more importantly, they were unmotivated and uninterested in doing the work. I suspected Detlev or Chrissy had begun talking bad about me behind my back. As Gonzalez would always say, "A band could take down your career quicker than any manager could."

Even Jimmy, who was one of my favorite backup singers, started distancing himself and taking sides with Chrissy and Detlev in little spats that created conflict and confusion. It was the divide and conquer game, and things worsened. This type of behavior was not new to me.

I began to insist that Chrissy and Detlev help me get an apartment because I was so annoyed with what was happening around me. I even called Gonzalez hoping his guilt would get the better of him. I kept conversations going with him, and he never stopped asking about booking me ever since we parted ways. If he was willing to send me the right contract, I was open to working with him, but he never changed, and he's still sending me contracts with his company name at the top and not from promoters.

Eventually, Detlev found me an apartment in Koln. He claimed it was in his name, and I never saw any lease agreement, so I didn't know for sure. He and Chrissy told me I could not get my own place because of the insolvency. The apartment was a two-bedroom unit across the street from a park. It wasn't the best neighborhood, but it wasn't the worst. I finally moved in, and we all remained as civil as possible because concerts were coming in, and there was still business to handle in producing the new album that I labeled, "*Tricks and Tracks.*" This was the second attempt to create a project on my own, "*Humanology*" was the first.

Then Detlev began playing games with the concert money, and things came to a breaking point before one of the concerts when the band waited for the tour bus at a local McDonald's in Koln. I was aware that Detlev had gotten the deposit for the show we were scheduled to do that day. I asked Detlev to pay me before the bus left for the concert. Normally, I'd get my portion of the funds several weeks before the concert day. While standing in McDonald's, Detlev said, "Okay, I'll pay you your money, but what happens next is on you."

I had no idea what he was talking about. Shortly after Detlev walked out of the McDonald's, the entire band came and surrounded me. Chris, the drummer, said, "We want more money, or we are not doing the show."

"Your money comes after tonight's performance."

"We also want a nightliner for this performance, so we don't have to sleep somewhere uncomfortable." Nightliners are buses that also allow band members to sleep while traveling.

"C'mon guys, Detlev is supposed to pay you out of the concert money, not out of my money, and this is not a show where we can afford a sleeper."

They weren't budging, and they acted like a pack of thugs. In the end, I pulled out the money and handed it over, keeping only five hundred euros, which wasn't enough to pay my rent. A few hours later, the bus came, and they loaded the bus. Detlev was driving to the concert, so I rode with him and cussed up a storm all the way to the concert.

"What is going on, Detlev? Why are they acting like this? Tell me what you said to make them turn on me!"

Detlev barely said a word, and I eventually had to let it go to be in the right mindset for delivering a good show, which was more important than dealing with a bunch of disrespectful band members. I performed a kick-ass show that night because in the back of my mind, I knew this band would be fired. It was time to clean my house again.

I needed to make sure that the album I was producing was in my hands before I did anything that could stop it. Things were already looking shady with the production because I only went to the studio to lay down my voice one song at a time. Despite the many times I asked when I was going back into the studio, I never got an answer from Detlev.

After several weeks, I was asked to go to a different studio to lay down tracks. It was an awkward session, but a few days afterward, I had lunch with Andy, one of my drummers, and I got some answers. Andy seemed concerned, and when I asked again what was going on, he looked me dead in my eyes.

"I think Detlev is going to take over the album. It's not right."

"Take it over? What the hell does that mean?"

"He told us we all are going to get credits for the music instead of being paid for studio work. He said we can get paid a lot more money."

"Why didn't you tell me this before?"

"Marla, I tried. When I asked him after the last concert if we could meet you to talk about it, he said it would be a ticking time bomb, and he threatened to fire us all."

I was shocked at what I was hearing and wasn't sure if Andy was telling the truth, but there were no other answers. I may never know what happened, but I do know that things weren't right. I really needed to get this situation with "*Tricks & Tracks*" under control. It was really bothering me. I called the last studio engineer to see if I could talk to him, but he didn't return my calls. I found out that Detlev registered the songs without my permission, and he refused to turn over the masters for the album.

I could not believe how deep the betrayal was until this happened. I went to Karlsruhe and hired an engineer on my own. My only recourse was to re-record my own songs with different arrangements and different beats. I didn't know how else to move on it, and I refused to sit back and do nothing. In the end, it was never released.

It was the end of 2014, and I still needed to get rid of these band members and find a way out of this situation. I had a few gigs and a television appearance coming up and I was still frustrated with this band. During rehearsals at my apartment, one of the background singers, a girl named Amaka, told me that she could refer someone, a keyboard player and potential bandleader, and I told her to call who she knew. I trusted her because she came on board as a background singer after all the drama happened.

One night in November, when the bus showed up for one of the final gigs with the current band, a few of the band members had already left. I got on board and didn't really talk much. I was frustrated, and I'm sure it showed. We stopped to picked up a few remaining band members, and Amaka boarded, along with her friend Bruno, and she introduced us.

"Bruno Seletkovic, this is Marla Glen."

We shook hands, and I said, "Nice to meet you. You're going to be my next band leader!"

Bruno laughed and said, "Well, okay."

He seemed shocked, but I was serious. At this point, I was beyond my wits' end.

We arrived at the studio and started preparing for the show. Bruno seemed to be misinformed, and as I was in my dressing room getting set up, he came in.

"I thought I was coming to a rehearsal."

"No. This is an actual show. You ready?"

"I don't know anything. I'm not sure if I'll be able to keep up."

"You will be fine. I will ensure you get some sheet music, so jump in and make it work."

Bruno jumped in reluctantly, but he learned the songs quickly and pulled off the show without any problems, and that told me how great he was. It was a lot like meeting a brother from a different mother and reminded me of when I met Crosio. After the show, we exchanged numbers and began to talk over the next few days. There weren't many shows in December, and in preparation for 2015 shows, I began having rehearsals again at my Köln apartment in January. During this time, I began to tell Bruno all my problems with the current band, and he agreed to help me replace everyone.

He was indeed knowledgeable about the music business, reminding me of Michele Crosio, but better. At this point, there was no doubt in my mind that Bruno was indeed going to be my band leader. Now that the situation with the band looked like it was going be resolved I began having other problems. I went out to the store one afternoon to get beer and weed papers, and when I arrived home, there was an official-looking notice on my apartment door. It was in German, and I had no idea what it said, so I placed it on the table and turned on the television.

# CHAPTER 50

# Out With The Old

It was barely daylight. Everything was quiet as I slept with my new girlfriend, Cathy. She was one of the few African women I had dated, and she was a bit younger than me, small- framed and cute as a button. Originally from Kenya. I met her in a local African shop, and our friendship became flirtatious and then interesting. She moved in with me after I got my own apartment in Koln. That morning I was tired when I was awakened by someone hammering on the door. They were frantic. Cathy had a look of concern on her face yet didn't utter a word. I grabbed my robe and headed to the door as the knocking persisted.

*"Who is it!?"*

There was murmuring on the other side of my front door, but I could not make out what they were saying over the loud knocking.

I shouted again, "Who is it!?"

I peeked out of the peephole, and a tall German woman was standing there with the police.

"Es ist die Polizei. Du musst raus!"

I opened the door. Initially, they began speaking in German.

"What are you talking about? Please, I don't understand."

The woman began speaking in English.

"You have not paid the rent. You must go!"

I looked at the paper she was handing me; it was in German. Now I was frantic.

"I don't know what you are talking about. I did not sign anything to get into this apartment. Detlev handled everything. My road manager."

The police officer interjected, "You have to leave."

I began pleading, "Why do I have to leave? I have been paying. Everything is paid, and it's coming straight out of my bank account!"

The German woman replied, "There were notices. We have not received payment for several months. You must go."

I looked her in the eyes and said, "The money came out of my bank account. I can show you my bank statements."

I went to grab a nearby box that had all my statements in it.

"It's in here. I have proof."

The woman sighed and seemed annoyed.

"None of that matters. Detlev says you owe him money, but the rent here is what I'm concerned about. There were notices. You have to go; it's not been paid."

I couldn't believe this was happening. As my voice went up an octave, I said, "What are you talking about? What notices?"

The police officer became agitated, then said, "We cannot continue this conversation. It's too late; you have to be out. I will give you until the end of the day."

I shouted, *"What?! C'mon!"*

Cathy stood in the background silently as I stood pleading.

*"I have proof. I can show you my bank statements!"*

The woman walked away, and the officer stood there. He said it again, firmly, "You have till the end of the day. That is all you have."

There was no choice but to leave. The last thing I needed was to be put in jail again. It was clear Detlev had me in some sort of situation that I could not fix. I didn't know where my rent money was going; I never met the people I had been paying my rent to. Detlev just told me to make sure the right amount was put in the bank so it could be withdrawn every month. On my bank statements was the name of a German company withdrawing the exact amount monthly. I had no idea who was behind that company.

Shortly after they left, I gathered my things as quickly as I could, taking the important things, grabbing clothes, and picking up all my instruments. I left to go to the bank, and luckily, I had enough to help with the move. Cathy made some phone calls, and she got a truck and movers to get the furniture, and one of the band members came to help. This was embarrassing, insulting, and frustrating, and I was beyond pissed.

I had almost 5000 Euros, just enough to get a truck and maybe put a down payment on another apartment. Cathy helped me to find a storage place, and within a few hours, my things were safe. I called my friend, Tollman, who lived in Dusseldorf, and he arranged a room at an inexpensive hotel. Cathy and I stayed there for about three months and then moved into a friend's small studio apartment. The place was only big enough for one person, but Cathy and I made it work.

We were still booking gigs, but they weren't coming quickly enough, and being displaced didn't help the situation. It was the end of the year, and many promoters had already booked their clubs and festivals. Cathy was still acting as my booking agent, but she was mostly taking phone calls that came through and making them on my behalf. She was smart about handling things, but I needed a real booking agent, not my girlfriend. We began to argue a lot, and I could tell we weren't going to make it as a couple. I kept trying, but Cathy had her own set of issues, and as much as I wanted to help her, I knew I couldn't. During the course of our relationship, Cathy had been keeping her best friend Irene updated on everything happening with us. I hadn't met Irene, but I was aware she was also from Kenya. I try to stay out of conversations when women are talking. One afternoon in the middle of Cathy and Irene's conversation, Cathy turned to me and said, "Irene's says her boyfriend can help you."

I responded, "Oh yeah? How?"

She said, "By investing in what you are doing."

I gave her a look and said, "What does he do? And, what's his name?"

She said, "Ingo. And he owns a Driving School."

I paused and said, "Okay, let's set it up."

I met Ingo and Irene at a hotel where Irene worked. During this time, Cathy and I lived with them for a few months until I landed a private concert with a longtime fan from Switzerland who was kind enough to pay me early, so I could have enough money to put down on an apartment. Everything worked out, and Irene and Ingo were instrumental in getting me a cozy two-bedroom place close to them in Oppenheim, and I lived in the quaint town for about two and a half years. Ingo never invested, but he acted as a road manager for the time I spent there, and Irene handled my wardrobe needs.

The apartment he found had a cozy feel to it, and it was within walking distance of a few wineries and a nice shopping area. The town was quiet, but they had festivals, nice walking trails, a few good restaurants, and it allowed me to relax and focus on my next moves. Oppenheim wasn't my destination of choice; for some reason, God put me there, and I just rolled with it. The neighborhood's peace allowed me to focus enough to write new music to prepare for my next CD. I would travel by train back and forth to work on things with Bruno. Our first project was collaborating on a "Marla Glen Live" CD. It was an easy task because we had concerts coming that would let us effectively record the sound on stage. All the songs were tunes I had been doing for years, so the timing just made sense. While working on that project, I began writing songs even without knowing where money would come from to complete the next project. I knew I needed to make up for lost time. The good thing about my past with Vogue Records was that they showed me that I needed to have something to release every two years, and I tried to live by that. I never wanted an entire year to go by without me working towards releasing something else. I felt good to be making new music with Bruno. He's a fantastic arranger, and we are so musically connected that oftentimes it feels like we share the same brain. Bruno would send me a beat, "Hey man, check this out."

The moment I heard it, lyrics would begin coming to me.

"This is a hit, Bruno. Let's work on it."

I'd listen to the tune countless times, then work on creating lyrics and the melody.

After that is done, it becomes a complete song, then Bruno goes into the studio and uplifts it with instruments. When he's working, I give Bruno all the space he needs to do his part, and he does the same for me. We have the type of working relationship that I always wanted to have with Crosio. Unlike working with Michele Crosio, working with Bruno feels more like a partnership. Almost every day we talk about how to create music and work tirelessly doing it.

Ultimately my relationship with Cathy ended, and after chatting for some time on Facebook, in 2015 I reconnected with and began dating a young German woman from Hamburg, who I met earlier in my career when I lived in France. Her name was Stevie. She was much too young to date back then, and I had no time for serious relationships. Stevie is older now, and our relationship has grown over the past six years. She is a twin, and when we talked on Facebook, I asked her, "Are you the good twin or the bad one?"

With a smiley face, she responded, "The bad one!"

We have been talking ever since, and she was the inspiration for a few new songs on the *Unexpected* CD I released in February 2020.

One of the tunes I wrote was based on a conversation we had while I was writing music. Stevie interrupted the flow by asking me to go to the park and do other lovely things. I called the song *Ordinary*. I was trying to explain that I had work to do and that I was on a mission. When I was done with the music, we spent plenty of time together.

### Ordinary
By Marla Glen
If I was an ordinary person
I would walk on the beach with you
If I was an ordinary person
I would go on Vacances Avec Toi

If I was an ordinary Person
If I was an ordinary Person
If I was an ordinary Person
I would walk in the park with you

If I was an ordinary person
I would live anywhere with you
If I was an ordinary person
I would clean up your house for you

If I was an ordinary person
If I was an ordinary person
If I was an ordinary person
I would do what you want me to
Ordi -nary - we will carry
Ordi- nary - let's find Harry

If I was an ordinary person
I could ride on a bike with you
If I was an ordinary person
I could go to the movies with you

If I was an ordinary person
If I was an ordinary Person
If I was an ordinary Person
I would always make love to you

Ordi-nary, Where Is Harry
Ordi-nary, Who Is Perry

Ordi-nary, We Will Carry
Ordi-nary, Let's Find Harry

Ordi-nary
Who Is Perry
Ordi-nary, Let's Find Mary

Ordi-nary. We Will Carry
Ordi-nary
Let's Find Harry
Ordi-nary, Where Is Harry

Ordi-nary, Who Is Perry
Wait!! Stop!
I found Mary
Oh, there is Harry
I still don't know who Perry is

From the moment Bruno and I connected, things began to look up. Songs were coming to me like crazy. It's incredible how having a roof over your head, while reading the Bible and smoking weed allows my mind to come up with new music. So, I continued writing and completed enough songs for the CD. When I was done, I asked a few friends for the money. Within weeks of asking, a couple of angel investors stepped up to the plate and became financial backers. They were a Godsend because, between Bruno and me, we only had about one hundred euros in our pockets. With the funds I received, I completed the mastering of the CD and hired Stacey to direct the music video for *I Don't Care*, which was the first single I wanted to release. The band and my girlfriend were involved in making the video, and we all had a lot of fun doing it. The lyrics were based on a lot of the myths that followed me from the past, which included chasing women, smoking cigars, and drinking whiskey, all of which I really don't do. This song, like many of the others I wrote, is therapeutic, and at this point, I had gotten to a stage where I just didn't care anymore, and that is how the lyrics came to me. I have several songs about my past experiences, but some, like *Believer,* are about world issues. The tune *Who's to Blame?* is about the problems children are having in Africa. I'm very grateful to have completed a CD on my own, and I decided to call it, *Unexpected.* It was a long time coming, but I finally did it!

# CHAPTER 51

# Finding Freedom

The moment Bruno and I completed the last song, we sat in his apartment, smiling and enjoying the feeling of having a great sense of accomplishment. We opened up a couple of beers, clinked the bottles, and said to each other, "Congratulations motherfucker! We did it!"

Bruno turned to me and said, "Well, next, you will have to register all your songs for the CD."

I looked at him and said, "You know how to do that?"

He responded, "I looked it up. The process is easy."

I had learned that Bruno if he didn't know something, he'd study it and find a way to get it done. He's resourceful as well as genuine.

Never in my entire career had I registered my own songs. It was always done for me or behind my back with someone else's name on them. I stood there speechless almost with tears in my eyes as Bruno, step by step, walked me through the entire process. It was the best I have felt since the beginning of my career. I was excited to submit each song and receive the paperwork back with my name on them as song-writer and producer and Bruno as co-producer and arranger. I was right about him, and very grateful that we met because it was always a dream to have a bandleader that I can trust and who is amazing at everything he does.

I knew that Bruno and I could not do the music as well as the paperwork involved to make everything work so we needed a secretary. I connected with one of my Facebook friends, a woman who looked very professional by the name of Susan, and we would chat from time to time. After about six months of chatting, I had a concert coming up in and I asked her to come around. She arrived with a friend to the concert, and after the show, we all hung out on the tour bus and drank Champagne, afterwards I introduced her to Bruno. We began talking business.

"We really could use a secretary for what Bruno and I are doing," I said,

"I'm in management, so I would not be interested in doing that," she responded.

I was persistent because Susan had a great vibe.

"Maybe there is another way I could help," she responded.

We continued to talk and eventually scheduled future meetings.

After months and several meetings later, Susan's participation turned out to be so much more, and Mohr Publishing was born. She came on board and began working hands-on with the publishing portion of the company. She is not only a great asset but a much-needed part of the team.

Bruno and I began looking for distributors to help get the CD out into the marketplace, and we ultimately landed on a company called *Soulfood*. I was super excited. *Soulfood* became involved in the way that I've always wanted. As a Mohr publishing partner and distribution company, they listened to me, and respected me, and I was included on every email, every conversation, and every decision that had to do with me and my career. For the first time in a while, I began to hear my music on the radio again. What an amazing feeling and sense of accomplishment.

After about three years in Oppenheim, it was time to drift again. Instead of being forced to move, I left on my own, and this time, it was with intention and purpose. In November 2019, I moved within walking distance of Bruno. It's centrally located, and many of the band members are close, so laying down tracks is easy and effortless. The band that Bruno put together when we first met still has some of the same members, and their loyalty is refreshing and heartwarming. We are like a family; we get the work done but play and goof off while doing it. With a great band, Bruno as a musical partner, and Susan taking the weight, I feel really good about this team.

With everything in place, I was excited about making things happen and getting my new CD out into the market when the pandemic hit. After we got over the initial shock of it all, Bruno and I realized that we had something hard to come by, uninterrupted "time." We went to work to create music. I didn't get many concerts, but I got a great start on archiving songs we keep in the vault until we package future CDs. Thanks to Bruno, Susan, and the band, I now have six projects in the works, and we owe a part of that to the Covid pandemic. I learned a lot during this process because in addition to helping me with the music part of this business, I also have help with the business aspect of my life. It feels good to know where money is going, who rent and bills are being paid to, with a transparency that I needed. There is no doubt in my mind that Bruno and I have each other's back. This makes my job as a performer easy, and I love the process, unlike in the past, where things were going so fast, and I always felt like I had to watch people around me, not knowing what the next problem would be. I make my music for the fans; it's a bittersweet feeling, and I'm a lot happier now and much calmer than I used to be. Making music has always been like therapy to me and I know it shows in my lyrics.

When we aren't working, Bruno and I go to dinner with our girl-friends, share the occasional meal, and just relax and chill. During Covid, I also went over a lot of old business and had boxes of paper-work to go through, and Bruno helped with this as well. In following the paper trail from my past, he explained to me the steps people took to rip me off. Just like I was told, it took me a long time, but I finally figured it out, and with this team, I'm protected, and I feel like I will never be put in that situation again. I can see the transparency and loyalty of my team. I've created a good foundation, and I've always done it for the fans, so I feel good about finishing the projects we have been working on.

Sometimes not so nice experiences would pop back up, and I am learning to deal with the unpleasantries. I've had conversations with Menges, politely and sometimes not so politely asking for my rights back for "*Humanology.*" As of 2022, Menges has remastered, re-released it, and still claims I owe him money. Every time we chat on WhatsApp, I've asked him to take me off his website and stop living off of my name, but he continues to insist that his production cost of 20k has not been paid. I've asked for invoices and receipts and he refuses to give me anything or stop distributing the album. Ironically, the title of the album is opposite in the fact that Menges is being inhuman and unsympathetic based on his greed. I take comfort from the fact that the word of God says, "revenge is mine," and I'm being very patient until I get a good lawyer. It's been eleven years, and I deserve to get my rights back, and clearly — he's been paid. I simply keep myself busy to keep my mind off of it. Despite everything, I am at peace with it all, and I still feel like someday I will get some kind of justice. In the meantime, I'll keep making music and touring the world.

I still chat with Gonzalez from time to time; we are cordial and respectful. When he calls me on WhatsApp, I usually answer by saying, "Hey Mr. Gonzalez, how are you doing?"

He is always busy with something or even in court with clients. He's very firm on how he works.

"I'm getting too old for some of the games out there today," he said recently.

I responded, "Is that right?" and moved on with the conversation.

We laughed and talked about the business and even joked about the past.

In 2022, there was an article in a Swiss Magazine where he was on the cover. He stated in the article that I sold two million records. In private, he'd always mentioned to me that I made millions but never gave me exact numbers. That last time we spoke, he offered to book concerts as a promoter and management. Bruno and Stacey were shocked that I'd even consider it, but I insisted I'm not that naïve kid he worked with in the 90s anymore, and I know a lot more about this business. I told Stacey, "I'd be open to working with him again, but this time it will be on my terms."

"Are you sure?" she asked.

"Gonzalez is good at what he does. And maybe I do feel a little like Ms. Simone in understanding that dealing with the devil you know is better than dealing with the one you don't know," I replied.

I introduced him to Bruno, and over a few weeks they went back and forth discussing how we could work together. Even though I know he did a lot of shady things in the past, I was hoping that Gonzalez would find a way to make things right by me. However, after several months of trying to work things out, Gonzalez and I could not get on the same page of how we could work together, so we both moved on, and somehow managed to remain friends.

As much as that chapter of my life is closed, I live everyday with unanswered questions. In the Summer of 2023, Stacey had one last interview with Gonzalez, and Nataf. Menges did not respond to requests. Their conversations left me just as baffled and frustrated as I was when we were working together. Gonzalez, of course does not admit to taking any money from me, and when questioned about my taxes, and how much I grossed while working with him, he stated,

"Marla was never in tax trouble with me. My accountant would go through Marla's finances, and made a suggestion for Marla to keep a certain amount aside for taxes. Stacey asked,

"How did you get paid?"

He calmly responded,

"I had access to Marla's account, and sometimes I would take my commission, and sometimes Marla would just give it to me. Sometimes checks from Vogue went to Marla, and sometimes they would go to me."

He further stated,

"I have nothing to hide. If Marla wanted to go back through my accounts, it may be found that Marla owes me money."

He chuckled. After hearing these words, I could only shake my head. Same ol' Gonzalez. Stacey probed further,

"Did you do Marla's taxes?" Without hesitation, Gonzalez replied,

"Yes, I did. It was a part of what I did for Marla."

"Well, did Marla get a copy of his taxes?"

Gonzales quickly replied,

"I don't think Marla ever got a copy of his taxes, but if Marla didn't get them, it's because Marla didn't ask."

Of course, I asked about my taxes. Whenever I asked, he said, it wasn't any of my business. The bottom line is I've never seen them. While I probably would not have known how to do them, it would have been nice to at least see them, and to this day have I seen a copy of my taxes from him. This may mean nothing to most, but I've always wanted to be involved in every part of my career, even if it's simply getting copies of my own taxes.

The conversation Stacey had with Nataf revealed he didn't remember nearly as much as I did from my past, he was asked, "What was it like working with Marla?" He raised an eyebrow, and was hesitant to reply, he said,

"Marla was a great performer. He did the job as an artist in the noble sense of the word, but it wasn't easy to work with Marla." He continued,

"The beginning was fine, but as time went on, Marla felt like people were attacking him. Marla was always in a very defensive state of mind."

He was right, after the first year, I was defensive, upset, and frustrated with how things were unfolding.

Fabrice claim to not know the extent of Gonzalez's involvement in handling my career. I don't know how he thought I managed things by myself, with no family around, barely speaking the language, and no one to really explain things. He smirked,

"Marla didn't know how to do the job successfully. He didn't play the game."

He then quoted a French saying,

"To be talented is a gift, but to be successful is a job."

Despite it all, success to me, is the fact that I was able to walk away with my sanity. Most of it, anyway.

He didn't remember when I stormed into his office, asking for my money. How does one forget something that? He did not remember telling me "We sold you to Germany." He explained there is no such way to sell and artist to just one region, but these words I remember like it was yesterday. Whether it was something that was lost in translation, or if I misunderstood the context of the conversation, or perhaps he forgot he said these words to me, this statement was one of the determining factors for me moving to Germany, and in my mind it happened. Regarding how I was paid, Nataf stated,

"It is highly impossible that Marla didn't get any checks from Vogue, BMG. It was illegal for us to pay anyone except the artist. Unless the artist signs something saying to pay someone else."

Illegal as it may have been, it happened. I would have never signed anything knowingly to turn over my royalties, or any money due to me. I feel like it was very possible that Gonzalez could have intercepted those payments, much like Mr. Bryant did, and that could explain why I never saw a great deal of my money. While the past is the past, some of the memories stay with me, some I've managed to let go. What brings me the most peace is that I sleep good at night, knowing that I am still here, capable of performing and creating good music.

I have learned a great deal on this journey, and recently while in a meeting, someone asked, "Why did you name your recent CD "Unexpected?"

I responded, "I've had so many ups and downs, and I know that people had written me off as a musician thinking I would get eaten up by the wolves of this industry and quit. So, to have produced my very own CD was not only a job I needed to get done for myself, but I also realized that it was unexpected for me to have survived the music business this long.

It was unexpected for me to believe I could continue doing this work and still thrive in this business without losing my mind. I owe it all to God, and there is no way I could have done it without Him and knowing all along that He was watching over me. It's been well worth The Cost of Freedom. By His grace, expect more from me in the future.

The End

www.ingramcontent.com/pod-product-compliance
Lightning Source LLC
Chambersburg PA
CBHW020432130626
46549CB00001B/96